Praise for

Uprooting Racism

Paul Kivel ... presents a powerful yet accessible vision, informed by research and reflection on racism in the US. ...This book provides the best concrete guidance for the new or perplexed would-be white ally that I have ever seen in print. For the individual explorer, the self-study exercises are amazing. As a resource for the educator or trainer's library, *Uprooting Racism* is indispensable and unique. I have personally used many of the exercises in the book in my own teaching. Paul's support and guidance for educators and trainers in his books and on his website is outstanding.

— Victor Lee Lewis, Progressive Life Coach,
founder/director of the Radical Resilience Institute,
Co-Editor with Hugh Vasquez of Lessons from "The Color of Fear."

Uprooting Racism gives the student, activist and practitioner something for their social justice tool box. The expanded edition is challenging, informative and practical. You'll finish the book and want to get right to work.

— Dr. Eddie Moore Jr., Founder/Director,
The White Privilege Conference

Uprooting Racism continues to be a powerful and wonderful book, a major contribution to our understanding of racism as white people. ... Not only does Kivel address tough issues related to whiteness and racism, ... he also identifies specific ways that whites can be allies for change — all done with honesty, forthrightness, respect, and from the heart. For any white person who is sincere about working for social justice, here's the source.

— Judith H. Katz, Ed. D., author of *White Awareness: Handbook for Anti-Racism Training*; and *The Inclusion Breakthrough: Unleashing the Real Power of Diversity*

This expanded volume is even more comprehensive, heart-felt and easy to use. The book ... is a must for anyone who wants to create settings in which respectful, fair and trusting relations are the norm.

— Margo Adair, author of *Meditations on Everything Under the Sun* and founder of Tools for Change

Paul Kivel writes with clarity and depth in a style that is adequately complex for understandings of racism in our time. He uses his writing power to illuminate all the systems, inner and outer, which lead to inequitable distribution of power, respect, money, safety, security, and opportunity in the world....

— Peggy McIntosh, founder and co-director,
National SEED Project on Inclusive Curriculum,
author *White Privilege: Unpacking the Invisible Knapsack*

...a courageous, accessible and practical guide for those who are interested in ending racism. With great wisdom and compassion, Paul asks each of us to take responsibility for our part in maintaining a system that is catastrophic for all. I appreciate that he does so without blaming or shaming, and that he gives clear and useful tools for ending oppression. As an African-American, I am delighted to have a book to recommend to white (as well as other) folks interested in creating a world wherein racism is obsolete. Read this book!

— Akaya Windwood, consultant on diversity and organizations

Uprooting Racism is a fact-filled resource for teachers and parents to use in educating ourselves and our young people about the history and the hidden costs of racism in our communities. Kivel presents simple, meaningful actions we can all take to build a more just and healthy society.

— Jackie Shonerd, parent and Coordinator for Conflict Resolution Programs,
Oakland, (CA) Unified School District

As a woman of color actively engaged in social justice movements for over 25 years, I have often longed for a book like *Uprooting Racism* to help white people understand the institutional, systematic, and persistent character of racism in our world. Paul Kivel has written a handbook to critically examine racism in our lives, and in our work for peace and justice.

— Luz Guerra, activist, consultant/writer

Uprooting Racism is a uniquely sensitive, wise, practical guide for white people struggling with their feelings about race.

— Howard Zinn, author of *A People's History of the United States*

...the 'how-to manual' for whites to work with people of color to create an inclusive, just world in the 21st century. *Uprooting Racism* succinctly describes how intricately racism is tied to all institutions and our daily lives. ... It should be in the toolbox of anyone who is working for an anti-racist society.

— Maggie Potapchuk, Senior Program Associate, Network of Alliances, Bridging Race and Ethnicity (NABRE), a program of the Joint Center for Political and Economic Studies

Those of us who commit to the life-long journey of being anti-racist whites need lots of help. The revised edition of *Uprooting Racism* offers a clear vision of the journey's destination, an invaluable and accessible map and a set of tools for the steps we must take to get there. ...I recommend it highly and plan to use it in my own work.

— Louise Derman-Sparks, co-director, of the Early Childhood Equity Alliance. Author of *Teaching/Learning Anti-Racism: A Developmental Approach*

How
White People
Can Work
for Racial
Justice

UPROOTING RACISM

REVISED AND EXPANDED 3RD EDITION

PAUL KIVEL

NEW SOCIETY PUBLISHERS

Cover design by Diane McIntosh.
Image copyright iStock (porcorex)

Printed in Canada. Third printing August 2016.

Paperback ISBN: 978-0-86571-688-9
eISBN 978-1-55092-495-4

Inquiries regarding requests to reprint all or part of *Uprooting Racism* should be addressed to New Society Publishers at the address below.

To order directly from the publishers, please call toll-free (North America) 1-800-567-6772, or order online at www.newsociety.com

Any other inquiries can be directed by mail to:
New Society Publishers
P.O. Box 189, Gabriola Island, BC V0R 1X0, Canada
(250) 247-9737

Library and Archives Canada Cataloguing in Publication

Kivel, Paul

Uprooting racism : how white people can work for racial justice / Paul Kivel. -- 3rd rev. and expanded ed.

Includes bibliographical references and index.
ISBN 978-0-86571-688-9

1. Racism--United States. 2. Race awareness--United States. 3. Whites--Race identity--United States. 4. United States--Race relations. I. Title.

E184.A1K58 2011   305.800973   C2011-904335-1

New Society Publishers' mission is to publish books that contribute in fundamental ways to building an ecologically sustainable and just society, and to do so with the least possible impact on the environment, in a manner that models this vision. We are committed to doing this not just through education, but through action. Our printed, bound books are printed on Forest Stewardship Council-certified acid-free paper that is **100% post-consumer recycled** (100% old growth forest-free), processed chlorine free, and printed with vegetable-based, low-VOC inks, with covers produced using FSC-certified stock. New Society also works to reduce its carbon footprint, and purchases carbon offsets based on an annual audit to ensure a carbon neutral footprint. For further information, or to browse our full list of books and purchase securely, visit our website at: www.newsociety.com

NEW SOCIETY PUBLISHERS

To my family — Micki, my love
Ariel, Shandra and Ryan, Amanda,
Niko and Mateo, my inspiration
and to all those fighting for justice

Join the Conversation

Visit our online book club at NewSociety.com to share your thoughts about *Uprooting Racism*. Exchange ideas with other readers, post questions for the author, respond to one of the sample questions or start your own discussion topics. See you there!

Contents

Lists, Diagrams and Exercises

Acknowledgments

I ACKNOWLEDGE THE CREATIVE SPIRIT that is the source of life and connects us to each other and to all life. I acknowledge the earth that nurtures and sustains us. I acknowledge the Native Peoples whose land I am on. And I acknowledge all those whose work makes my life possible.

North America has a long and distinguished history of white people who have fought against racism and racial violence. This history began in the days of Antonio de Montesinos and Bartolomé de Las Casas, Spanish priests who documented and protested against the atrocities that Columbus and other early conquistadores committed against the Native Americans in the West Indies. It continues today with white people fighting against hate crimes, police brutality, housing and job discrimination and the recent attacks against immigrants and poor people of color. These efforts by white people have been inspired by the constant, unrelenting fight by people of color for survival, for justice and for an end to the political, economic and cultural exploitation they have experienced in the United States.

My deepest gratitude goes to the multitudes of people of color who have challenged racism in both small and large ways over the centuries, and who have demonstrated by their lives that the lies of racism are untrue, inhumane and violate the integrity of each person who colludes with injustice.

I am also proud to be Jewish and to be able to contribute to the historic struggle of Jewish people to survive waves of anti-Jewish oppression and create our lives anew in the framework of freedom and justice that Judaism provides. I want to acknowledge my Jewish foreparents and the many Jews who are still on the front lines of the battle for racial justice because they understand the connections between anti-Jewish oppression (anti-Semitism) and racism.

There are many people who have inspired my work and writing, most of whom I have never met. I have read their words, heard their songs, witnessed their actions and strive to be true to their vision.

I want to acknowledge specifically those who I have learned from and who have supported my work in the last few years. They are Bill Aal, Margo Adair, Martin Cano, Jim Coates, Hari Dillon, Steve Falk, Isoke Femi, Margot Gibney, Luz Guerra, Sonia Jackson, Francie Kendall, David Landes, Nell Myhand, Namane Mohlabane, Daphne Muse, Ayana Morse, Kiran Rana, Bill Rosenfeld, John Tucker, Akaya Windwood, Shirley Yee and my mother, Betty Jean Kivel.

I also thank my wonderful "Jews schmooze" group: Alina Evers, Chaya Gusfield, Julie Nesnansky, Adee Horn, Ariel Luckey, Aurora Levins-Morales, Ilana Schatz, Richard Shapiro and Penny Rosenwasser.

Several people reviewed early drafts of the book and gave me support and feedback. Special thank yous to Robert Allen, Kostas Bagakis, Allan Creighton, Victor Lewis, Nell Myhand, Yeshi Neumann, Barry Shapiro and Hugh Vasquez.

It has been my great pleasure and challenge over the years to work with Robert Allen, Heru-Nefera Amen, Allan Creighton, Victor Lewis, Jackie Shonerd, Harrison Sims and others at the Oakland Men's Project and Nell Myhand, Hugh Vasquez and Shirley Yee at the Todos Institute. I have learned much from their passion for justice, their gentle caring and their fierce dedication to freedom.

My family has been particularly inspiring and supportive in many ways. My deepest love and appreciation go to Ariel Luckey, SAM Luckey, Ryan Luckey, Amanda Salzman, Kesa Kivel, Dana Kivel and our grandchildren Niko and Mateo. My life-partner, Micki, has been a loving support, insightful editor, wonderful co-parent and shares my vision of a just world.

My appreciation also goes to the staff at New Society Publishers who provided strong and consistent support to this project from their initial enthusiasm for the book through the final editing and production, and on to the second and now third editions. My special thanks to those who guided it through the entire process with skill and dedication. Judith and Chris Plant are the guiding light for the revised edition. Betsy Nuse has provided excellent editing, and the cover design is by Diane McIntosh.

Preface

BEFORE I WROTE THIS BOOK, I accumulated a long list of reasons why it was an important project. Racism is pervasive, its effects devastating, the need to fight against it urgent. People of color are being blamed for our social problems and attacked on all fronts. Recent immigrants, African American women on welfare, youth of color, Muslims and affirmative action programs are just some of the current targets of white anger. It seems like the civil rights and social justice gains we made in the 1960s and 70s are being rolled back.

I could also see the huge impact racism had on my relationships with other people, what my children learned in school, how we dealt with economic issues at the state and federal level and what sports and music I paid attention to. Racism is everywhere, influencing us at every turn. There is no shortage of immediate reasons why writing a book like this one needed to be done.

In the workshops my co-workers and I were facilitating, participants were eager to talk about these issues and anxious to become involved. Somehow, few of them were able to translate their understanding of the issues and their commitment to ending racism into concrete community action. When they asked me for resources, there were no guides for critical thinking and social action I could point them to. What was available about racism or white people was theoretical — interesting but not practical.

With all this in mind, I sat down to write this book. I suddenly accumulated a long list of reasons why I couldn't do it. I wasn't qualified. The subject was too big. The issue was too important. How could I add anything new? The connections between racism, religious oppression, gender and economic issues were too complex. People of color have addressed all the issues much more powerfully than I could. I would make mistakes. I would leave important pieces out. People of color would be angry at me. Other white people would call me racist. People would expect me to have all the answers.

The entire task felt formidable, scary, fraught with problems, and I felt ill-equipped to carry it out successfully.

I procrastinated. I hoped someone else would do it. "There must be some-one else who knows more, or writes better, or knows how to say it the right way." "There's certainly someone who could do it without making mistakes or looking foolish." These thoughts went through my mind as I waited for someone else to step forward.

Then one day I recognized these feelings. They were the same feelings that white people experience in our workshops — the same "reasons" they give for not doing more to stop racism. I knew that if I let these feelings stop me from taking the risk of writing this book I would be succumbing to the paraly-sis that often keeps white people from taking action against racial injustice. When confronting the reality of racism, we become sad, angry, overwhelmed, numb, anxious and passive. When faced with the need to intervene, speak up or take action against racism, we become tentative from questions and con-cerns, waiting for someone more qualified to step up.

There is no one who can take our place or do our part. I realized it was crucial for me to write what I could; that was my responsibility. Yes, it was scary. Yes, I would make mistakes. I didn't know all the answers; I wouldn't be able to cover everything; some people might not like what I write. But a book like this needed to be written, and I was in a position to write it.

Many white people have stood up against racism. They used their feelings to guide them to action, not to stop their involvement. I needed to call on their examples of risk taking, moral integrity and strategic action to realize that what I do makes a difference.

I'm sure you will experience many feelings as you read this book. Let them guide you, but don't let them stop you. It is easy to become overwhelmed by our feelings, by how much there is to do and by how confusing and risky it seems. I'm asking you to tap into another set of feelings to guide you — understand-ing and compassion for people of color, outrage at injustice, courage, passion and commitment to building a democratic, multicultural and just society. We need to concentrate on what it is we can do, how we can make a difference.

Whenever I become overwhelmed thinking about how much there is to do, I remind myself of a saying by Rabbi Tarfon. I hope it will guide you as well.

It is not upon you to finish the work.
Neither are you free to desist from it.

Preface to the Third Edition

WHEN I WROTE *Uprooting Racism,* I wanted to address the strongly entrenched institutional and organizational structures in our society that maintain and perpetuate racism. My hope was that if we, as white people, could better understand the injustice on which our lives and our society are based and could see the collaborative role that we play in maintaining racism, we would be more motivated to combat it and more effective at doing so. I also wanted my book to address the daily indignities and attacks that people of color experience.

When the first edition was published in the early nineties, there were books about racism, but few that documented how white people benefited from and participated in perpetuating it. Even fewer examined the way that racism influenced the workings of our institutions. But, perhaps as a legacy of the civil rights movement, there was still a vigorous discussion of racism in US society and a widespread acceptance of the fact that we had work to do to make racial justice a reality.

Fifteen years later there are a massive number of studies and other forms of documentation demonstrating the workings of racism in everything from its devastating impact on the lives and opportunities of people of color to how white people think, act and talk about racism, what benefits we gain from it and how it is perpetuated in the everyday practices and policies of our organizations and institutions.[1]

At the same time within the white community there is a culture of denial and minimization about the existence of racism. Despite pervasive segregation and discrimination in education, housing, healthcare and the job market; despite widespread surveillance, control and punishment of people of color through the welfare, child welfare, foster care, education, police, immigration and criminal/legal systems; despite hate crimes, police brutality, racial profiling and everyday forms of what has been called micro-aggression against people of color, a January 2009 poll showed that while most white people believe that acts of racism still occur, only 22% believe that racism is a major societal problem.[2]

In fact, I often hear references to a "post-racial" society, a belief that the civil rights movement and subsequent legislation "took care of all that," and a feeling that having a black man as president proves that we have moved beyond race in the United States. Any continuing racism must be residual from the past or the result of racist individuals who are the exception.

Yet the evidence of pervasive, life-destroying racism throughout our society persists. The evidence is not only in statistics and broad patterns of discrimination, exclusion and marginalization, but also in the everyday experiences of people of color. Last week, for example, three of the African American women who live in the apartment next door described how they have been harassed by a white resident in the apartment on the other side of them. This person not only drops trash and dog shit onto their driveway and parking spots, but also calls them "niggers" when they complain. When they call the police, the officers don't take down all the details of the situation, minimize the incident and discourage them from pursuing the matter.

Last night I was at a board meeting for a local organization with which I volunteer. One of the white members, referring to the newest group of board members most of whom are people of color, started out a sentence with "When we brought these people on board ...." When a board member who was a person of color objected to being called one of "these people," the white board member replied, "You know I didn't mean it like that."

Today one of the two African American women who are checkout clerks at my local grocery store (the other 15 or so checkout staff are white) told me about an incident that happened the day before. A customer had mistaken her for the other African American staff person. When the woman politely reminded the customer that she was not the other clerk, the customer replied, "Well it's an easy mistake to make. You know how all African Americans look alike." The woman I was talking with had barely been able to restrain herself from making an aggressive comeback to this customer's remarks and was still visibly upset as she recounted the incident to me. I looked down the aisle at the other African American checker and noticed immediately that she bore no physical resemblance to the woman I was talking with.

Every day I hear a new story, read a new report, witness the devastating impact of racism on our community. I don't ask for these stories, but I listen carefully when I hear them. I don't take them personally or try to defend white people. I know that these stories are not about me and that sometimes the white people involved have no conscious intention of hurting a person of color. These stories are about the everyday discrimination and disrespect towards people of color that racism produces and that people of color have to live with. What should I do when I hear these stories?

Sometimes listening is enough, especially if I am listening without offering excuses, defenses, explanations or minimizations. Often more is called for. I try to think of how I can respond to these incidents. I am sympathetic to the store clerk and affirm that she's justified in being upset. I call the board member and talk about the comment he made. I volunteer to be part of a group that confronts our racist neighbor. My actions never feel like enough, but I have learned that they do make a difference.

Since I wrote *Uprooting Racism,* I have become even more acutely aware of how interdependent our lives are and how dependent I am on the low-paid work of people of color in the United States and in other countries. I look at the label on my jeans, shirts or underwear; I track the work that produced my computer, TV and microwave; I learn more about who grows, picks, packages and prepares the food I eat; I notice who cleans the public buildings and classrooms I use. Often it is people of color in poorly paid, low-status jobs who allow me to enjoy the benefits of inexpensive clothes, low-priced electronic equipment, cheap food and clean and well-maintained public spaces.

Just walking down the street to the park makes me aware of this interconnection and dependency. I meet people like Renee, who maintains the flowers and trees in the park down the block from us. Now in his 50s, he emigrated here from the Philippines many years ago and has raised his children in this country. Or people like Dereje, an immigrant from Ethiopia who is on the city's mosquito abatement team. When the owners of the apartments next to the park call the city to complain about the mosquitoes, Dereje comes out and mixes the chemicals into the pond to control the bugs.

My daily life is interwoven with the lives of hundreds, if not thousands, of people of color. Yet so much of their lives, work and culture is ridiculed, exploited or rendered invisible by our society that often I don't see them, I don't make the connections. My ignorance and subsequent inaction contribute to their exploitation, discrimination and scapegoating. I become a partner in racism, a collaborator in injustice.

A few years ago I was hopeful that we were making some inroads in recognizing and addressing racism. However, watching the response to the September 11, 2001 World Trade Center and Pentagon bombings, the response to the disasters of Hurricanes Rita and Katrina and the collapse of the stock and housing bubbles, I fear we have suffered major setbacks. There has been an alarming increase in hate crimes against Arab Americans, against Muslims and even against those who are mistaken for members of these two groups, such as Sikhs, whose men traditionally wear turbans. African Americans, Latino/as, Native Americans and Asian Americans are threatened by racial profiling on our streets and at our borders. Mosques are being attacked across the US. The housing and financial meltdowns have disproportionately affected communities of color — transferring even more wealth to white communities.[3] And all of us face attacks on our civil liberties, increased police and military surveillance and the further shifting of resources from education, health and other social programs to war, surveillance and prisons.

On the other hand, in this time of increased insecurity and fear, I have been heartened by the number of white people (as well as many people of color) who have stood in solidarity with Arab Americans, Muslims, recent immigrants, African Americans, Native Americans and others under attack. They have challenged stereotypes and misinformation and confronted scapegoating and harassment. They have acted as allies in the best tradition of white people. I hope that this new edition of *Uprooting Racism* will continue to support that tradition of caring and social responsibility.

I know that many white people find it hard to read about racism. I have been told stories of how students, required to read this book, would read a chapter and then throw the book across the room because they were so upset at what I was saying and what it meant for their lives. But then they would go across the room, pick up the book and read another chapter. That is what it takes to confront racism. We need to keep going back and picking up the task no matter how uncomfortable, angry or frustrated we become in the process. Being an ally is like that. We keep learning, doing our best, leaving something out, making mistakes, doing it better next time.

Now, more than ever, we as white people need to put our shoulders to the task of working with people of color to uproot racism and build healthy, inclusive and sustainable communities. As I discuss in more detail in the book, it is inadequate to say "I am not prejudiced," and morally evasive to say "I treat everyone the same." In a world in which racism continues to be one of the bedrocks of our organizations and institutions, in which most people of color, every single day, are confronted with the repercussions of racial discrimination, harassment and exploitation, we must ask ourselves

What do I stand for?

Who do I stand with?

Do I stand for racial justice, the end of discrimination and racial violence and a society truly based on equal opportunity?

Do I stand with people of color and white allies in the struggle to uproot racism?

These are the challenging questions I offer to you as you begin to read this book. I hope *Uprooting Racism* helps you to be clearer and more effective in answering them.

Paul Kivel, June, 2011

Notes

1. See the bibliography.
2. Michael A. Fletcher and Jon Cohen. "Far Fewer Consider Racism Big Problem: Little Change, However, at Local Level." *Washington Post,* January 19, 2009. [online]. [cited March 4, 2011]. washingtonpost.com/wp-dyn/content/article/2009/01/18/AR2009011802538.html.
3. This transfer is estimated to be in the hundreds of billions of dollars. See Amaad Rivera et al. *Foreclosed: State of the Dream 2008.* United for a Fair Economy, January, 2008. [online]. [cited March 4, 2011]. faireconomy.org/files/StateOfDream_01_16_08_Web.pdf.

A Note to Readers
Outside the United States

MANY OF THE EXAMPLES used in the book are from the United States, where I live and about which I have more access to information. Many reports, studies and accounts of racism in other white majority societies — Great Britain, Canada, France, Germany, Australia and New Zealand — show similar patterns of racism against people of color. For example, the Parekh Report, *The Future of Multi-ethnic Britain*, documents extensive institutional and cultural racism throughout Great Britain.[4] If you live in a white majority country, talk with people of color, investigate the studies and reports and don't let yourself be complacent or indifferent simply because the situation is not exactly the same as that which I describe in the United States.

Notes

4. The Parekh Report. *The Future of Multi-Ethnic Britain*. Profile, 2000.

Introduction

"Only Justice Can Put Out the Fire" [1]

THIS IS A BOOK ABOUT RACISM FOR WHITE PEOPLE. In this book I want to talk to you personally about what racism means to those of us who are white and how we can make a difference in the struggle for racial justice.

For the last 35 years, my work has been driven by one powerful question: how can we live and work to sustain community, nurture each other and create a multicultural society based on love, justice and interdependence with all living things? I feel strongly that the challenge posed in that question is the most important one we face today.

Over the years, I have come to realize that racism is one of the systems of oppression that most keep us from working together to build such an inclusive, just and sustainable society.

There is fire raging across the United States — usually a series of brush fires erupting whenever conditions are right, sometimes a firestorm, always a smoldering cauldron. Whether it is major urban uprisings, intellectual debates or everyday conflicts in our neighborhoods and schools, racism is burning us all. Some of us have third-degree burns or have died from its effects; many others live in the charred wreckage. Most of us suffer first- and second-degree burns at some time in our lives. We all live with fear in the glow of the menacing and distorted light of racism's fire.

As white people we do many things to survive the heat. Some of us move to the suburbs, put bars on our windows, put locks on our hearts and teach our children distrust for their own protection. Some of us believe the enemy is "out there" — and that we can be safe "in here." When we don't talk about our fears, we are prevented from doing anything effective to put out the fire.

Poll after poll shows that most white Americans are scared. We are scared about violence; about the economy; about the environment; we are scared about the safety, education and future of our children.[2] Much of the time those fears are directed toward people of color — long-term residents or recent immigrants. It is easy for us to focus on them, and yet doing so devastates our ability to address critical national issues of economic inequality, war, social infrastructure, family violence and environmental devastation.

Since the bombing of the World Trade Center and the Pentagon in 2001, white people are even more afraid. We have been shown our vulnerability and our complicity.[3] Many of us wanted to do something, to pick up a bucket and throw water on the flames, but the size of the blaze seemed to make our individual efforts useless. Besides, many of us thought that we were too far away from the cause of the fire to make a difference. Arabs and Muslims were defined as the problem; the danger was anywhere and everywhere. Unending war was declared the only solution.

In fact, there are already flames in our (all too often predominantly white) schools, churches, neighborhoods and workplaces. Poverty, family violence, drugs and despair are not limited to somewhere "out there" nor to "those people." Our houses are burning too, and we need to pick up our buckets and start carrying water now. But just like the volunteer fire departments in rural communities and small towns, we need to be part of a fire line where everyone realizes that when the sparks are flying, anything can catch on fire. As a community we can be alert for sparks and embers so they can be put out before a bigger blaze develops.

We don't need scare tactics. They just reinforce the fear and paralysis. We don't need numbers and statistics. They produce numbness and despair. We need to talk with each other, honestly, simply, caringly. We need to learn how to talk about racism without rhetoric, which fans the flames; without attack or intimidation, which separates people from one another. We need to share firefighting suggestions, skills and experience so we can work together to put out the blaze.

Racism is often described as a problem of prejudice. Prejudice is certainly one result of racism, and it fuels further acts of violence toward people of color. However the assumption of this book is that racism is the institution-alization of social injustice based on skin color, other physical characteristics and cultural and religious difference. White racism is the uneven and unfair distribution of power, privilege, land and material goods favoring white people. Another way to state this is that white racism is a system in which people of color as a group are exploited and oppressed by white people as a group.

As we have witnessed many times in European and American history, the fires of racism include flames of anti-Jewish oppression⁴ and anti-Muslim oppression (Islamophobia), united by a history of Christian dominance that has always treated Muslims and Jews with suspicion and hostility. Most of the Jews in the United States are of European background. Sometimes these Jews are considered white and sometimes not, just as Asian and Arab Americans are sometimes considered white or not. Jewish people are vulnerable to the same kinds of violence, discrimination and harassment that most people of color have experienced; at the same time, Jews who are of European descent are buffered from racism's worst aspects by the benefits of being white. Because of this complex dynamic, understanding and confronting anti-Jewish oppression is a crucial link in the struggle to end racism. In this book, Jews of European descent will be referred to both as white and as targets of racism. Jews of color are always targets of racism from white people and even from Jews of European descent. They are also vulnerable to anti-Jewish oppression.

Originally called Moors or Saracens, Muslims have been labeled the unrelenting foe of the Christian West since the first crusade was declared in 1095. In fact, a European Christian identity was first established in this period by uniting people against the Moors as a common enemy. Muslims, like Jews, were one of the many groups treated as dangerous outsiders by Christians. Even though there are white Muslims in the US, they have never experienced the acceptance that white Jews have experienced. Even so, white people who are Muslims do retain some of the benefits of being white while being vulnerable to many of the penalties for being a person who is not Christian.

Anti-Jewish oppression and anti-Muslim oppression are similar to, different from and intertwined with racism. European Christian ruling classes have exploited, controlled and violated other groups of people based on religion, race, culture and nationality (as well as gender, class, physical and mental ability and sexual orientation) for many centuries. There is tremendous overlap in the kinds of violence that have been directed at these groups and the justifications used to legitimize it. Racism and anti-Jewish and anti-Muslim oppression are primary, closely related tools that the powerful have used to maintain their advantage.

When I wrote my book *Men's Work*, I quoted a statement from Alice Walker in the preface. The statement was about how the fear of not being perfect can inhibit committing oneself to public action about a particular issue. She was talking about speaking out against cruelty to animals even though she occasionally ate meat. I referred to writing about sexism even though I wasn't perfectly non-sexist.

I think it is crucial that each of us speaks up about issues of violence and injustice. It is true that our words would have more moral credibility if we were leading a mistake-free life and were totally consistent in what we say and do. We have to "walk the walk," not just "talk the talk."

However, issues of social justice are not fundamentally about individual actions and beliefs. This book is about racism, an institutionalized system of oppression. Although my actions can either support or confront racism, it is completely independent of me. In fact, even if most of us were completely non-racist in our attitudes and practices, there are many ways that unequal wages, unequal treatment in the legal system and segregation in jobs, housing and education could continue.

This book is about uprooting the system of racism. You may need to reexamine your individual beliefs and actions in order to participate effectively in that uprooting. This book will help you look at how you have learned racism, what effects it has had on your life, what have been its costs and benefits to you and how you have learned to pass it on. More importantly, this book will help you become a member of a network of people who are committed to racial justice. It offers you strategies and guidelines for becoming involved in the struggle.

Don't take it too personally. You did not create racism. You may have many feelings while reading this book. Confronting racism may trigger a range of feelings including guilt, defensiveness, sadness or outrage. Acknowledge the feelings, talk with others, but don't get stuck. If our feelings immobilize us, we cannot strategically plan how to transform the system.

This book is not about unlearning racism.[5] Unlearning racism makes it easier for people of color to live and work with us, but it doesn't necessarily challenge racist structures. Unlearning racism may or may not be a path toward eliminating racism. In a society where individual growth is often not only the starting place, but also the end point of discussion, strategies for unlearning racism often end in complacency and inaction.

This book does not document the existence of racism. There are many books and thousands of studies showing the direct, devastating impact of racism on the daily lives of the tens of millions of people of color in the US. That there are inequality and injustice in our educational, political, legal, medical, housing and employment systems is amply documented and indisputable. I will present few statistics and little information proving racism exists. There are excellent resources listed in the Bibliography and Other Resources sections where you will find such documentation.

Instead, this book provides some suggestions and starting points based on the fact that racism exists, it is pervasive and that its effects are devastating. Because of this devastation, we need to start doing everything possible to end racism. The first step is for us to talk together, as white people.

Notes

1. Ron Romanovsky and Paul Phillips. "Burning Angels" on *Let's Flaunt It!* Fresh Fruit Records, 1995.
2. Barry Glassner. *The Culture of Fear: Why Americans Are Afraid of the Wrong Things.* Basic, 1999, pp. xi-xxviii.
3. By complicity I mean the connections between interventionist US foreign policy in the Middle East in countries such as Iran, Iraq, Saudi Arabia, Afghanistan, Palestine and Israel prior to 9/11.
4. I use anti-Jewish oppression in place of the more common anti-Semitism for accuracy, clarity and to separate it from the recent use of anti-Semitism to describe critiques of policies of the State of Israel. Use of anti-Semitic to refer to Jewish oppression makes invisible the oppression of other Semitic people. It also misrepresents Jews because not all Jews are Semitic in geographic origin; the ancestors of many Jews converted to Judaism in other parts of the world. Anti-Jewish oppression is parallel to anti-Muslim oppression and helps to highlight the common history of systemic attack that Muslims and Jews have experienced within Christian-dominated Europe and the US.
5. Unlearning racism refers to "unlearning" the lies, myths and stereotypes about people of color and white people that foster racial prejudice.

Part I

What Color Is White?

Let's Talk

I AM TALKING TO YOU AS ONE WHITE PERSON to another. I am Jewish, and I will talk about that later in this book. You also may have an ethnic identity you are proud of. You likely have a religious background, a culture, a country of origin and a history. Whatever your other identities, you may not be used to being addressed as white.

Other people are African American, Asian American, Pacific Islanders, Native American, Latino/as or Muslims. *Other* people have countries of origin and primary languages that are not English. Rarely in the US do white people identify ourselves or each other as white. It is an adjective that is seldom heard explicitly, but is everywhere implied. People are assumed white unless otherwise noted, much as people (and animals) are assumed to be male.

Read the following lines:

> He walked into the room and immediately noticed her.
> This new sitcom is about a middle-aged, middle-class couple and their three teenage children.
> He did well in school but was just a typical all-American kid.
> Women today want to catch a man who is strong, but sensitive.
> She didn't know if she would get into the college of her choice.
> My grandmother lived on a farm all her life.
> I have a friend who has AIDS.
> He won a medal on the Special Olympics basketball team.

Are all these people white? Read the sentences again and imagine the people referred to are Chinese Americans or Native Americans. How does that change the meanings of these sentences? If you are of Christian background, what happens when you make them Jewish or Muslim?

8

We assume we are white. It may seem like I'm stating the obvious. Yet there is something about stating this obvious fact that makes white people feel uneasy, marked. Why notice? What's the point of saying "I'm white?"

White people have been led to believe that racism is a question of particular acts of discrimination or violence. Calling someone a name, denying someone a job, excluding someone from a neighborhood — that is racism. These certainly are acts of racism. But what about working in an organization where people of color are paid less, have more menial work or fewer opportunities for advancement? What about shopping in a store where you are treated respectfully, but people of color are followed around or treated with suspicion?

People of color know this racism intimately. They know that where they live, work and walk. Whom they talk with and how — what they read, listen to or watch on TV — their past experiences and future possibilities are all influenced by racism.

- For the next few days notice how rarely you see or hear the words *white, Caucasian* or *Euro-American.*
- Where is it implied but not stated specifically?
- Carry your whiteness with you. During the day, in each new situation, remind yourself that you are white. What difference has it made/does it make? Who is around you? What are they doing? Are they white or people of color? What difference does it make?
- Write down what you notice. Discuss it with a friend.
- Particularly notice whenever you are somewhere where there are only white people. How did it come to be that there are no people of color there?
- Are they really not there, or are they only invisible? Did they grow some of the food, originally own the land, build the buildings or clean and maintain the place where you are?

"I'm Not White"

R ECENTLY I WAS DOING A WORKSHOP ON RACISM. We wanted to divide the group into a caucus of people of color and a caucus of white people so that each group could have more in-depth discussion. Immediately some of the white people said, "But I'm not white."

I was somewhat taken aback because although these people looked white, they were clearly distressed about being labeled white. A white Christian woman stood up and said, "I'm not really white because I'm not part of the white male power structure that perpetuates racism." Next a white gay man stood up and said, "You have to be straight to have the privileges of being white." A white, straight, working-class man from a poor family then said, "I've got it just as hard as any person of color." Finally, a straight, white, middle-class man said, "I'm not white, I'm Italian."

My African American co-worker turned to me and asked, "Where are all the white people who were here just a minute ago?" I replied, "Don't ask me. I'm not white, I'm Jewish!"

Most of the time white people don't notice or question our whiteness and the benefits it brings. However, when the subject is racism, many of us don't want to be perceived as white because it opens us to charges of being racist and brings up feelings of guilt, embarrassment or hopelessness. Of course, there are others who proudly claim whiteness and deny or minimize the impacts of racism.

Those of us who are middle-class are more likely to take it for granted that we are white without having to emphasize the point, and to feel guilty when it is noticed or brought up. Those of us who are poor or working-class are more likely to have had to assert our whiteness against the effects of economic discrimination and the presence of other racial groups. Although we share the benefits of being white, we don't share the economic privileges of being middle-class, and so we are more likely to feel angry and less likely to feel guilty than our middle-class counterparts. Whatever our economic status, many white people become paralyzed with some measure of fear, guilt or defensiveness when racism is addressed.

In the US it has always been dangerous even to talk about racism. "Nigger lover," "Indian lover" and "race traitor" are labels that have carried severe consequences. You may know the names of white civil rights workers Goodman, Schwerner and Luizzo who were killed for their actions. Many of us have been isolated from friends or family because of disagreements over racism. A lot of us have been called "racist."

I want to begin here — with this denial of our whiteness — because racism keeps people of color in the limelight and makes whiteness invisible. To change this we must take whiteness itself, hold it up to the light and see that it is a color too. Whiteness is a concept, an ideology, which holds tremendous power over our lives and, in turn, over the lives of people of color. Our challenge will be to keep whiteness center stage. Every time our attention begins to wander off toward people of color or other issues, we will have to notice and refocus. We must notice when we try to slip into another identity and escape being white.

If, when you move down the streets of major cities, other people assume, based on skin color, dress, physical appearance or total impression, that you are white, then in US society that counts for being white. This is where we are going to start talking about what it means to say "I am white." I realize that there are differences between the streets of New York and Minneapolis, Vancouver and Winnipeg and between different neighborhoods within each city. But in US and Canadian society, there is a broad and pervasive division between those of

- What parts of your identity does it feel like you lose when you say aloud the phrase "I'm white?"
- Part of our discomfort may come from our own family's ethnic and class background and its complex relationship to whiteness.
- When they arrived in the United States or Canada, what did members of your family have to do to be accepted as white? What did they have to give up?
- Has that identification or pride ever allowed you or your family to tolerate poverty, economic exploitation or poor living conditions because you could say, "At least we're not colored?"

us who are treated as white people and those of us who are treated as people of color, and most of us learn at a very early age which side we are on.

Several studies have shown that young children between the ages of two and four notice differences of skin color, eye color, hair, dress and speech and the significance that adults give to those differences.[1] This is true even if parents are liberal or progressive. The training is too pervasive within our society for anyone to escape. Anthropology and sociology professor Annie Barnes recounts the following interview with a parent who noticed how early in their lives white children learn racism:

> I experienced it [racism] through my three-year-old daughter. One day at preschool, the students had a "show and tell." All the students had brought their toys to school. My daughter forgot her toys, so I had to go home and get them. My daughter told me specifically what to bring. She wanted her pretty black Barbie doll with the white dress. She loved this doll and thought that it was pretty and often said, "When I grow up, I want to look just like my Barbie."
>
> All the other children were white. While my daughter brought out her Barbie during show and tell, they screwed up their faces and said, "Yuck. That's not Barbie. She's ugly ...." She cried for hours and never carried her doll to school again, I couldn't believe those little children's actions. That was racism by babies, so to speak.[2]

Whiteness is about more than skin color, although that is a major factor. People of color, Muslims, Jews and others are also marked as different by dress, food, the smells of cooking, religious ceremonies, celebratory rituals and mannerisms. These features are all labeled racial differences, even though they may be related to culture, religion, class or country of origin. I'm sure you know whether you are treated as white or as a person of color by most of the people you meet.

• •

- Say "I am white" to yourself a couple of times.
- What are the "buts" that immediately come to mind?
- Do you defend yourself with statements such as "I have friends who are people of color" or "My family didn't own slaves?"

- Do you try to minimize the importance of whiteness ("We're all part of the human race")?

White people are understandably uncomfortable with the label *white*. We feel boxed in and want to escape, just as people of color want to escape from the confines of their racial categories. Being white is an arbitrary category that overrides our individual personalities, devalues us, deprives us of the richness of our other identities, stereotypes us and yet has no scientific basis. However, in our society being white is just as real and governs our day-to-day lives just as much as being a person of color does for African Americans, Latino/as, Asian Americans, Pacific Islanders, Native Americans, Arab Americans and others. To acknowledge this reality is not to create it or to perpetuate it. In fact, it is the first step to uprooting racism.

We may claim that we aren't white because we simply don't (or refuse to) notice race. I sometimes like to think that I don't. But when I'm in an all-white setting and a person of color walks in, I notice. I am slightly surprised to see a person of color, and I look again to confirm who they are and wonder to myself why they're there. I try to do this as naturally and smoothly as possible because I wouldn't want anyone to think that I wasn't tolerant. Actually what I'm surprised at is not that they are there, but that they are there as an equal. All of my opening explanations for their presence will assume they are not equal. "They must be a server or delivery person," I tell myself. It is usually not until another white person introduces me, or gives me an explanation, that my uneasiness is laid to rest. (And even then I may inwardly qualify my acceptance.) I think that most of us notice skin color all the time, but we don't *notice* race unless our sense of the proper racial hierarchy is upset.

Since I've been taught to relate differently to people who are African American, Latino/a, Asian or Arab American, I may need more information than appearance gives me about what kind of person of color I am with. I have some standard questions to fish for more information, such as: "That's an interesting name. I've never heard it before. Where's it from?" "Your accent sounds familiar, but I can't place it." "You don't look American. Where are you from?" And the all-too-common follow-up "No, I mean where are you *really* from?"

Sometimes I ask these questions of white Americans who have unusual names or unfamiliar accents. But I have noticed that most often I use these questions to clarify who is white and who isn't and, secondarily, what kind of person of color I am dealing with.

I was taught that it is not polite to notice racial difference. I also learned that racial difference is an artificial basis used to discriminate against and exploit people of color, and therefore sometimes I overcompensate by pretending to ignore it. Occasionally I hear white people say, "I don't care whether a person is black, brown, orange or green." Human beings don't come in orange or green. Those whose skin color is darker are treated differently in general, and we, in particular, respond differently to them. As part of growing up white and learning racial stereotypes, most of us have been trained to stiffen up and be more cautious, fearful and hesitant around people of color. These are physiological and psychological responses that we can notice in ourselves and see in other white people.[3] These responses belie our verbal assurances that we don't notice racial differences.

There's absolutely nothing wrong with being white or with noticing the differences that color makes. You are not responsible for being white or for being raised in a white-dominated, racist society in which you have been trained to have particular responses to people of color. You are responsible for how you respond to racism (which is what this book is about), and you can only do so consciously and effectively if you begin by realizing that it makes a crucial difference that you are perceived to be and treated as white.

Notes

1. See Kathleen McGinnis and Barbara Oehlberg. *Starting Out Right: Nurturing Young Children as Peacemakers.* Crossroad, 1988 and Louise Derman-Sparks and the A.B.C. Task Force. *Anti-Bias Curriculum: Tools for Empowering Young Children.* National Association for the Education of Young Children, 1989.
2. Annie S. Barnes. *Everyday Racism: A Book for All Americans.* Sourcebooks, 2000, p. 38.
3. For a more detailed discussion about how racism is lived in our bodies see George Yancy. *Black Bodies, White Gazes: The Continuing Significance of Race.* Rowman & Littlefield, 2008.

"I'm Not Racist"

WHETHER IT IS EASY OR DIFFICULT to say that we're white, the phrase we often want to say next is "But I'm not racist." There are lots of ways we have learned to phrase this denial:

I'm not racist.

I don't belong to the Klan.

I have friends who are people of color.

I don't see color, I'm colorblind.

I do anti-racism work.

I went to an unlearning racism workshop.

This book is not about whether you are racist or not, or whether all white people are racist or not. We are not conducting a moral inventory of ourselves, nor creating a moral standard to divide other white people from us. When we say things like "I don't see color," we are trying to maintain a self-image of impartiality and innocence (whiteness). Ultimately, this disclaimer prevents us from taking responsibility for challenging racism because we believe that people who see color are the problem.

The only way to treat all people with dignity and justice is to recognize that racism has a profound negative effect upon all of our lives. Noticing color helps to counteract that effect. Instead of being color neutral, we need to notice much more acutely and insightfully exactly the difference that color makes in the way people are treated.

Just as it's not useful to label ourselves racist, it is not useful to label each other. White people have committed some very brutal acts in the name of whiteness. We may want to separate ourselves from them by claiming that they are racist and we are not. But because racism operates institutionally, to the benefit of all white people, we are connected to the acts of other white people.

Of course you're not a member of the Klan or other extremist groups. Of course you watch what you say and don't make rude racial comments. But dissociating from white people who do is not the answer. You may want to dissociate yourself from their actions, but you still need to challenge their beliefs. You can't challenge them or even speak to them if you have separated yourself from them, creating some magical line with the racists on that side and you over here. This division leads to an ineffective strategy of trying to convert as many people as possible to your (non-racist and therefore superior) side. Other white people will listen to you better, and be more influenced by your actions, when you identify with them. Then you can explore how to work from the inside out together.

Perhaps most importantly, people who are more visibly saying or doing things that are racist are usually more scared, more confused and less powerful — or they are trying to increase their own power by manipulating racial fears. It is amazing how, when we feel scared, confused or powerless, we can do and say the very same things. Since racism leads to scapegoating people of color for social and personal problems, white people are all susceptible to resorting to it in times of trouble. Notice the large number of white people who are blaming immigrants of color for our economic problems. Visible acts of racism are, at least in part, an indication of the lack of power that a white person or group of people have. More powerful and well-off people can simply move to segregated neighborhoods or make corporate decisions that are harder to see and analyze as contributing to racism. Since the racism of the wealthy is less visible to us, those of us who are middle-class can inadvertently scapegoat poor and working-class white people for being overtly racist.

We do need to confront words and actions that are racist when we encounter them because they create an atmosphere of violence in which all of us are unsafe. We also need to understand that most white people are doing the best they can to survive. Overtly racist people are scared and lack the information and skills to be more tolerant. We need to challenge their behavior, not their moral integrity. We also need to be careful that we don't end up carrying out an upper-class agenda by blaming poor and working people for being racist when people with wealth control the media, the textbooks, the housing and job markets and the police. Staying focused on institutions and decision makers challenges societal racism.

What Is Whiteness?

RACISM IS BASED ON THE CONCEPT OF WHITENESS — a powerful fiction enforced by power and violence. Whiteness is a constantly shifting boundary separating those who are entitled to certain benefits from those whose exploitation and vulnerability to violence is justified by their not being white.

Racism itself is a long-standing characteristic of many human societies. For example, justifying exploitation and violence against other peoples because they are *inferior* or different has a long history within Greek, Roman and European Christian traditions. The beginnings of biological racism go back to the Spanish Inquisition. Trying to root out false Muslim and Jewish converts to Christianity but unable to reliably do so, the courts ruled that anyone with a Jewish or Muslim parent or grandparent was not a Christian. Soon, the courts were ruling that any person with any Muslim or Jewish blood was incapable of being a righteous Christian because they did not have clean blood (*limpieza de sangre*).[1]

In more recent historical times in Western Europe, those with English heritage were perceived to be pure white. The Irish, Russians and Spanish were considered darker races, sometimes black and certainly non-white. The white category was slowly extended to include northern and middle European people, but still, less than a century ago, it definitely excluded eastern or southern European peoples such as Italians, Poles, Russians and Greeks. In the last few decades, although there is still prejudice against people from these geographical backgrounds, they have become generally accepted as white in the United States.[2]

The important distinction in the United States has always been binary — first between those who counted as Christians and those who were pagans. As historian Winthrop Jordan has written:

> Protestant Christianity was an important element in English
> patriotism .... Christianity was interwoven into [an Englishman's]
> conception of his own nationality, and he was therefore inclined
> to regard the Negroes' lack of true religion as part of theirs. Being
> a Christian was not merely a matter of subscribing to certain doc-
> trines; it was a quality inherent in oneself and in one's society. It
> was interconnected with all the other attributes of normal and
> proper men.[3]

As Africans and Native Americans began to be converted to Christianity, such a simple distinction was no longer useful, at least as a legal and political difference. In addition, because Europeans, Native Americans and Africans often worked and lived together in similar circumstances of servitude, and resisted and rebelled together against the way they were treated, the land-owning class began to implement policies to separate European workers from African and Native American workers. Even in this early colonial period, racism was used to divide workers and make it easier for those in power to control working conditions. Drawing on already established popular classifications, whiteness, now somewhat separate from Christianity, was delineated more clearly as a legal category in the United States in the 17th century, and the concept of lifelong servitude (slavery) was introduced from the West Indies and distinguished from various forms of shorter-term servitude (indenture). In response to Bacon's Rebellion and other uprisings, the ruling class, espe-cially in the populous and dominant territory of Virginia, began to establish a clear racial hierarchy in the 1660s and 70s.[4] By the 1730s racial divisions were firmly in place legally and socially. Most blacks were enslaved, and even free blacks had lost the right to vote, the right to bear arms and the right to bear witness. Blacks were also barred from participating in many trades during this period.

Meanwhile, whites had gained the right to corn, money, a gun, cloth-ing and 50 acres of land at the end of indentureship; they could no longer be beaten naked and had the poll tax reduced. In other words, poor whites "gained legal, political, emotional, social, and financial status that was directly related to the concomitant degradation of Indians and Negroes."[5] Typically, although poor whites gained some benefits vis-à-vis blacks and Indians, because of the increased productivity from slavery, the gap between wealthy whites and those who were poor widened considerably.

Although racism was legally, socially and economically long established in US society, it was only defined "scientifically" as a biological/genetic characteristic about 150 years ago with the publication of Darwin's theory of species modification. People combined Darwin's ideas with systems of human classification developed by Linnaeus, Blumenbach and others into a pseudo-scientific theory, eventually called Social Darwinism, which attempted to classify the human population into distinct categories or races and put them on an evolutionary scale with whites on top.

The original classifications consisted of 3, 5, up to as many as 63 categories, but a standard became one based on Caucasoid, Negroid and Mongoloid races. These were not based on genetic differences, but on differences that Europeans and European Americans perceived to be important. They were in fact based on stereotypes of cultural differences and (mis)measures of physiological characteristics such as brain size.[6]

From the beginning, the attempt to classify people by race was fraught with contradictions. Latin Americans, Native Americans and Jewish people did not fit easily into these categories so the categories were variously stretched, redefined or adapted to meet the agenda of the people in Europe and the US who were promoting them.

For example, in the 19th century Finns were doing most of the lowest-paid, unsafe mining and lumbering work in the upper Midwestern US. Although logically, having light skin, they were white, in terms of political, cultural and economic "common sense" they were considered black because they were the poorest and least respected group in the area besides Native Americans. The courts consistently ruled that they were not white, despite their skin color, because of their cultural and economic standing.[7] In another case, the courts ruled that a Syrian was not white, even though he looked white and had the same skin color as Caucasians, because "common sense" dictated that a Syrian was not white.

On the West Coast during the constitutional debates in California in 1848–49, there was discussion about the status of Mexicans and Chinese. There were still Mexicans who were wealthy landowners and business partners with whites, while the Chinese were almost exclusively heavily exploited railroad and agricultural workers. It was eventually decided that Mexicans would be considered white and Chinese would be considered the same as blacks and Indians. This decision established which group could become citizens, own land, marry whites and have other basic rights.[8]

There was a complex and dynamic interplay between the popular conception of race and the scientific categories, neither of which was grounded in physiological or biological reality, but both of which carried great emotional import to white people and devastating consequences to people of color, regardless of how they were being defined.

Although a few scientists still try to prove the existence of races, most scientists have long ago abandoned the use of race as a valid category to distinguish between humans. There is such tremendous genetic difference between these arbitrary groupings and such huge overlap between them that no particular racial groupings or distinctions based on skin color or other physical characteristics are useful or justified.[9] The Human Genome Project has found that all humans share 99.9% of the same genes and has confirmed there are no human "races." Of the .1% of the human genome that varies from person to person, only 3 to 10% is associated with geographic ancestry or "race" as classically defined.[10]

Yet despite the conclusions of the Human Genome Project, some are reasserting that there are important racial differences. These assertions are driven by political and economic motivations, not scientific research. For example, the first racially marketed drug, BiDil, was about to lose its patent protection as a drug for the treatment of heart disease. Even though the drug had failed to perform better than other products in tests and works with patients of all ethnic backgrounds, the company claimed that the drug was effective for African Americans and was able to extend its lucrative patent monopoly on the basis of the claim. It is now marketed extensively on that basis, which reinforces the common misperception that there are significant biological differences based on race.[11]

Genomic research has demonstrated that people have what has been labeled "ancestry groups." These are the genetic markers indicating geographic root areas or origin areas. Most individuals have mixed ancestry groups, and certainly, "knowing a person's geographical origin[s] does not give us enough information to predict his or her genotype" because the majority of genomic variation occurs within, not across, ancestry groups.[12] For example, a person perceived as, or self-identified as, African American in the United States would have anywhere between 1 and 90% ancestry in either Europe or Africa.[13]

There is likewise no scientific (i.e., biological or genetic) basis to the concept of whiteness. There is nothing scientifically distinctive about it except skin color, and that is highly variable. All common wisdom notwithstanding, the skin color of a person tells you nothing about that person's culture, country of origin, character or personal habits. Because there is nothing biological about whiteness, it ends up being defined in contrast to other labels, becoming confused with ideas of nationality, religion and ethnicity.

For example, Jews are not a racial group. People who are Jewish share some cultural and religious beliefs and practices but come from every continent and many different cultural backgrounds. Jews range in skin color from white to dark brown. Because race was falsely assumed to be a scientific category, being Jewish has often been falsely assumed to mean that a Jew is genetically different from non-Jewish people.[14]

I grew up learning that racial categories were scientifically valid and gave us useful information about ourselves and other people. In other words, racism had a scientific stamp of approval. It is difficult for me to let go of the certainty I thought I had gained about what racial difference meant. And, of course, there are always new attempts to prove to us that race means something.[15]

• •

- What residual doubts do you have that there may be something genetic or biological about racial differences? ("But, what about ...?")
- How can you respond to people who say that there are specific differences between races?

• •

I began to understand the artificial nature of racial categories more clearly when I examined how moral qualities were attached to racial differences. This confirmed my suspicion that there was a political, not a scientific agenda at work in these distinctions.

These moral qualities have, in turn, been used to justify various forms of exploitation.

From the old phrases referring to a good deed — "That's white of you" or "That's the Christian thing to do" to the new-age practice of visualizing oneself surrounded by white light — white has signified honor, purity, cleanliness and godliness in white western European, mainstream US and Canadian culture. Because concepts of whiteness and race were developed in Christian Europe, references to whiteness are imbued with Christian values. We have ended up with a set of opposing qualities or attributes that are said to define people either as white or as not white.

Qualities not associated with whiteness have been given negative meanings. They have become associated not only with people of color, but also with children, workers, lesbians, gays, bisexuals, Jews and heterosexual white women — just those groups excluded from the political and scientific institutions that define what normal should be.

Not all white people had an equal voice in defining racial differences. Those with most power — who had the most to gain or preserve — set the terms. White landowners, church leaders — the educated and successful — systematically defined whiteness in ways that extolled and legitimized their own actions and sanctioned the actions of others.

Dark and White Qualities	
Dark	**White**
pagan	Christian
godless	god-fearing, wholesome
animal-like	god-like
primitive, wild, uncivilized	civilized
less than human	human
superstitious	scientific
subjective	objective, detached, neutral
immoral	moral
sinful	innocent
soulless, damned	saved
abnormal	normal
emotional, angry	calm
rude	polite
crude, brutish	refined
impulsive, irrational	thoughtful, rational
present time oriented	future oriented
low class	middle-class
manipulative	sincere
undignified	respectable
devious	straightforward
malicious	loving
prone to dishonesty	well-intentioned, honest
dirty, contaminated	clean, pure
sexual, promiscuous	chaste, committed
intellectually inferior	intelligent
weak link	strong specimen
traditional	modern
un-American, traitor	American, patriot
needing permission	authorized
colorful	bland
impatient	patient
self-righteous	righteous
rhythmic	stiff

- Which words in each pair do you associate with white people?
- Which words on the left do you use to discount people of color's demands for fair and equal treatment ("they are too ... "), or to blame them for how they are treated in our society ("They would be successful if they weren't so ... ")?

It is difficult for any of us to dissociate positive qualities from white people and negative ones from people of color, no matter how colorblind we would like to be because the emotional resonances of these dichotomies are passed on to us by parents, schools and the media. As sociologists Picca and Feagin observe, "when given a test of unconscious stereotyping, nearly 90 percent of whites quickly and implicitly associate black faces with negative words and traits (for example, evil character or failure). They have more difficulty linking black faces to pleasant words and positive traits than they do white faces."[16]

White people who have challenged racism and the false dichotomies upon which it is based have been labeled to show that they don't really belong to the white group. Labels such as "nigger lover," "race traitor," "un-American," "feminist," "liberal," "Communist," "unchristian," "Jew," "fag," "lesbian," "crazy," "illegal alien," "terrorist" and "thought police" have all been used to isolate and discredit people, to imply that they are somehow outside the territory of whiteness and therefore justifiably attacked. We can see from the moral virtues attached to whiteness that only those who are white are able to speak with authority. A powerful way to discredit any critique of whiteness or racism is to discredit the speaker by showing that they are not really white. This is a neat, circular convention that stifles any serious discussion of what whiteness means and what effect it has on people.

This leaves most of us who are white on pretty shaky ground. If we bring attention to whiteness and racism, we risk being labeled not really white or a "traitor to our race." These accusations discredit our testimony and potentially lose us some of the benefits of being white such as better jobs and police protection from violence. Behind the names lies the threat of physical and sexual violence such as ostracism, firing, silencing, condemnation to hell, institutionalization, incarceration, deportation, rape, lynching and other forms of mob violence that have been used to protect white power and privilege.

We could usefully spend some time exploring the history and meaning of any particular pair of words on the list above. I encourage you to do so. Each one reveals some vital aspect of whiteness and racism. Here I want to point out three concepts that many of these words cluster around: Christian, American and male.

One cluster of concepts and practices of whiteness grows out of dominant Western Christianity. Whiteness has often been equated with being a *Christian* in opposition to being a pagan, infidel, witch, heathen, Jew, Muslim, Native American, Buddhist or atheist. Racial violence has been justified by a stated need to protect Christian families and homes. Pogroms, crusades, holy wars and colonial conquests have been justified by the need to save the souls of uncivilized and godless peoples (often at the cost of their lives).

Jewish people have lived within Christian-dominated societies (when permitted to) for nearly 1,700 years since Christianity became the official religion of the Roman Empire. There is substantial history of Christian teaching and belief that Jewish people are dangerous and evil. These beliefs have been sustained even during periods of hundreds of years when Jews were not living near Christians.[17] Jews, along with Muslims, have become symbols to many Christians of the infidel. This anti-Jewish oppression, originally based on religious and cultural differences, has become racialized as Christian values were combined with racial exploitation and an ideology of white superiority. It has exposed Jews to the same harsh reality of violence that pagans, Roma,[18] witches and Muslims have experienced.

In addition, anti-Jewish and anti-Muslim hatred has been passed on to Christians of color. Religious leaders of both Eastern Orthodox and Catholic branches of Christianity, as well as most Protestant denominations, have accused the Jews of killing Jesus, using the blood of Christian children for Passover ritual, refusing to recognize the divinity of Jesus and consorting with the devil. Muslims were accused of colonizing the Holy Land, attacking Europe and being mortal foes of Christendom. As Christianity was spread by Western colonialism and missionary practice, these teachings were incorporated into the beliefs of many Christians of color.

At the same time, there are core Christian values of love, caring, justice and fellowship that have inspired some Christians to work against racism. For example, many white abolitionists were Christians inspired by religious teachings and values.

Yet another cluster of meanings centers on the concept of *American*.[19] In the United States the idea of who is an American is often conflated with who is white. In fact, *all-American* is often used as a thinly disguised code word for *white*. A third-generation Swedish or German American child is considered an all-American kid in a way that a third-generation Japanese or Chinese American child is not.

In the same way, the patriotism of anyone with darker skin color is routinely questioned. During World War II, US citizens of Japanese heritage were interned in concentration camps and US citizens of Italian or German heritage were not.[20] Even when they fought in the armed services in wartime, the loyalty of Asian American, Latino/a, Native American, Arab American and African American soldiers was challenged.

As the definition of who was white was broadened over time to include virtually all people of European descent, the boundaries keeping people of color out were firmly maintained. Immigration policies and quotas consistently favored Europeans and much of the time completely excluded people who were not considered white. Today, even when they have legally arrived here, non-Native American people of color are routinely asked where they came from and told to go back home. For example, even though many Spanish-speaking citizens have roots in the Southeast, Southwest and California going back more than three centuries, native-born Latino/as in these areas are often stopped by police and immigration officials and asked to show proof of citizenship. The passage of an Arizona law in April, 2010 that mandates police to stop anyone who looks like they could be in the country illegally — in other words racial profiling anyone who looks Latino/a — is just the most recent manifestation of racist targeting of the entire Latino/a community.[21] The reluctance of many white people to fully accept people of color as patriotic Americans has meant that many feel forever foreign and wonder what it would take for them to be accepted as "all-American."

Finally, whiteness strongly leans toward male virtues and male values. While terms of whiteness apply to men and women, there are also significant differences in which qualities are associated with each.

White women are held to higher standards of chasteness, cleanliness and restraint than white men. The basis of their rationality, righteousness and authority is supposed to lie with the white men they are related to. For example, white women are presumed to carry white authority over women and men of color. White women hold onto whiteness by the authority and protection of white men or by their willingness to adapt to male roles and exert authority in traditionally male spheres to protect their white privilege as employers, supervisors or teachers. They can also be cast out of the circle of white male protection by being rebellious or by violating racial or gender norms. White women have both colluded with and resisted their role and the violence it has justified.[22]

In most discussions of masculinity, we underestimate the role that racism plays. Training in white male violence against people of color starts early. White male bonding at work, at school or in the extended family includes significant levels of racism toward men of color ranging from sitting around joking about men of color (or lesbians or gays of all colors), to bonding as a team against an opposing team of color, to participating in an attack upon a specific person of color, to joining an explicit white supremacist group. Not participating in such "rites of passage" makes white men vulnerable to physical and sexual aggression from their white peers.

White men also bond with others and "prove" their heterosexuality by verbally and sexually assaulting women of color, Muslim and Jewish women. The ability to have sex with, but not to be undermined or entrapped by, exotic and dangerous women is a sign of sexual prowess and reaffirms that a man is in control, is one of the (white Christian) boys and that he knows the sexual and racial order.

When a young man is pushed by white male peers to assault or harass women or men of color, a lot is riding on the line — and he knows it. It is hard for most young men to avoid responding to such pressure because the threat of violence from other white men is real and immediate. We can help young men refuse to participate in white male violence by giving them tools for resisting white male socialization and that would make the entire community safer.[23]

Racism is a many-faceted phenomenon, slowly and constantly shifting its structures, dynamics and justifications. But at its core, it is a system that maintains a racial hierarchy and protects white power and wealth. It is a powerful construct with wide-ranging effects on our lives and on the lives of people of color. It is our challenge to let go of the construct and work to end such a destructive system.

Notes

1. James Carroll. *Constantine's Sword: The Church and the Jews.* Houghton Mifflin, 2001, pp. 374-375.
2. In some northern and western European countries, there are still strong and abusive patterns of racism against southern and eastern Europeans.
3. Quoted in Ronald Takaki. *Strangers From a Different Shore: A History of Asian Americans.* Penguin, 1989, p. 47.

4. This separation of white from Christian occurred officially in Virginia in 1667 when legislators passed a law which stipulated that "The conferring of baptisme doth not alter the condition of the person as to his bondage or freedom." Quoted in Bill Bigelow and Bob Peterson, eds. *Rethinking Columbus: The Next 500 Years.* Rethinking Schools, 1998, p. 26.
5. Thandeka. *Learning to be White.* Continuum, 1999, p. 43.
6. Stephen J. Gould. *The Mismeasure of Man.* Norton, 1981.
7. Ian F. H. Lopez. *White by Law: The Legal Construction of Race.* New York University, 1999.
8. Tomas Almaguer. *Racial Fault Lines: The Historical Origins of White Supremacy in California.* University of California, 1994, pp. 9–10, 54.
9. Sandra Harding, ed. "Science Constructs Race," section 2 of *The "Racial" Economy of Science: Toward a Democratic Future.* Indiana University, 1993.
10. Barbara A. Koenig. "Which Differences Make a Difference?: Race, DNA, and Health" in Hazel Rose Markus and Paula M.L. Moya, eds. *Doing Race: 21 Essays for the 21st Century.* Norton, 2010, p. 165.
11. There are no medical conditions or vulnerabilities that are exclusive to one "race" although there are medical conditions that people within specific genetic subgroupings are more likely to experience.
12. Marcus W. Feldman. "The Biology of Ancestry" in Markus and Moya, p. 151.
13. Ibid., p. 144.
14. See Sholomo Sands. *The Invention of the Jewish People.* Verso, 2009, particularly pp. 256-280, for an historical account of the creation of the story that Jews are a racial or biological grouping.
15. See Steven Fraser, ed. *The Bell Curve Wars: Race, Intelligence and the Future of America.* Basic, 1995; R. Lewontin et al. *Not in Our Genes: Biology, Ideology and Human Nature.* Pantheon, 1984; Stephen J. Gould, *Ever Since Darwin: Reflections in Natural History.* Norton, 1977 and *The Mismeasure of Man.*
16. Leslie Picca and Joe Feagin. *Two-Faced Racism: Whites in the Backstage and Frontstage.* Routledge, 2007, p. 12.
17. Bernard Glassman. *Anti-Semitic Stereotypes Without Jews: Images of the Jews in England 1290–1700.* Wayne State University, 1975.
18. *Roma* is the name of those European peoples commonly referred to as gypsies, a racially derogatory term.
19. Throughout the book I will not use *American* except in this context because the word refers to people from anywhere in the Americas but has been racially appropriated by white people in the US.
20. There was anti-German and anti-Italian sentiment during the war and some people from both groups were harassed, discriminated against or attacked.
21. See the chapter "Recent Immigrants" in Part IV for more discussion of this and similar anti-immigrant legislation.
22. See the chapter "Exotic and Erotic," especially pages 91-92. 62 near eradication.
23. See Creighton and Kivel, *Helping Teens Stop Violence;* Allan Creighton and Paul Kivel. *Young Men's Work: Stopping Violence & Building Community.* Hazelden, 1998; Paul Kivel. *Boys Will Be Men: Raising Our Sons for Courage, Caring, and Community.* New Society, 1999.

Words and Pictures

SINCE WHITENESS HAS BEEN A DEFINING PART OF OUR CULTURE for hundreds of years, we have embedded the ideas that white people are good and people of color are bad and dangerous into our everyday language. Most phrases containing *black* have negative meanings, while those containing *white* have positive meanings. Looking more deeply at our words and their current meanings, we can find hundreds that imply people of color and people of different cultures and ethnicities are dangerous, threatening, manipulative, dishonest or immoral. In fact, anything foreign or alien has connotations of being not white, not pure, not American and not Christian. We reinforce racism every time we use such language.

My goal in the following exercise is not to enforce some kind of political correctness. We are trying to understand how racism becomes embedded in our culture, our language, the way we see the world. And we are trying to develop ways of talking with each other that are respectful and counter historical patterns of exploitation and domination.

We also need to challenge racially demeaning usage in visual images. Advertisements, movies and TV images develop images of darkness to convey danger and to provoke white fear. Disney movies provide many examples of color-coding in popular culture. Throughout *The Lion King*, lightness is associated with good, darkness with evil. Everything from the coloring of the manes of the lions, the color of different animals to the sunshine in the lions' kingdom versus the murky land of the hyenas reflects the racial and moral hierarchy of the film. This is reinforced by the language of the characters: the lions talk in middle-class "white" English and the hyenas in a more colloquial street dialect. *Aladdin* is also racially coded: Jafar, Kazim and the bazaar merchants each have exaggerated stereotypical "Arab" features and speak in heavy accents while Aladdin, Jasmine and the Sultan have "European" features and no trace of an accent.[1] These racial, color-coded values can be found consistently in Disney movies going back to *Sleeping Beauty* and *Dumbo* (remember the crows).

Pictures, movies and video games also convey images of the ideal white body against which everyone in our society is judged. The white male body, whether upper-class or working-class, is *handsome* — fit, tall, with hair, blue eyes, fair skin and strong features. It speaks with authority, dominates others

---

Each of the following words and phrases contains a derogatory racial meaning in its definition or derivation or puts a positive spin on whiteness, white people or white culture. Can you list alternative, racially neutral words you could use in their place?

Racially Charged Words	
blacklist_____	gypsy blood_____
blackmail _____	macho _____
black market_____	manana _____
black sheep_____	tribal warfare_____
white lie _____	natives _____
white knight_____	peace pipe_____
black magic_____	feather in your cap _____
Dark Ages _____	on the warpath _____
to gyp (from gypsy) _____	banana republic _____
yellow peril_____	china doll_____
red menace_____	Chinese fire drill _____
to scalp _____	far east, near east, _____
to Jew down _____	middle east _____
war paint (referring _____	dark continent_____
to women's makeup)_____	third world_____
Indian giver_____	red-blooded _____
whitewash _____	wandering Jew _____
pure/white as snow _____	grandfather clause _____
that's white of you _____	call in the cavalry_____
the dark side_____	Byzantine_____
to be in the dark_____	blue blood _____
to be dim-witted_____	assassin _____
wampum _____	_____

What other words or phrases can you think of that are racially derogatory?

- What films have you seen where the use of images of white and black, light and dark, or the racial casting of the heroes and villains was used to reinforce white = good and dark = bad?

and is muscular/athletic and competitive. It stands or sits in postures of strength that command respect and attention. It is a body that is under control and controls others. It is also a body that can be roused to anger and violence to protect the innocent (usually white women) and pursue the guilty.

The ideal white female body is portrayed as the standard of beauty. Blond, blue-eyed, thin, sexually inviting and even fairer than her male counterpart, this female body is portrayed in postures and roles that convey submission, availability and seductiveness.

Whiteness represents pure, Christian goodness. White people are almost always central characters, hero or heroine, consistently juxtaposed to images of darker-skinned men and women representing, dirt, animality, danger and moral corruption.[2] The marketing of the normalness, naturalness and essential goodness of idealized whiteness prompts millions of women and men, both white and people of color, to spend endless amounts of time and money bleaching, dyeing or straightening their hair, lightening their skin color, losing weight, using cosmetics or having cosmetic surgery.

If we pay attention to the images around us, we will notice the pervasive influence that racism has on our everyday lives. Racial difference and racial hierarchy, like gender hierarchy, are built into our language, our visual imagery and our sense of who we are.

Notes

1. John Tehranian. *White Washed: America's Invisible Middle Eastern Minority.* New York University, 2009, p. 75.
2. For an extended discussion of how white people are generally portrayed in movies as moral heroes with beautiful bodies while people of color are portrayed as either dangerous, immoral or marginalized see Hernan Vera and Andrew M. Gordon. *Screen Saviors: Hollywood Fictions of Whiteness.* Rowman & Littlefield, 2003.

White Benefits, Middle-class Privilege

IT IS NOT NECESSARILY A PRIVILEGE TO BE WHITE, but it certainly has its benefits. That's why so many of our families gave up their unique histories, primary languages, accents, distinctive dress, family names and cultural expressions. It seemed like a small price to pay for acceptance in the circle of whiteness. Even with these sacrifices, it wasn't easy to pass as white if we were Italian, Greek, Irish, Jewish, Spanish, Hungarian or Polish. Sometimes it took generations before our families were fully accepted, and then it was usually because white society had an even greater fear of darker-skinned people.

Privileges are the economic extras that those of us who are middle-class and wealthy gain at the expense of poor and working-class people of all races. *Benefits*, on the other hand, are the advantages that all white people gain at the expense of people of color regardless of economic position.[1] Talk about racial benefits can ring false to many of us who don't have the economic privileges that we see others in this society enjoying. But though we don't have substantial economic privileges, we do enjoy many of the benefits of being white.

We can generally count on police protection rather than harassment. Depending on our financial situation, we can choose where we want to live and choose safer neighborhoods with better schools. We are given more attention, respect and status in conversations than people of color. Nothing that we do is qualified, limited, discredited or acclaimed simply because of our racial background. We don't have to represent our race, and nothing we do is judged as a credit to our race or as confirmation of its shortcomings or inferiority.

These benefits start early. Others will have higher expectations for us as children, both at home and at school. We will have more money spent on our education, we will be called on more in school and given more opportunity and resources to learn. We will see people like us in textbooks. If we get into trouble, adults will expect us to be able to change and improve and therefore will discipline or penalize us less harshly than children of color.

These benefits accrue and work to the direct economic advantage of every white person in the United States. First of all, we will earn more in our lifetime than a person of color of similar qualifications. We will be paid $1.00 for every $.60 that a person of color makes.[2] We will advance faster and more reliably and, on average, accumulate eight times as much wealth. A white family will, on average accumulate $170,000 in assets, a black family $17,000, and a Latino/a family $21,000.[3] The gap for single women-headed households is even more stark — in 2007 a white female-headed household had on average $41,000 in assets, a black female-headed household $100, and a Latina-headed household $120.[4]

There are historically derived economic benefits too. All the land in the US was taken from Native Americans. Much of the infrastructure of this country was built by slave labor, incredibly low-paid labor or by prison labor performed by men and women of color. Much of the housecleaning, childcare, cooking and maintenance of our society has been done by low-wage-earning women of color. Today men and women and children of color still do the hardest, lowest-paid, most dangerous work throughout the US. And white people enjoy plentiful and inexpensive food, clothing and consumer goods because of that exploitation.

We have been taught history through a white-tinted lens that has minimized our exploitation of people of color and extolled the hardworking, courageous qualities of white people. For example, many of our foreparents gained a foothold in the US by finding work in such trades as railroads, streetcars, construction, shipbuilding, wagon and coach driving, house painting, tailoring, longshore work, bricklaying, table waiting, working in the mills or dressmaking. These were all occupations that blacks, who had begun entering many such skilled and unskilled jobs, were either excluded from or pushed out of in the 19th century. Exclusion and discrimination, coupled with immigrant mob violence against blacks in many northern cities (such as the anti-black draft riots of 1863), meant that recent immigrants had economic opportunities that blacks did not. These gains were consolidated by explicitly racist trade union practices and policies that kept blacks in the most unskilled labor and lowest-paid work.[5]

It is not that white Americans have not worked hard and built much. We have. But we did not start out from scratch. We went to segregated schools and universities built with public money. We received school loans, Veterans Administration (VA) loans, housing and auto loans unavailable to people of color. We received federal jobs, apprenticeships and training when only whites were allowed.

Much of the rhetoric against more active policies for racial justice stem from the misconception that all people are given equal opportunities and start from a level playing field. We often don't even see the benefits we have received from racism. We claim that they are not there.

Notes

1. See the important work on privilege done by Peggy McIntosh. *White Privilege and Male Privilege: A Personal Account of Coming to See Correspondences Through Work in Women's Studies.* Wellesley College, Center for Research on Women, 1988 as well as material from Allan Creighton with Paul Kivel. *Helping Teens Stop Violence*, rev. ed. Hunter House, 2011; and George Lipsitz. *The Possessive Investment in* Whiteness: How White People Profit from Identity Politics. Temple University, 1998.

2. In 2007 black families earned 59 cents, Latino families earned 62 cents, and American Indian/ Alaska Native families made 59 cents for every dollar in income earned by a white family. For women-headed households the gaps were even larger. Nationally, Asian American income was $1.10 but was highly variably based on geography and ethnicity. *Check the Color Line: 2009 Income Report.* Applied Research Center, 2009. [online]. [cited February 8, 2011]. colorlines. com/pdf/2009_Check ColorLineIncome.pdf.

3. Insight Center for Community Economic Development. *Laying the Foundation for National Prosperity: The Imperative of Closing the Racial Wealth Gap.* March, 2009. [online]. [cited February 8, 2011]. insightcced.org/uploads/CRWG/ LayingTheFoundationForNationalProsperity-MeizhuLui0309.pdf.

4. Insight Center for Community Economic Development. *Lifting As We Climb: Women of Color, Wealth, and America's Future.* Spring, 2010. [online]. [cited February 8, 2011]. insightcced.org/ uploads/CRWG/LiftingAsWeClimb-WomenWealth-Report- InsightCenter-Spring2010.pdf.

5. For an extended history of the relationship between the white working class and workers of color, see David R. Roediger. *The Wages of Whiteness: Race and the Making of the American Working Class.* Verso, 1991.

White Benefits? A Personal Assessment

WHEN I BEGAN TO TAKE CAREFUL STOCK of my family's history, I began to see the numerous ways that my father and I, and indirectly the women in my family, have benefited from policies that either favored white men, or explicitly excluded people of color and white women from consideration altogether. Of course, the fact that my foreparents were considered white enough to immigrate to the United States during a period that most people of color could not was a monumental white benefit and provided the foundation for all the future ones.

My father had an overseas desk job in the military during World War II. When he returned he was greeted by many government programs specifically designed to reintegrate him into society and help him overcome the disadvantage of having given his time to defend the country.

The benefits from these programs were primarily available to white men. As one study explained, "Available data illustrate clearly that throughout the post-WWII era the benefits provided by each and every component of the MWS [militarized welfare state] disproportionately accrued to whites. Jim Crow and related overt exclusionary policies ensured that African Americans' proportion of WWII veterans [benefits] was significantly less than their portion of the total population. In the Korean War veterans population, they were nearly as underrepresented."[1]

During most of World War II, the armed services had been strictly segregated. After the war, many people of color were denied veterans' benefits because they had served in jobs that were not considered eligible for such benefits. Many more were deliberately not informed about the benefits, were discouraged from applying when they inquired about them or simply had their applications for benefits denied. The report cited above concluded, "Thus, not only were far fewer blacks than whites able to participate in these programs, but those blacks who could participate received fewer benefits than their white counterparts."[2]

My father was able to continue his education on the GI Bill (attending the nearly all-white and largely male University of Southern California). He was not unique; 2.2 million men received higher education benefits from the GI Bill. In fact, by 1947, half of all college students were veterans.[3]

My father applied for a training program to become a stockbroker — just one of many lucrative professions reserved for white men. When my father completed his training and joined the firm, he was on the road to economic success with all the resources of a national financial corporation behind him. Besides the immediate income from his wages and commissions as a stock-broker, there were other financial benefits he had privileged access to. The company had a generous pension plan. That had a significant effect later on in our family's life, but at the time it meant that my parents could save money for a car and for their children's college education because they knew their retirement was secure.

My father was also able to contribute to Social Security, which had been set up primarily to benefit white male workers during the Depression. My father (and mother and, indirectly, their children) benefited from the program when he retired. Although many people with jobs were eligible to contribute to Social Security, millions more were not. US President Franklin Roosevelt knew he could not pass the Social Security bill without the votes of southern agricultural and western mining interests that controlled key Congressional committees. These interests were unwilling to support the bill if people of color, particularly agricultural workers, were included.[4] Their compromise was to create a system in which the benefits were specifically set up to exclude large numbers of people of color (and, incidentally, white women) by exclud-ing job categories such as agricultural and domestic work. Many hundreds of thousands more people of color were in job occupations that qualified for Social Security, but earned too little to be able to participate.[5]

My father had secured a good job and was eligible for a housing loan because of affirmative action. Of course, he still had to find a house that could be both a shelter for his family and an investment. Like most white people of the period, he wanted to live in a white suburban neighborhood with good schools, no crime and rising property values. Many people, however, were excluded from buying houses in precisely those areas because they were not white males.

For example, the FHA specifically channeled loans away from the central city and to the suburbs, and its official handbook even provided a model restrictive covenant (an agreement not to sell to people of color or, sometimes, Jews) to prospective white homebuyers and realtors.[6] The FHA and the VA financed more than $120 billion worth of new housing between 1934 and 1962, but less than 2% of this real estate was available to non-white families.[7]

In addition, the federal home-mortgage interest tax deduction meant that the government subsidized my father's purchase of a house at the direct expense of people who did not have affirmative action programs or other means to help them buy a house and therefore were renters. This provided my father additional tens of thousands of dollars of support from the government over his adult lifetime. Researchers estimate that these affirmative action housing programs for white men have cost the current generation of African Americans alone approximately $82 billion.[8]

The results of all of this affirmative action provided my family with more than just financial benefits. For me, specifically, I was able to go to a public school with many advantages. These included heavy investments in science programs, sports programs, college preparatory classes and leadership programs. There were no students or teachers of color at my school, so these advantages were only for white people. And most of these programs were designed for the boys; girls were discouraged from participating or straightforwardly refused the opportunity.

Meanwhile the government was subsidizing suburban development, and my family enjoyed parks, sports facilities, new roads — an entire infrastructure that was mostly directed to the benefit of white men and their families, even though the entire population paid taxes to support it.

Of course my mother and my sister enjoyed substantial benefits as long as they stayed attached to my father. They did not receive these benefits on their own behalf or because they were felt to deserve them. They received them because they supported and were dependent on a white man. Even though my father was verbally and emotionally abusive towards my mother, she did not contemplate leaving him, partly because she did not have the independent financial means to do so nor did she have access to the kinds of affirmative action that he did.

Growing up as the son of a white male who had access to so much, I viewed these benefits as natural and inevitable. I came to believe that because

I lived in a democracy where equal opportunity was the law of the land, white men must be successful because they were superior to all others. They must be smarter and work harder; my father must be a much superior person. No one ever qualified his success to me by describing all the advantages he had been given or labeled him an affirmative action baby.

My father made good, sound decisions in his life. He worked hard enough and was smart enough to take advantage of the social support, encouragement and direct financial benefits that were available to him. Many white women, and men and women of color, were just as smart and worked just as hard and ended up with far, far less than my father.

As a result of all of these white benefits, my father retired as a fairly wealthy and successful man at the age of 50. By that time, I was already enjoying my own round of affirmative action programs.

My parents could afford private college tuition, but just in case they could not, my father's company offered scholarships for white males, the sons of employees. There was a more specific affirmative action program offered at many of these schools — legacy admissions. Children of alumni were given special preferences. I was told that if I wanted to go to my father's alma mater, USC, I had an excellent chance of getting in regardless of my qualifications because my father had gone there.[9]

I attended Reed College in the mid 1960s, a school that had no faculty of color, only one white woman faculty member and barely a handful of students of color until my senior year. During my college years, I was strongly encouraged in my studies and urged to go on to graduate school, which I could see was even more clearly a white male preserve.

By the late 1960s the United States was fully engaged in the Vietnam War. The US government reinstated the draft and developed yet another affirmative action program for white males — especially white males from affluent families — the college draft deferment. Proportionately few students of color were attending college in those years, and large numbers of white males were. This deferment naturally resulted in fewer young men being eligible for the draft, so the armed forces lowered its standards in order to recruit more men of color who had previously been rejected. The results of these policies were that, in 1964, 18.8% of eligible whites were drafted, compared to 30.2% of eligible blacks. By 1967, when there was larger-scale recruitment, still only 31% of eligible whites were inducted into the military compared to 67% of eligible blacks. I was able to avoid the draft entirely because of affirmative action for white men and what Michael Eric Dyson has called the affirmative retroaction policies of the military, which targeted men of color for recruitment.[10]

If I had wanted to serve in the armed forces, I could have used my education to get a non-combat job, or I could have applied to West Point or Annapolis and been assured that, as a white man, I wouldn't have to compete with women or with most men of color for a position as an officer.

When I graduated from college, I was presented with a wide variety of affirmative action options. In fact, corporate recruiters were constantly at my predominantly white college offering us job opportunities. Many of my working-class friends had to take any job they could get to support themselves or their parents or younger siblings. Since I had no one else to support, I could pursue the career or profession of my choice.

When I eventually became involved in a long-term relationship and my partner and I wanted to buy a house, we were given preferred treatment by banks when we applied for loans in the form of less paperwork, less extensive credit checks and the benefit of the doubt about our financial capacity to maintain a house. Our real estate agent let us know that we were preferred neighbors in desirable communities and steered us away from less desirable areas (neighborhoods with higher concentrations of people of color). In addition, because of my parents' secure financial position, they could loan us money for a down payment and cosign our loan with us.[11]

Most of the government programs and institutional policies described above were not called affirmative action programs. Programs that benefit white men never are. They are seen as race and gender neutral, even though most or all of the benefits accrue to white men. These programs were not contested as special preferences nor were the beneficiaries stigmatized as not deserving or not qualified.

Your parents probably did not own slaves. Mine did not even arrive in the US until after slavery. Nor were my parents mean bosses, exploiting workers in factories or otherwise discriminating against people of color. Nevertheless, they and I benefited directly and specifically from public and private policies — various forms of white male affirmative action at the expense of people of color. And these benefits continue to accrue to me and my family.

The purpose of this checklist is not to discount what we, our families and foreparents have achieved. But we do need to question any assumptions we retain that everyone started out with equal opportunity.

Think about your grandparents and parents and where they grew up and lived as adults. What work did they do? What are some of the benefits that have accrued to your family through your foreparents and to you directly because of racism?

Look at the following checklist.[12] Put a check beside any benefit that you enjoy that a person of color of your age, gender and class probably does not. Think about what effect not having that benefit would have had on your life. (If you don't know the answer to any of these questions, do research. Ask family members. Do what you can to discover the answers.)

White Benefits Checklist
❑ My ancestors were legal immigrants to this country during a period when immigrants from Asia, South and Central America or Africa were restricted.
❑ My ancestors came to this country of their own free will and have never had to relocate unwillingly once here.
❑ I live on land that formerly belonged to Native Americans.
❑ My family received homesteading or landstaking claims from the federal government.
❑ I or my family or relatives receive or received federal farm subsidies, farm price supports, agricultural extension assistance or other federal benefits.
❑ I lived or live in a neighborhood that people of color were discouraged or discriminated from living in.
❑ I lived or live in a city where red-lining prevents people of color getting housing or other loans.
❑ My parents or I went to racially segregated schools.
❑ I live in a school district or metropolitan area where more money is spent on the schools that white children go to than on those that children of color attend.
❑ I live in or went to a school district where children of color are more likely to be disciplined than white children, or are more likely to be tracked into non-academic programs.
❑ I live in or went to a school district where the textbooks and other classroom materials reflected my race as normal and as heroes and builders of the United States, and where there was little mention of the contributions of people of color.
❑ I was encouraged to go on to college by teachers, parents or other advisors.
❑ I attended a publicly funded university or a heavily endowed private university or college, and/or I received student loans.
❑ I served in the military when it was still racially segregated, achieved a rank where there were few people of color or served in a combat situation where there were large numbers of people of color in dangerous combat positions. ☛

White Benefits Checklist *cont.*

❑ My ancestors were immigrants who took jobs in railroads, streetcars, construction, shipbuilding, wagon and coach driving, house painting, tailoring, longshore work, bricklaying, table waiting, working in the mills, dressmaking or any other trade or occupation where people of color were driven out or excluded.

❑ I received job training in a program where there were few or no people of color.

❑ I have received a job, job interview, job training or internship through personal connections of family or friends.

❑ I worked or work in a job where people of color made less for doing comparable work or did more menial jobs.

❑ I have worked in a job where people of color were hired last or fired first.

❑ I work in a job, career or profession or in an agency or organization in which there are few people of color.

❑ I received small business loans or credits, government contracts or government assistance in my business.

❑ My parents were able to vote in any election they wanted without worrying about poll taxes, literacy requirements or other forms of discrimination.

❑ I can always vote for candidates who reflect my race.

❑ I live in a neighborhood that has better police protection and municipal services and is safer than one where people of color live.

❑ The hospital and medical services close to me or which I use are better than those of most people of color in the region in which I live.

❑ I have never had to worry that clearly labeled public facilities, such as swimming pools, restrooms, restaurants and nightspots, were in fact not open to me because of my skin color.

❑ I see people who look like me in a wide variety of roles on television and in movies.

❑ My skin color needn't be a factor in where I choose to live.

❑ A substantial percentage of the clothes I wear are made by poorly paid women and children of color in the US and abroad.

❑ Most of the food I eat is grown, harvested, processed and/or cooked by poorly paid people of color in this country and abroad.

❑ The house, office building, school, hotels and motels or other buildings and grounds I use are cleaned or maintained by people of color.

❑ Many of the electronic goods I use, such as TVs, cellphones and computers, are made by people of color in the US and abroad.

❑ People of color have cared for me, other family members, friends or colleagues of mine either at home or at a medical or convalescent facility.

❑ I don't need to think about race and racism every day. I can choose when and where I want to respond to racism. ☛

What feelings come up for you when you think about the benefits that white people gain from racism? Do you feel angry or resentful? Guilty or uncomfortable? Do you want to say "Yes, but ....?"

You may be thinking at this point, "If I'm doing so well, how come I'm barely making it?" Some of the benefits listed above are money in the bank for each and every one of us. Some of us have bigger bank accounts — much bigger. According to 2007 figures, 1% of the population controls about 43% of the net financial wealth of the US, and the top 20% own 93%.[13] In 2009, women generally made about 80 cents for every dollar that men made in an average week of full-time work. African American women made 69 cents and Latinas 60 cents.[14] In studies looking at a 15-year period, women's income averages just 35-40% of men's.[15]

Benefits from racism are amplified or diminished by our relative privilege. People with disabilities, people with less formal education and people who are lesbian, gay or bisexual are generally discriminated against in major ways. All of us benefit in some ways from whiteness, but some of us have cornered the market on significant benefits to the exclusion of others.

Notes

1. Bristow Hardin. "Race, Poverty and the Militarized Welfare State." *Poverty & Race* (January/February 1999). [online]. [cited February 9, 2011]. prrac.org/full_text.php?text_id=193&item_id=1862&newsletter_id=42&header=Search Results.
2. Ibid. There were few women of any color who were eligible for veterans' benefits, although women served in many capacities vital to the war effort. Many white women and men and women of color were, in fact, displaced from manufacturing, clerical and sales jobs after the war by affirmative action programs for white men.
3. For more on the disproportionate impact of the GI Bill, see Chapters 1 and 8 in Edward Humes. *Over Here: How the GI Bill Transformed the American Dream.* Houghton Mifflin Harcourt, 2006.
4. Eric Foner. "Hiring Quotas for White Males Only." *The Nation,* June 26, 1995, p. 24.
5. Dalton Conley. *Being Black, Living in the Red: Race, Wealth, and Social Policy in America.* University of California, 1999, p. 36.
6. Melvin L. Oliver and Thomas M. Shapiro. *Black Wealth/White Wealth: A New Perspective on Racial Inequality.* Routledge, 1997, p. 39.
7. Lipsitz. *The Possessive Investment in Whiteness,* p. 6.
8. Oliver and Shapiro, p. 151.
9. Legacy admissions were started in the 1920s by elite eastern schools to give the children of old monied white families clear preference over the children of Jewish and other recent immigrants

who were outscoring them on entrance exams. As recently as the late 1980s, legacies were three times more likely to be accepted to Harvard than non-legacies, and on average, 20% of Harvard's freshmen class were legacy admissions. At Yale the ratio was two times more likely to be accepted, and Dartmouth admitted 57% of its legacy applicants, compared to 27% of non-legacies. The University of Pennsylvania even has a special office of alumni admissions that actively lobbies for alumni children. Legacy admissions are clearly preferences for less-qualified students. The Office of Civil Rights found that the average admitted legacy at Harvard between 1981 and 1988 was significantly less qualified than the average admitted non-legacy. See John Larew. "Who's the Real Affirmative Action Profiteer?" *The Washington Monthly,* June 1991, reprinted in Nicolaus Mills, ed. *Debating Affirmative Action: Race, Gender, Ethnicity, and the Politics of Inclusion.* Delta, 1994, pp. 247–258. For up-to-date information and arguments against legacy admissions, see Richard D. Kahlenberg, ed. *Affirmative Action for the Rich: Legacy Preferences in College Admissions.* Century Foundation, 2010. He argues in part that legacy admissions are white admissions.

10. Michael Eric Dyson. *I May Not Get There With You: The True Martin Luther King Jr.* Free Press, 2000, pp. 60–61.
11. This generational advantage of affirmative action is quite common. The Los Angeles Survey of Urban Inequality, for instance, indicates that white homebuyers are twice as likely to receive family assistance in purchasing a home as blacks (Oliver and Shapiro, p. 145).
12. This checklist works well as an exercise in a workshop or other group situation. As each item is read by a facilitator, all the people in the group to whom the item applies stand up or raise their hands silently for a moment, then sit down (or lower their hands) before the next item is read. Discussion in pairs or as a whole group can follow.
13. *Financial wealth* refers to land, stocks, bonds, buildings — everything that can be owned minus debt but excluding people's personal possessions, cars and houses. Percentages are from 2007 and drawn from Edward N. Wolff. *Recent Trends in Household Wealth in the United States: Rising Debt and Middle-Class Squeeze, an Update to 2007.* Levy Economics Institute Working Paper #589 (March 2010). [online]. [cited February 9, 2011]. levy.org/pubs/wp_589.pdf.
14. Institute for Women's Policy Research. *The Gender Wage Gap 2009.* Fact Sheet # IWPR C350 (September 2010). [online]. [cited February 9, 2011]. iwpr.org/pdf/C350.pdf.
15. Stephen J. Rose and Heidi I. Hartmann. *Still a Man's Labor Market: The Long-Term Earnings Gap.* Institute for Women's Policy Research Report #C355, 2004. [online], [cited February 9, 2011]. iwpr.org/pdf/C355.pdf.

The Economic Pyramid

AS THE ECONOMIC PYRAMID SHOWS, wealth is tremendously concentrated in the US.[1] People of color are preponderantly on the bottom and in the middle of the pyramid. The top of the pyramid is primarily white. There are also large numbers of white people in the middle and on the bottom of the pyramid. With wealth so concentrated at the top, most white people have much to gain from working with people of color to redistribute wealth and opportunity. However racism often keeps poor, working- and middle-class white people from identifying their common struggles with people of color. Feelings of intra-racial solidarity keep many white people focused on our racial connections with people at the top rather than our economic connections with others lower down. The small amount of benefit we receive from being white can distract us from recognizing the large amount of exploitation we experience at the hands of those economically on top. For example, many poor and working-class southern white men fought in alliance with landowning whites in the US Civil War, and tens of thousands died to protect white supremacy. However the landowning class of the South used the slave-based economy to ensure poor whites remained disenfranchised, to keep their wages low and to dramatically curtail their civil rights.[2]

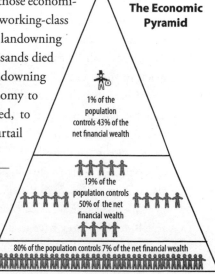

The Economic Pyramid

1% of the population controls 43% of the net financial wealth

19% of the population controls 50% of the net financial wealth

80% of the population controls 7% of the net financial wealth

Notes

1. Percentages are from 2007 and drawn from Wolff. "Recent Trends in Household Wealth."
2. Michael Goldfield. *The Color of Politics: Race and the Mainsprings of American Politics.* New Press, 1997.

The Costs of Racism to People of Color

T HE OPPOSITE OF A BENEFIT is a *disadvantage*. People of color face distinct disadvantages. If we were to talk about running a race for achievement and success in the US and white people and people of color lined up side by side as a group, then every white benefit would put white runners steps ahead of the starting line and every disadvantage would put people of color steps backwards from the starting line before the race even began.

The disadvantages of being a person of color in the United States today include personal insults, harassment, discrimination, economic and cultural exploitation, stereotypes and invisibility, as well as threats, intimidation and violence. Not every person of color has experienced all these disadvantages, but they each have experienced some of them, and they each experience the vulnerability to violence that being a person of color here entails.

Institutional racism is discussed in detail in Parts IV, V and VI, but personal acts of harassment and discrimination committed directly by individual white people can also take a devastating toll.[1] People of color never know when they will be called names, be ridiculed or have jokes and comments made to them or about them by white people. They don't know when they might hear that they should leave the country, go home or go back to where they came from. Often these comments are made in situations where it isn't safe to confront the person who made the remark.

People of color also have to be ready to respond to teachers, employers or supervisors who have stereotypes, prejudices or lowered expectations about them. Many have been discouraged or prevented from pursuing academic or work goals or have been placed in lower vocational levels because of their racial identity. They have to be prepared to receive less respect, attention or response from a doctor, police officer, court official, city official or other professional. They are likely to be mistrusted, accused of stealing, cheating or lying or stopped by the police because of their racial identity. They are also likely to have experienced employment or housing discrimination or know someone who has.

There are cultural costs as well. People of color see themselves portrayed in degrading, stereotypical and fear-inducing ways in the media. They may have important religious or cultural holidays that are not recognized where they work or go to school. They have seen their religious practices, music, art, mannerisms, dress and other customs distorted, "borrowed," ridiculed, exploited, used as mascots or otherwise degraded.

If they protest they may be verbally attacked by whites for being too sensitive, too emotional or too angry. Or they may be told they are different from other people of their racial group. Much of what people of color do or say, or how they act in racially mixed company, is judged as representative of their race.

On top of all this, they have to live with the threat of physical violence. Some are survivors of racial violence or have close friends or family who are. Perhaps even more disheartening, they have to teach their children at a young age how to respond to this as well.

Although all people of color have experienced some of the disadvantages mentioned above, other factors make a difference in how vulnerable a person of color is to the effects of racism. Economic resources help buffer some more egregious effects. Depending upon where one lives, women and men with different racial identities are treated differently. Discrimination varies in form and ranges from mild to severe depending on one's skin color, ethnicity, level of education, location, gender, sexual orientation, physical ability, age and how white people and white-run institutions respond to these factors.

Most of us would like to think that today we have turned the tide and that people of color can run the race equally with white people. We now have an African American president and some people of color who are wealthy or in positions of power. But, if we honestly add up the benefits of whiteness and the disadvantages of being a person of color, we can see that existing affirmative action programs still don't put everyone at the same starting line.

- Is it hard for you to accept that this kind of pervasive discrimination still occurs?
- Which of the above statements is particularly hard to accept?

There are no biological, physiological or psychological attributes that people of color possess that make them different from white people. They don't bring housing, educational and employment discrimination, hate crimes or racial profiling on themselves. These disadvantages are perpetrated by white people (like you and me) and white-run institutions.

Notes

1. See Ellis Cose. *The Rage of a Privileged Class.* HarperCollins, 1993; Joe R. Feagin and Vera Hernan. *White Racism: The Basics.* Routledge, 1995; Annie S. Barnes. *Everyday Racism;* Philomena Essed. Everyday Racism. Hunter House, 1991, and *Understanding Everyday Racism: An Interdisciplinary Theory.* Sage, 1991.

The Culture of Power

WHY DON'T WHITE PEOPLE see white benefits? Whenever one group of people has benefits at the expense of another group, the privileged group creates a culture that places its members at the center and other groups at the margins. People in the in-group are accepted as the norm; if you are in that group, it can be very hard to see the benefits you receive.

Since I'm male and I live in a culture in which men have more social, political and economic power than women, I often don't notice that women are treated differently than I am. I'm inside a male culture of power. I expect to be treated with respect, to be listened to and to have my opinions valued. I expect to find books and newspapers that are written by people like me, that reflect my perspective and that show me in central roles. I don't necessarily notice that the women around me are treated less respectfully, ignored or silenced; that they are not visible in positions of authority nor welcomed in certain spaces and that they are not always safe in situations where I feel perfectly comfortable.

• •

- Remember when you were a young person entering a space that reflected an adult culture of power — a classroom, store or office where adults were in charge?
- What let you know that you were on adult turf — that adults were at the center of power?

• •

Some of the things I remember are that adults were in control. They made the decisions. They might be considerate enough to ask me what I thought, but they did not have to take my concerns into account. I could look around and see what was on the walls, what music was being played, what topics were being discussed and most importantly, who made those decisions.

I felt I was under scrutiny. I had to change my behavior — how I dressed, how I spoke, even my posture ("Sit up, don't slouch") — so that I would be accepted and heard. I couldn't be as smart as I was, or I'd be considered a smart aleck. Sometimes I had to cover up my family background and religion in order to be less at risk from adult disapproval. And if there was any disagreement or problem between an adult and myself, I had little credibility. The adult's word was almost always believed over mine.

The effects on young people of an adult culture of power are similar to the effects on people of color of a white culture of power. As an adult, I rarely notice that I am surrounded by an adult culture of power. Similarly, as a white person, when I'm driving on the freeway I am unlikely to notice that people of color are being pulled over based on skin color. Or when I am in a store, I am unlikely to notice that people of color are being followed, not being served as well or being charged more for the same items. In a society that proclaims equal opportunity, I may not even believe that other people are being paid less than I am for the same work, or being turned away from jobs and housing because of their surname, the color of their skin or their accent. Most of the time, I am so much inside the white culture of power that it is invisible to me, and I have to rely on people of color to point out to me what it looks like, what it feels like and what impact it has on them.

We can learn to notice the culture of power around us. I was giving a talk at a large Midwestern university and was shown to my room in the hotel run by the university's hotel management department. When I had put my suitcase down and hung up my clothes, I looked around the room. There were two pictures on the wall. One was of a university baseball team from many years ago — 22 white men wearing their team uniforms. The other picture was of a science lab class — 14 students, 13 white men and 1 white woman — dressed in lab coats and working at lab benches. In total I had 35 white men and 1 white woman on the walls of my room. "This clearly tells me who's in charge at this university," I said to myself, and it would probably send a message to many people of color and white women who stayed in that room that they could expect to be excluded from the culture of power in this institution. I mentioned the composition of the pictures to the hotel management and referred to it again in my talk the next day.

The pictures themselves, of course, were only symbolic. But as I walked around the campus, talked with various officials and heard about the racial issues being dealt with, I could see that these symbols were part of the construction of a culture of power from which people of color and women were mostly excluded. I have learned that noticing how the culture of power works in any situation provides a lot of information about who has power and privilege and who is vulnerable to discrimination and exclusion, and this university was no exception.

The problem with a white culture of power is that it reinforces racial hierarchy. As white people, many of us expect to have things our way, the way we are most comfortable with. We may go through life complacent in our monoculturalism, not even aware of the limits of our perspectives, the gaps in our knowledge, the inadequacy of our understanding. Of course a white culture of power also dramatically limits the ability of people of color to participate in an event, a situation or an organization. They are only able to participate on our terms, at our discretion, and this puts them at an immediate disadvantage. They often have to give up or hide much of who they are to be accepted. And if there are any problems, it becomes very easy to identify people of color as the source of those problems and blame or attack them rather than the problem itself.

It is important that we learn to recognize the white culture of power in our society so that we can challenge the hierarchy of power it represents and the confinement of people of color to its margins. Use the previous paragraphs and the questions below to guide you in thinking about the white culture of power around you.

The Culture of Power

1. Is there a white culture of power, and if so, what does it look like
   a. In your office or area where you work?
   b. In your school or classroom?
   c. In your living room or living space?
   d. In your congregation?
   e. Where you go out to eat?
   f. Where you shop for clothes?
   g. In agencies whose services you use?

2. Some questions you might ask yourself to identify the culture of power and its appearance include:
   a. Who is in authority?
   b. How is the space designed?
   c. What is on the walls?
   d. What languages are used? Which are acceptable?
   e. What music and food is available?
   f. Who is treated with full respect?
   g. Whose experience is valued?
   h. Who decides?

(These questions may be used to identify cultures of power based on gender, class, sexual orientation, religion, age or physical ability as well as race.)

In your workplace, insofar as you have control over it, what changes can you make to diminish the impact of the white culture of power on people of color?

••

When we talk about the culture of power and the unequal distribution of benefits and disadvantages, we may feel uncomfortable about being white. It is probably inevitable that, when faced with the reality of the unequal distribution of benefits and harm of racism, we will have many strong feelings. These feelings are healthy and need to be acknowledged. Recognize and accept your feelings and any resistance you have to the information presented above. For too long we have ignored or denied the realities of racism. In order to make any changes, we have to start by facing where we are and making a commitment to persevere and overcome the injustices we face.

We can support each other through the feelings. We need a safe place to talk about how it feels to be white and know about racism. It is important that we turn to other white people for this support.

You will find more information about racism in the Bibliography and Other Resources sections at PaulKivel.com. The exercises in this book will also help you begin to think more clearly about racism, about typical white reactions and about how to respond to them. Many organizations and websites can provide further information about particular issues. Be creative and don't become discouraged — later chapters of this book offer more advice about how to be a strong anti-racist ally to people of color.

- Who are white people you can talk with about racism?
- When people say, "We all have it hard," or "Everyone has an equal opportunity" or "People of color just want special privileges," how can you use the information in this book to respond? What might be difficult about doing so?
- What additional information or resources will you need to be able to do this with confidence? How might you find those resources?

Entitlement

HAVING BENEFITS AND BEING PART OF THE CULTURE OF POWER often encourages a person to develop a sense of entitlement to special treatment. *Entitlement* is the sense that you are owed certain rights, privileges, services or material goods because of who you are. In Western countries a person's race, class and gender strongly influence what that person feels entitled to.

Of course, there are some entitlements that we might all agree are legally or morally good. A right to a decent job, to food and housing, to free speech, to be able to vote — we might call these basic rights or entitlements.

But I use entitlement here in a different way. When people grow up in a society where, despite rhetoric about equal opportunity, they are given more access to power, goods and services, they will come to think that they deserve more than others. And they may become upset, bitter and resentful if they don't receive what they see as their due. When you don't expect to have to wait your turn or wait in line or take a number, when you do have to do these things and you see other people being served ahead of you, you may feel angry at these people for being given preference. In fact, it is simply your sense of entitlement that is being challenged.

A sense of entitlement is also visible when people don't acknowledge the humanity and worth of the people who serve them. When I was younger, there were times when I would walk past a receptionist and into my office without saying anything to her. There were times when I did not acknowledge or talk with the people maintaining the building in which I went to school, or the people who cleaned my dorm room in college or my motel room when I traveled. When this behavior was pointed out to me and I began to notice it in myself, I realized that I felt entitled to other people's services and assumed that they were there to take care of my needs. At first I thought that to correct this

I had to become friends with people who provided services for me. However, I soon saw that what was required from me was not friendship, but acknowledgement of and respect for people who were contributing to my well-being and the well-being of the community. I needed to see them differently, as full human beings, rather than as support staff for my life and activities.

How does this sense of entitlement show itself? I have noticed it in the following ways. (I have put the word *white* in parentheses because although I think that it is usually white people exhibiting these behaviors, with people of color or people of a lower class on the receiving end, this is not always the case. There are certainly people of color, especially those with economic means, who do these things as well.)

> (White) People cutting in line in front of others because they think their needs have a priority.
>
> (White) Drivers cutting in front of other cars because they are in a hurry.
>
> (White) People walking by or ignoring people like receptionists, maintenance staff or cleaning staff.
>
> (White) People feeling okay about paying childcare workers, au pairs, gardeners, in-home attendants and other workers less than a living wage.
>
> (White) People who become impatient when they don't receive the prompt service or the attention they feel entitled to and direct abusive comments at the staff who are dealing with them.
>
> (White) People who leave a paltry tip when they can well afford to tip generously.
>
> (White) People quickly judging the motives and behavior of people they don't know and holding their own group up for comparison.
>
> (White) People taking up more time and attention than their fair share in conversations, classrooms, meetings and public events.
>
> (White) People speaking for others, about others or using phrases like "we," "they" or "that group" rather than "I think," "I feel," "in my opinion."

A clear sign of entitlement is indicated when white people use possessive adjectives in such phrases as "They are taking *our* jobs, invading *our* country, destroying *our* neighbourhood or disrupting *our* workplace." It may appear to be ours because discrimination and violence have kept other people out, but is it really legitimate to claim exclusive rights to something we have acquired or maintained by force?

I know that I have often acted from a sense of entitlement, but because I grew up believing in equal opportunity and equal rights, I had to develop a rationale for my behavior. I had to explain to myself why I deserved better treatment, quicker access, prompter service and more air time in meetings. As a result, I have consciously or unconsciously told myself that I deserve this preference because:

> I am better educated
> I have more experience
> I am more rational
> My time is more valuable
> I worked hard to get to where I am
> They probably don't need as much to live on
> I don't actually have direct contact with them so I am not
> responsible
> I need to get there on time

I have only just begun to see the sense of entitlement that these excuses mask and the degree to which they are rationalizations for inequality.

Besides lessening our own sense of entitlement, we can also challenge the behavior of those around us. In a public place, we can ask people to wait their turn. In a meeting, we can ask those who have spoken not to speak again until everyone has had a turn. We can ask people to use "I" statements and not make generalizations about others. And we can challenge people's

Entitlement

1. Look over the list of entitlements above and note the ones that you have felt at times.
2. Which others would you add to the list?
3. Which rationalizations have you used to explain the preference you felt you deserved?
4. Has your sense of entitlement ever led you to ignore the needs or rights of others?
5. What impact does it have on others and on the community when you act out of a sense of personal entitlement?
6. How can you better notice the impact of entitlement on your family, work and school environments?

rationalizations for unequal and inadequate wages, benefits, tips and other forms of monetary compensation. In public discussions, we can challenge people about their sense of entitlement to jobs, education or housing when past policies of discrimination have given preference to white people or restricted access to people of color.

When we challenge behavior based on a sense of entitlement in white people, we counter the negative impact such behavior has on people of color. We also counter one of the costs to white people of racism, a mistaken belief that white people and their culture are superior to all others. This is only one of many costs that white people pay for the racial benefits we receive.

The Costs of Racism to White People

W<small>E TEND TO THINK OF RACISM</small> as a problem for people of color and something we should be concerned about for their sake. It is true that racism is devastating to them, and if we believe in justice, equality and equal opportunity for all, then we should try to end it. However, as we've seen in previous chapters, although racism produces material benefits for white people, its costs are devastating, especially to those without the money and power to buffer the effects. We have been trained to ignore, deny or rationalize away the significant costs of racism to us. It is sobering for us to talk together about what it really costs to maintain such a system of division and exploitation in our society. We may even find it difficult to recognize some of the core costs of being white in our society.

For example, one of the conditions of assimilating into white mainstream culture is that people are asked to leave behind the languages, foods, music, games, rituals and the expressions parents and/or grandparents used. We lose our own families' cultures and histories. Sometimes this loss leads us to romanticize the richness of other cultures.

White people have a distorted and inaccurate picture of history and politics because the truth about racism has been excluded, the contributions of people of color left out and the roles of white people cleaned up and modified. We also lose the presence and contributions of people of color to our neighborhoods, schools and relationships. Our experiences are distorted, limited and less rich the more they are exclusively or predominantly white.

There are many ways that racism affects our interpersonal relationships. We may have lost relationships with friends, family members and co-workers to disagreements, fights and tension over racism. At the same time, we may have lost relationships with people of color because the tensions of racism make those relationships difficult to sustain.

Racism distorts our sense of danger and safety. We are taught to live in fear of people of color. We are exploited economically by the ruling class and unable to fight or even see this exploitation because we are taught to scapegoat people of color. On a more personal level, many of us are brutalized by family violence and sexual assault. We are less able to resist it effectively because we have been taught that people of color are the real danger, never the white men we live with.

There are also spiritual costs. Many of us have lost a connection to our own spiritual traditions, and consequently have come to romanticize those of other cultures, such as Buddhist or Native American beliefs.

Our moral integrity is deeply damaged as we witness situations of discrimination and harassment and do not intervene. Our feelings of guilt, shame, embarrassment or inadequacy about racism and about our responses to it lower our self-esteem. Because racism makes a mockery of our ideals of democracy, justice and equality, it leads us to be cynical and pessimistic about human integrity and about our future, producing apathy, blame, despair, self-destructive behavior and acts of violence.

It can be hard for us to be honest with ourselves about the costs of racism in our own lives. The following is a checklist you can use to evaluate the costs of racism to white people. Check each of the items that apply to you.

When I use this list in an exercise with a white group and every person answers "yes" to a substantial number of the questions, I can clearly see that we have all paid some of the costs of racism. Realizing what those costs are can easily make us angry. If we are not careful, we can turn that anger toward people of color, blaming them for the problems of white racism. Sometimes we say things like "If they weren't here, we would not have these problems." But racism is caused by white people, by our attitudes, behaviors and institutions. How is it that white people in general can justify retaining the benefits of being white without taking responsibility for perpetuating racism?

Costs of Racism to White People Checklist [1]

❑ I don't know exactly what my European American heritage is, what my great-grandparents' names were, or what regions or cities my ancestors are from.

❑ I grew up, lived or live in a neighborhood, or went to school or a camp, which, as far as I knew, was exclusively white.

❑ I grew up with people of color who were servants, maids, gardeners or babysitters in my house.

❑ I did not meet people of color in person, or socially, before I was well into my teens.

❑ I grew up in a household where I heard derogatory racial terms or racial jokes.

❑ I grew up in a family or heard as a child that people of color were to blame for violence, lack of jobs or other problems.

❑ I have seen or heard images, in magazines, on TV or radio, on CDs or in movies of (check all that apply):

    ❑ Mexicans depicted as drunk, lazy or illiterate

    ❑ Asians depicted as exotic, cruel or mysterious

    ❑ South Asians depicted as excitable or "silly"

    ❑ Arabs depicted as swarthy, ravishing or "crazed"

    ❑ African Americans depicted as violent or criminal

    ❑ Pacific Islanders depicted as fun-loving or lazy

    ❑ American Indians depicted as drunk, savage or "noble"

    ❑ Muslims depicted as fanatics and terrorists

    ❑ Women of color portrayed as exotic, erotic or dangerous

    ❑ Any character roles from non-white cultures depicted by white actors

❑ I was told not to play with children of particular other ethnicities when I was a child.

❑ I have sometimes felt that "white" culture was "wonderbread"[2] culture — empty and boring — or that another racial group had more rhythm, more athletic ability, was better at math and technology or had more musical or artistic creativity than mine.

❑ I have felt that people of another racial group were more spiritual than white people.

❑ I have been nervous and fearful or found myself stiffening up when encountering people of color in a neutral public situation (for example, in an elevator, on the street).

❑ I have been sexually attracted to a person from another racial group because it seemed exotic, exciting or a challenge.

❑ I was in a close friendship or relationship with a person of color, where the relationship was affected, stressed or endangered by racism between us or from others.

❑ I am not in a close significant relationship with any people of color in my life right now.

❑ I have been in a close friendship or relationship with another white person where that relationship was damaged or lost because of a disagreement about racism.

❑ I have felt embarrassed by, separate from, superior to or more tolerant than other white people.

❑ I have worked in a job where people of color held more menial jobs, were paid less or were otherwise harassed or discriminated against and I did nothing about it. ☞

❑ I have participated in an organization, work group, meeting or event which people of color protested as racist or which I knew to be racist and did nothing about it.

❑ I have had degrading jokes, comments or put-downs about people of color made in my presence and did not protest or challenge them.

❑ I have felt racial tension or noticed racism in a situation and was afraid to say or do anything about it.

❑ I have seen a person of color being attacked verbally or physically and did not intervene.

❑ I am concerned that there is not enough attention paid to family violence and sexual assault in my community because of the focus of police and criminal justice resources on communities of color.

❑ I am concerned that drug abuse in my white community is not taken seriously enough because disproportionate attention is on drug use in communities of color.

❑ I experience a heightened and intrusive state of surveillance and security in my neighborhood, where I shop, in my school, when I cross borders or when I use airports because of social fears of the dangers of people of color.

❑ I have had to accept unnecessary limits on my basic civil liberties because of social fears that people of color are dangerous.

❑ I have felt angry, frustrated, tired or weary about dealing with racism and hearing about racial affairs.

❑ I live in a community where, for whatever reason, no people of color are present, so that some of these questions don't apply.

Notes

1. Original version copyright the Oakland Men's Project, 1990. Adapted from Creighton and Kivel, *Helping Teens Stop Violence.* Reprinted with permission.
2. I borrow this word from Margo Adair and Sharon Howell. *The Subjective Side of Politics and Breaking Old Patterns, Weaving New Ties: Alliance Building, and Democracy at Work.* Tools for Change, 1995.

Retaining Benefits,
Avoiding Responsibility

WE HAVE SEEN HOW PEOPLE OF COLOR experience acts of violence such as rape, battery, economic discrimination, lack of police protection, police brutality and poor healthcare due to racism. Money and other accoutrements of power afford some protection, but not completely and not always.

During the first few years that I worked with men who are violent, I was continually perplexed by their inability to see the effects of their actions and their ability to deny the violence they had perpetrated. I only slowly became aware of the complex set of tactics that men use to make their violence invisible and to avoid taking responsibility for their actions. These tactics are listed below in the rough order that men employ them.

These tactics are part of a cycle in which these claims, particularly those of blame, counterattack and competing victimization, can justify further violence. As I began to understand the interconnection between the systems of gender, race, class and sexual orientation, I came to see how these tactics are used,

List of Tactics to Avoid Responsibility	
Tactic	**Typical Statement**
Denial	"I didn't hit her."
Minimization	"It was only a slap."
Blame	"She asked for it."
Redefinition	"It was mutual combat."
Unintentionality	"Things got out of hand."
It's over now	"I'll never do it again."
It's only a few men	"Most men wouldn't hurt a woman."
Counterattack	
Competing victimization	"She controls everything."
	"Everybody is against men."

consciously and unconsciously, by those in power to cover over their violence. They are the tactics of those who seek to retain their power and privileges.

Although these tactics follow a logical progression from outright denial to competing victimization, they are often used in combinations that make it confusing to argue against them. Although they may appear to be based on logical reasoning, they are part of a strategy for explaining or justifying already existing injustice and violence.

We can learn to recognize and counter these tactics. I am going to use the history of the relationship between white Europeans and Native Americans to illustrate how these tactics have been (and still are) used to cover up the violence that white people commit toward people of color. There is more detailed information about that history in Part IV.

Denial

Denial is usually the first tactic employed and works very simply. The batterer says, "I didn't hit her."

White people say that Columbus was just looking for a trade route, the Pilgrims found a vast wilderness and the early colonists befriended the Indians and exchanged presents with them. At this level there is absolute denial that violence occurred and therefore of any responsibility for it.

Today we are using the tactic of denial when we say, despite all evidence to the contrary, "It's a level playing field," "Discrimination is a thing of the past" or "This is a land of equal opportunity." White people can also deny the existence of racism by claiming that class or some other factor is really the issue.

Minimization

If the denial doesn't hold up because of the evidence — for instance, she has a broken arm — then the violence is minimized. The batterer says, "I didn't hit her. Well, it was only a slap."

White people killed Native Americans and took their land. In response we say, "A few Indians died because they didn't have immunity to European diseases." We try to minimize the presence of the 12 to 15 million Native Americans in North America prior to 1492 and to minimize the violence we committed against them.

Today we continue to minimize racism by saying, "Personal achievement mostly depends on personal ability," "Racism isn't prevalent anymore" or (about slavery) "There were a lot of kind slave owners."

Blame

If the minimization doesn't hold up because the victim is in the hospital, then the batterer's effort shifts to a combination of justifying the violence and blaming the victim: "She asked for it" or "She should have known not to say that to me." If the discussion is more general, then men might make statements like "Women are too emotional/manipulative/backstabbing."

Similarly, we know that millions of Native Americans died, not only from intentional transmission of diseases, but also because white people shot, tortured and enslaved them. Since the blame has to fall on entire societies, we make statements like "Indians were primitive." "They had not developed the technology to compete." "They were not physically able to resist the diseases, hold up under slavery [they didn't make good slaves!]." "They were naive, simple heathens."

Historically there have been continual attempts to explain away white violence against people of color as the inevitable result of genetic/biological, physiological or psychological differences. These differences often do not exist. Where they do, they are seldom related to real differences in behavior. In any case, they never justify injustice and violence.

When we describe the agency of people with power, explanations become clearer: He hit her. He broke her arm. He put her in the hospital. Columbus invaded, killed and enslaved the Taino/Arawak peoples. The US Army at Fort Clark deliberately distributed smallpox-infected blankets to the Mandan in order to kill them.[1]

Today we blame people of color for racism by saying, "Look at the way they act," "If they weren't so angry ...," "They have different cultural values" or "They are immoral, lazy, dumb or unambitious."

Redefinition

We want to hold adults responsible for what they do. Therefore we must carefully and accurately investigate what happened so that we can stop violence. If we don't look at the overall context and take differentials of power into account, we can be susceptible to the tactic of redefinition. For example, he says, "It was mutual combat." "She hit me first." "It takes two to fight."

If we can no longer claim that Columbus innocently discovered America, we try to redefine that event too. The 1992 quincentennial museum exhibit in New York was called "Encounter," a word implying some level of mutuality, equality and neutrality. In the same vein we say, "The settlers had to protect themselves from Indian attacks."

Today we redefine racism as a mutual problem by saying, "This country is just a big melting pot," "Anybody can be prejudiced" or "People of color attack white people too." The popular movie *Crash* was an example of redefinition of the "anybody can be prejudiced" variety. In the film all the characters — white and people of color — act with prejudice. The filmmakers make racism appear to be just a problem of prejudiced people not treating each other with respect.[2]

It Was Unintentional

At this point the group or individual with more power, who has clearly done something that resulted in some kind of devastation, might claim that the damage was unintentional and therefore their responsibility was minimal. The batterer says, "I didn't intend to hit her." "I didn't mean to hit her so hard." "Things got out of hand."

First of all, claims of innocence by someone who has hurt you are always suspect. Adults are responsible for their actions and for the results of those actions. "I didn't mean to" is not an acceptable legal or moral excuse for being violent toward another person. Secondly, actual intent is often discernible from the pattern of action. When a man systematically tries to control a woman and then says, "I didn't mean to hit her," he is saying that he hoped to control her by non-physical means. When all else failed, he resorted to hitting. The issue is power and control. Intent is clearly evident in the entire pattern of behavior.

We have said that the near eradication of Native Americans and their food supplies, hunting areas and natural resources was the unintended result of European immigration. We now know that the complete elimination of Native Americans from the United States was government policy as well as part of the general, everyday discourse of white Americans (see Part IV for details).

Today we continue to claim racism is unintentional by saying, "Discrimination may happen, but most people are well intentioned." "She probably didn't mean it like that." "It was only a joke."

It's All Over Now

Another way to defuse responsibility is by claiming that the violence happened in the past and is no longer an issue. The batterer says, "It's over with" or "I'll never do it again." He may finally claim responsibility (often indirectly), but he asserts that things have changed. Part of his claim is that the trauma, pain and vulnerability should just be forgotten. This discounts the seriousness of the violence, blames the survivor for not being able to let go of it and move on and focuses on the perpetrator's words, not his actions. All he offers is a promise that it won't happen again.

White people often claim that genocide, land grabbing and exploitation are things of the past. Most of our images of Indians reinforce that belief by focusing on Native Americans who lived 100 to 300 years ago. The reality is that effects of colonial violence are still readily apparent today. The small number of remaining Native Americans, the poor economic conditions, the alcoholism, the shattered traditions and devastated communities are the direct result of 500 years of systematic oppression.

Furthermore, the same policies exist today as they did hundreds of years ago. Across the US and Canada, land is still being taken; treaties are still being broken; Native culture, religion and artifacts are still being stolen and/ or exploited; Native American nations are still denied sovereignty; Native Americans are still being killed by whites with some degree of impunity; their land, including their sacred sites, is still being exploited and laid waste on a massive scale. Some of the violence takes different forms than it did a hundred years ago. It is important that we not use those differences to claim that we are not responsible for the violence that occurs today. When we are dealing with structural violence, the proof of change is structural change, not claims of innocence.

Today we claim racism is all over by saying, "Slavery was over a long time ago." "The days of land grabbing are long gone." "That was before the civil rights era." "There aren't any Indians left."

It's Only a Few People

If we are unable to maintain that the violence was all in the past, we may switch to another tactic to make a current situation seem isolated. We might say that it's really only a few people who are like that — it is not systemic or institutionalized. In the case of domestic violence, we contend that only a few men are batterers; most men treat women well. However, if 25% of all women experience at least one incident of intimate partner abuse from a man — 2-3 million such incidents a year — then we are clearly talking about a social issue, not the isolated anger of a few men.[3]

Similarly, it wasn't just rogue officers like Custer disobeying orders, or cruel, greedy men like Columbus or a few cowboys who killed Native Americans.

Slavery, genocide and racism were built into the structure of all the institutions of our society and were everyday occurrences. We have inherited, perpetuated and benefited from these actions. All of us are implicated.

Today we continue to use this tactic when we say, "Housing and job discrimination are the result of a few bigoted people." "The Far Right is behind the scapegoating of immigrants." "It's only neo-Nazis and Skinheads who do that sort of thing," or "Some people may be prejudiced but ...."

Counterattack and Competing Victimization

When all else fails and responsibility for the violence is inexorably falling on the shoulders of those who committed the acts themselves, there is a counterattack, an attempt to claim a reversal of the power relationships. This approach is usually combined with the final tactic, competing victimization. An individual batterer might say, "She really has all the power in our family." "If I didn't hit her she would run all over me." On a national level, there are more and more claims that women batter men too, that women win child custody and men don't when divorce occurs and that there is too much male-bashing.

To counter this tactic, we must go back to what happened, who has power and what violence is being done. Who ended up in the hospital, and who remained in control of the family resources? In the claims above, we find that in more than 90% of intimate partner abuse involving systematic, persistent and injurious violence, women are the victims.[4]

We now have a national debate about multiculturalism which claims that people of color and women have so much power that US society itself is threatened. We are told that Muslims, recent immigrants and other people of color are a danger and a threat to our national unity and way of life. White people are filing lawsuits against affirmative action, claiming to be the victims of racism.

We need to ask ourselves who was killed and who ended up with the land base of this country? Today, who has the jobs, who gets into the universities, who earns more pay and who gets more media attention for their concerns — white people or people of color?

Some white people are counterattacking by saying, "Political correctness rules the universities." "We just want our rights too." "They want special status." "They're taking away our jobs." Some of the things we say when we claim to be victims include: "White males have rights too." "I have it just as bad as anybody." "White people are under attack."

Even though all of these statements are demonstrably untrue, those with power have many resources for ensuring their view of reality prevails, and they have a lot at stake in maintaining the status quo. They will employ the tactics described above to defend their interests. We must be aware of these tactics and able to counter them.

Our strongest tools are a critical analysis of who has power and an understanding of the patterns and consequences of present actions and policies. Parts IV, V and VI of *Uprooting Racism* will help sharpen your analysis and increase your understanding of how racism plays out in current institutional and interpersonal practices.

Notes

1. Ward Churchill. *Indians Are Us? Culture and Genocide in Native North America.* Common Courage, 1994, p. 35.
2. *Crash.* Lion's Gate Entertainment, 2005. For excellent discussions of the film, see Michael Benitez Jr. and Felicia Gustin eds. *Crash Course: Reflections on the Film Crash for Critical Dialogues About Race, Power and Privilege.* Institute for Democratic Education and Culture — Speak Out, 2007.
3. Will Dunham. "Quarter of US Women Suffer Domestic Violence: CDC." *Reuters,* February 7, 2008. [online]. [cited February 11, 2011]. reuters.com/article/idUSN0737896320080207.
4. Michael S. Kimmel. "'Gender Symmetry' in Domestic Violence: A Substantive and Methodological Review." *Violence Against Women,* Vol. 8#11 (November 2002), pp. 1332–1363.

"Thank You for Being Angry"

A PERSON OF COLOR WHO IS ANGRY about discrimination or harassment is doing us a service. That person is pointing out something wrong, something that contradicts the ideals of equality set forth in the US Constitution and Bill of Rights. They are bringing our attention to a problem that needs solving, a wrong that needs righting. We could convey our appreciation by saying, "Thank you, your anger has helped me see what's not right here." What keeps us from responding in this way?

Anger is a scary emotion in our society. In mainstream, white Christian culture we are taught to be polite, never raise our voices, be reasonable and calm. People who are demonstrative of their feelings are discounted and ridiculed. We are told by parents to obey "because I said so." We are told by bosses, religious leaders and other authorities not to challenge what they say, "or else" (you'll be fired, go to hell, be treated as crazy). When we do get angry, we learn to hold it in, mutter under our breath and go away. We are taught to turn our anger inward in self-destructive behaviors. If we are men, we are taught to take out our frustrations on someone weaker and smaller than we are.

When we have seen someone expressing anger, it has often been a person with power who was abusing us or someone else physically, verbally or emotionally. We were hurt, scared or possibly confused. Most of us can remember a time from our youth when a parent, teacher or coach was yelling at us abusively. It may have made us afraid when those around us became angry. It may have made us afraid of our own anger.

Relationships between people of color and whites often begin as friendly and polite. We may be pleased that we know and like a person from another cultural group, pleased they like us. We are encouraged because, despite our fears, it seems that it may be possible for people from different cultures to get along together. The friendship may confirm our feeling that we are different from other white people.

But then the person of color becomes angry. Perhaps he or she is angry about something we said or did, or about a comment or action by someone else or about racism in general. We may back off in response, fearing that the relationship is falling apart. We aren't liked anymore. We've been found out to be racist.

For a person of color, this may be a time of hope that the relationship can become more intimate and honest. The anger may be an attempt to test the depths and possibilities of the friendship. The person may be open about their feelings to see how safe we are, hoping that we will not desert them. Or the anger may be a more assertive attempt to break through our complacency to address some core beliefs or actions.

Many white people have been taught to see anger and conflict as signs of failure. They may instead be signs we're becoming more honest, dealing with the real differences and problems in our lives. If it is not safe enough to disagree, express anger and struggle with each other, what kind of relationship can we have?

We could say, "Thank you for pointing out the racism because I want to know whenever it is occurring," or "I appreciate your honesty. Let's see what we can do about this situation." More often white people get scared and disappear or become defensive and counterattack. In any case, we don't focus on the root of the problem, and racism goes unattended.

When people of color are angry about racism, it is legitimate anger. It is not their oversensitivity but our lack of sensitivity that causes this communication gap. People of color are vulnerable to the abuse of racism every day. They are experts on it. Most of us rarely notice it. In fact, white people consistently deny the existence of racism. Even before the civil rights gains of the mid-1960s, polls consistently showed that white people did not consider racism a problem and believed that African Americans had opportunities equal to whites in the United States.[1] Recent polls confirm high levels of denial among white people of the impact of racism.[2]

It is the anger and actions of people of color that call our attention to the injustice of racism. It is tremendously draining, costly and personally devastating for people of color to have to rage about racism. They often end up losing their friends, their livelihoods, even their lives. Rather than attacking them for their anger, we need to examine the layers of complacency, ignorance and privilege we have put into place which require so much outrage to get our attention.

The 1965 riots in Watts, as never before, brought attention to the ravages of racism on the African American population living there. In 1968 a national report by the Kerner Commission warned of the dangers of not addressing racial problems. Yet in 1992, when there were new uprisings in Los Angeles, we focused again on the anger of African Americans, on containing that anger, protecting property and controlling the community rather than on solving the problems that cause poverty, unemployment, crime and high dropout rates. African Americans, Latino/as, immigrants, other people of color and their allies are frequently out in the streets protesting police brutality, cutbacks in human services, racial profiling, attacks on immigrants and other forms of racism. The only way to break this cycle of rage is for us to seriously address the sources of the anger, the causes of the problems. And in order to do that, we need to talk about racism directly with one another.

Notes

1. Tim Wise. *Speaking Treason Fluently: Anti-Racist Reflections from an Angry White Male.* Soft Skull, 2008, p. 82.
2. Mark R. Warren. *Fire in the Heart: How White Activists Embrace Racial Justice.* Oxford, 2010, p. 3.

It's Good to Talk about Racism

RACISM HAS GREAT POWER partly because we don't talk about it. Talking about racism lessens its power and breaks our awful, uncomfortable silence. Talking about it makes it less scary.

Talking about racism is an opportunity to learn about people of color and to reclaim our lives and true histories. We can ask questions, learn and grow in exciting ways previously denied us.

Talking about racism helps make our society safer for people of color and safer for us as well. Talking about it keeps us from passing racism on to our children. Talking about it allows us to do something about it.

We actually talk about race all the time, but we do it in code. Much in our discussions about economics, military issues, neighborhood affairs, public safety and welfare, education, sports and movies is about race — but using code words. These words allow white people to speak about race or about people of color because we can count on the *implications* of the words to convey our meaning without having to state things explicitly. We don't have to risk being accused of racism; we don't have to worry about being accountable for what we say. In order to be allies of people of color, we need to break this subterfuge and collusion between white people. Dealing with racism is not just talking — but talking openly, intentionally, with the goal of ending it. It calls for us to demystify and analyze our coded interactions.

I want to look briefly at eight words and phrases to decipher the meanings they contain, including the ways that class perceptions are intertwined with racial ones. This analysis should help us challenge other white people when they fall back on racial code words.

Underclass

Underclass generally stands for African Americans who are poor. It suggests they are a separate group from other poor people, a class by themselves that is below the rest of us. It connotes hopelessness, desperation and violence, implies that this group lives by values that are different from ours and that they have no ability to change their economic circumstances.

This word operates, like most racially coded words, by labeling a particular group and then creating or exaggerating its characteristics so that we feel completely separate from the group's members. The negative qualities attributed to this group then become justifications for our treatment of "them."

African Americans have no monopoly on poverty in the US. There are twice as many poor whites as poor blacks or Latino/as.[1] Nor is there a special "culture of poverty" (another racially coded phrase). There are certainly significant negative effects of poverty, but well-paying jobs, access to decent housing and schooling have been shown to mitigate most of these effects very quickly.

Welfare Mothers

This is another phrase that seems to have a clear definition but actually has several layers of racial meaning. For most white people, our image is of an African American woman with several children who lives rather well for long periods of time on welfare to avoid working for a living. In turn, the expense of providing for welfare mothers is said to be draining our country financially, contributing to the national deficit and providing a disincentive for African American teens to work. The reality is quite different. The majority of welfare recipients are white. Welfare recipients are primarily women who have, on the average, two children and stay on welfare for less than two years. Only 20% of welfare recipients had stayed on welfare for five years or more, and the percentage of African American women on welfare had actually dropped in the last two decades before the welfare system was drastically restructured in 1996.[2]

Welfare does not provide more than poverty-level support. The average payment in 2006 for a family of three was $372 per month, or $4,464 per year.[3] If you had two children, would you give up a job for this amount of money? With these meager payments, currently being cut back further, we can see why welfare accounts for less than 1% of the federal budget. Military spending, in contrast, accounts for about 54%.[4]

Inner City

Both of the terms examined above come together in this phrase. For most white people, *inner city* means anywhere there are large concentrations of people of color, regardless of their economic status. The central sections of most large metropolitan areas in the US are highly diverse economically and racially. In many cities, there are now neighborhoods of upper-income whites in gentrified houses and condos. Poor people in general, and welfare mothers in particular, can be found throughout the country, not just in urban areas. For example, there are poor white Appalachian communities that have long histories of poverty and as severe impediments to economic recovery as inner city areas.

Illegal Aliens

The use of the word *illegal* in this context is racist. No one is intrinsically illegal, and white people would never be described this way. When someone robs a bank or commits a murder, we do not say they are illegal; we say that they have committed an illegal act. In addition, the word *alien* makes it seem like immigrants are from another planet.

Which immigrants are legal or illegal at any particular time has always been a function of racially determined immigration policies. Today, discussion about illegal aliens (undocumented residents, or immigrants without papers) focuses on Mexicans, Central and South Americans and Asians but not on Canadians or Europeans. This justifies extending discriminatory policies such as racial profiling to legal residents and long-standing US citizens who are Spanish-speaking, while claiming that this is a legal and non-racial issue.

Terrorist

Terrorist has become a code word for Arabs and Muslims. When using it, we can mask Islamophobic and anti-Arab statements and policies while ignoring the terrorist acts of white people and the US government, such as the bombings of civilian areas in Bosnia, Afghanistan, Pakistan and Iraq.

Politically Correct

People of color and white allies have long been challenging language that is disrespectful and abusive as well as policies and practices that are discriminatory. People opposed to racial progress use *politically correct* to divert attention from racism by counterattacking the people who are challenging it. The people who use these words claim to be concerned about freedom of speech but avoid addressing issues of discrimination and harassment.

Invasion

Why don't we ever say that Europeans invaded North America? Didn't the US invade Afghanistan and Iraq? Most of the time, we use the word *invasion* to set ourselves up as victims, describing how we — white Americans — are being invaded by Japanese investment, Chinese imports, people of color moving to the suburbs or Haitian refugees. We avoid the word when it might accurately focus attention on our role in attacking others.

Model Minority

White people use this phrase the way we refer to well-behaved children. Implicit in the statement is a comparison to badly behaved children. Groups labeled *model minority*, often Asian Americans, are judged by white people to behave well by white standards and are contrasted with groups that are unruly, ungrateful or unsuccessful by our standards. This label, while seemingly positive, is still a stereotype applied indiscriminately to an entire community. It overlooks the complexity of Asian American communities, judges the entire group by white standards of obedience, docility and accommodation and is used to berate, by implication, African Americans or Latino/as for not being as successful.

We can only develop effective strategies for uprooting racism with language that reflects reality. The use of racially coded words allows white people to define people of color as the problem, ourselves as the victims and to avoid taking responsibility for ending racism. In effect, code words excuse us from being allies to people of color.

- *Crime, busing, taxes, quotas, state's rights* and *reverse racism* are other code words and phrases. How would you decipher them to another white person?
- What are other code words that you have heard white people use to talk about people of color without making an overt racial reference?

Notes

1. American Community Survey S1701. "Poverty Status in the Past 12 Months Data Set: 2006-2008 American Community Survey 3-Year Estimates." US Census Bureau. [online]. [cited February 12, 2011]. factfinder.census.gov/servlet/STTable?_bm=y&-geo_id=01000US&-qr_name=ACS_2008_3YR_G00_S1701&-ds_name=ACS_2008_3YR_G00_.
2. Farai Chideya. *Don't Believe the Hype: Fighting Cultural Misinformation about African Americans.* Plume, 1995, pp. 37-45.

3. US Department of Health and Human Services, Administration for Children & Families. *Temporary Assistance to Needy Families* (TANF). Eighth Annual Report to Congress, 2007. [online]. [cited February 12, 2011]. acf.hhs.gov/programs/ofa/data-reports/annualreport8/chapter10/chap10.htm.

4. War Resister's League. *Where Your Income Tax Money Really Goes: US Federal Budget 2009 Fiscal Year.* [online]. [cited February 12, 2011]. warresisters.org/sites/default/files/2009_piechart-BW.pdf.

Who Is a Victim?

SOME OF US BELIEVE that there is a certain glamour to being a victim. We may think victims get more attention, more respect or simply have some inherently virtuous quality. We may even believe that some people prefer to be victims and take active steps to achieve victim status. And sometimes, those of us with more power or privilege or less vulnerability to violence may think that the way to redirect attention, resources or virtue back to ourselves is to claim that we are victims too.

Men do this in custody cases, counter-harassment and discrimination suits and in charges of reverse discrimination. White people do this routinely when they protest affirmative action and reparative programs for people of color.

There is nothing, absolutely nothing, good about being a victim. Being a victim means you were not powerful enough to protect yourself from some-one else's abuse. Those who have been raped, robbed, battered, harassed or discriminated against know how painful and long-lasting the effects of abuse can be. Nor is it necessarily safe to step forward and describe one's victimiza-tion. Survivors of abuse are routinely blamed, not believed and revictimized.

Claiming to be victimized is not the same as being victimized. Who is the victim and who is the perpetrator of abuse in any particular situation depends on what actually happened and who has the power. In order to understand clearly who was victimized, we must ask the questions "Who has the power?" and "Who did what to whom?"

Actual reverse discrimination is rare, and many claims lack merit. Every year there are thousands of discrimination cases brought forward, many of them class action suits involving tens of thousands of plaintiffs. There are typically far less than a hundred cases of reverse discrimination initiated in a given year, and very few are determined to have merit by the courts.[1] Charges of reverse racism are usually a white strategy to deny white racism and to counterattack attempts to promote racial justice.

What is going on when white people claim reverse racism or claim to be victimized by people of color? Often we are being victimized, but not by people of color. We may be economically exploited by white-owned corporations that move jobs overseas, leaving our communities stranded and some of us unemployed. Deceived about the true cause of our exploitation, we are incited to blame people of color, Jews and recent immigrants.

An individual white person can be abused by a person of color. This is unfair and needs to be addressed. Any person can decide to hurt other people. We have seen in the chapters on white benefits and the costs of racism that whites are not victims of people of color in any way similar to how people of color are hurt by racism every day, in every aspect of their lives.

Notes

1. For example, a 1995 Labor Department draft report reviewing opinions by US District Courts and Courts of Appeal found that, between 1990 and 1994, of the 3,000 discrimination cases brought forward, only 100 were charges of reverse discrimination. Of the 100, only 6 were found to have merit. Relief was provided in those 6 cases. *Oakland Tribune,* March 31, 1995, p. A–9.

Part II

The Dynamics of Racism

The Enemy Within

ONE OF THE PURPOSES OF RACISM AND RELIGIOUS-BASED OPPRESSION is to keep people of color, Muslims, Jews and others at the center of attention while keeping white people in general, and white male Christians in particular, at the center of power and at the top of the economic pyramid. The majority of people in the US have been abused, economically exploited and discriminated against. We experience tremendous physical, economic and emotional loss from social inequity and personal abuse. Like the proverbial thief who points off in the distance to get you to look away and then deftly picks your pocket, systems of oppression divert our attention from those who have the power to rob and hurt us. In our pain and anger, we often turn against traditional scapegoats and blame people who are less powerful than we are.

People of color, immigrants and people who are not Christian have long been portrayed as economic threats to white Americans. We have heard and perhaps used phrases like "They take away our jobs." "They are a drain on our economic system, eating up benefits." "They drive wages down and unemployment up." Or, about Jewish people in particular, "They control everything." "They rob us blind."

In fact, these are not the groups of people who make the economic decisions that affect our communities. Corporate leaders lower wages, inflate prices and sell us shoddy and dangerous products with impunity. There has been an enormous redistribution of income toward the rich in the last 30 years, while the standards of living for the rest of us have decreased. Simultaneously, our national infrastructure has deteriorated, living wage jobs and affordable housing are beyond the reach of millions, and our schools are falling apart. We are being ripped off, not by welfare mothers earning $6,000 a year, but by corporate executives earning $10 million a year. We hurt ourselves and make it impossible to solve our social problems when we don't understand the economic basis of racism. And the rich keep getting richer.

In order to address racism effectively, we need to become better at analyzing where real power lies. Which groups are making important political and economic decisions and which are being blamed or scapegoated? The questions below can guide you in making such an analysis.

Where Does Economic Power Lie?

1. In your community, which corporations are the largest employers?
2. What decisions has this group made in the last few years that have affected employment levels and wages (e.g., opening or closing offices or plants, downsizing or moving production abroad)?
3. Which companies were taken over or bought out? Who took over and what happened to jobs, wages and working conditions after the takeover?
4. How would you describe the people who own these companies? Are they mostly or exclusively white? Are they primarily Christian? Are they men? (The fact that those who gain most are well-off Christian white men does not mean that most Christian white men benefit from their actions.)
5. Which particular racial groups are being blamed for economic and social problems in your local area? In your state?
6. How much money have businesses put into promoting this scapegoating through political contributions, lobbying, political ads or public campaigns?
7. How do you benefit and what do you lose from their actions?

The relationship between these issues is complex, and I have only sketched the briefest outline here.[1] Even so, it should be clear that effective action against racism makes the white community stronger and safer, and allows us to join as allies with people of color in the struggle for economic justice. Most white people have as much to gain as people of color from the struggle to redistribute wealth to poor, working- and middle-class people. Most white people have as much to gain as people of color from making our families and communities safer. Rather than letting racism divide us, we need to work together.

Notes

1. For a more detailed analysis of how the US economic system works, see Paul Kivel. *You Call This a Democracy?: Who Benefits, Who Pays and Who Really Decides*, rev. ed. Apex Press, 2006.

Fear and Danger

MANY OF US IN THE UNITED STATES today are afraid. We worry about crime, drugs, our children's future and our own security. Our fear, a result of many social and personal factors, is also linked to violence and messages of danger in the media.

In a society where we are constantly told how vulnerable we are, it is not surprising that most of us are fearful. Racism produces a fear-based society in which no one feels safe. However, *being afraid is not the same as being in danger*.

For example, white people often fear people of color, and most people of color fear white people. White people are not usually in danger from people of color. People of color are in danger of individual acts of discrimination, hate crimes and police brutality at the hands of white people, as well as of institutional practices that kill people due to lack of healthcare, lack of police protection and unequal legal prosecution. White people are rarely killed, harassed or discriminated against by people of color.

- Have you ever been in your car when a person of color drove past? Did you reach over to lock your car door?
- When a man of color walks by, do you touch your wallet or purse or hold it tighter?
- Have you ever watched suspiciously, closed a window, pulled a blind or locked a door when you saw a person of color in your neighbourhood?
- Have you ever had an adult or young person of color in your house and wondered, ever so briefly, if valuables were out?
- Have you ever seen a person of color with quality clothes, an expensive car or other valuable items and wondered how they got the money to buy them?

I have done all of these things. I was taught to fear people of color. I was told that they were dangerous and that they would steal, cheat or otherwise grab whatever I had. I grew up playing cowboys and Indians, always wanting to be the brave cowboy who protected the innocent homesteaders and settlers from the vicious (male) Indians ready to sweep down and destroy white outposts. I was learning that as a man I would have to protect (white) womanhood and (white) civilization.

Growing up in Los Angeles in the 1950s and early 1960s, I heard repeated stories about the "masses of Mexican and Central American people pushing against our borders, pressing to get in and overwhelm us." I remember a discussion with my parents in which I said I didn't think I ever wanted to have children because there were already so many people in the world. My parents tried to convince me that it was important that I have kids because I was smart and educated and we needed more of our kind. I understood "our kind" to be white. Again I was getting the message that we had to defend ourselves, reproduce ourselves and protect what was ours because we were under attack.

The patterns I learned have a long history. Individual white settlers who took Native American land feared retaliation. But many white people lived in cities and were not worried about Indian attack. White settlers, in conjunction with the US government which wanted to "open up" Native American land, had to convince the public that Native Americans were dangerous and needed to be exterminated. A campaign, using books, pictures and the media, created images of Indians as primitive, cruel savages who wanted to kill white men and rape white women. There was even a special genre of story called *captivity narratives* (accounts of white women abducted, raped and tortured by Indians) which built anti-Indian sentiment in white people.[1] This campaign made it easier to justify the appropriation of Native American lands and the killing or removal of Native Americans themselves. In the process, generations of us learned to fear Indians. Many children growing up today still do, even though there are only about 4.5 million Native Americans in the United States or about 1.5% of the population.[2]

Over the course of 240 years of slavery, white slave owners created the illusion that African Americans were dangerous to justify the harshness of their treatment and to scare other white people into supporting their subjugation. White people feared African Americans even though they were so thoroughly dominated and brutalized as to offer little threat to whites. Slaves were brutalized publicly and routinely. Some fought back, but most were more interested in escape than retaliation.

The constant reinforcement of white fear continues today. We still see selected news coverage that presents men of color, particularly African American, Latino, Native American and Arab American men, as the embodiment of danger itself, making it difficult for any white person not to have an immediate feeling of fear in their presence. This fear, in turn, has justified massive and continuous control of communities of color through the schools, police, legal system, jails, prisons and the immigration system. This control starts in preschool or elementary school. It limits educational opportunities, jobs, skills and access to healthcare. It is enforced by police brutality and various forms of discrimination. These conditions produce stress, despair and desperation for young men of color, leading to their killing each other and themselves at high rates, living several years less than white men on average.[3] White violence leads to fear, which is used to justify further white violence. Communities of color, not white people, are the victims of this cycle of violence.

Similarly men of Middle East origin are portrayed as fanatical terrorists who will stop at nothing to kill us. On the one hand, Arab Americans are victims of discrimination, stereotyping and hate crimes. On the other hand, the US government continues to use military force to disrupt the lives of Iraqis, Afghanis and Pakistanis, resulting in the deaths of tens of thousands. While Arab Americans and Muslims are under attack in the US, white Americans are in comparatively little danger. But white fear is used to justify the scapegoating, abuse and violence directed against Arabs, Arab Americans and Muslims. The misrepresentation and demonization is so extreme that I cannot remember the last time I saw a positive image of an Arab or Arab American in the US media.

Jewish people have likewise been portrayed as dangerous — economically dangerous. Stereotypes that Jews own the banks and are crafty, unscrupulous and untrustworthy contribute to such anti-Jewish fears. Age-old Christian teachings that Jews killed Jesus and false documents like the "Protocols of the Elders of Zion" are additional currents in this river of fear.

Economically, most banks, major corporations and other institutions that make the financial decisions about jobs, pensions and healthcare are owned by Christians. Christian fear works, like all racial fear, to divert people from the source of danger — people inside the mainstream who hold political, economic and social power. Jews are blamed for economic problems for which they are not responsible, and they become the targets of further anti-Jewish violence.

Jewish people in the United States have been subject to verbal and physical attack, bombings, desecration of cemeteries, intimidation and murder by white Christians. Jews have not attacked Christians for being Christian. Again we can see that, although the fear is mutual, Jewish people are in some danger from Christians whereas Christians are in no danger of being attacked by Jews.

Jews who are white are feared and are taught to fear people of color. Many white Jewish concerns about violence focus on danger from African Americans, even though most anti-Jewish violence is committed by white Christians. The focus by white Jews on external danger from people of color also helps conceal the significant levels of domestic violence, sexual assault and child abuse within the Jewish community. When Jewish family violence is denied and minimized and Jewish family values are held up as better than those of African Americans, then racism is perpetuated. This racism justifies violence against African Americans while obscuring violence against Jewish women and children.

Many times we use stories to justify the fear that we feel toward people of color. We might introduce them by such phrases as "I was attacked once by ... "I don't want to sound prejudiced, but I know someone who had a bad experience with ..." or "It's unfortunate, but my one negative experience was ...." We then use these single examples to reinforce a stereotype about a whole category of people and to prove our fear of them is legitimate. Even if true (and many are not), these stories don't counter the fact that people of color are many times more likely to experience violence from white people than the reverse.

• •

- Is there a story that you use to justify your fears of people of color?
- What are stories that you've heard other white people use?

• •

These shared stories can be a way to strengthen white solidarity by implying that we share a common danger. They reinforce our desire to be with white people and to avoid people of color. They also raise the stakes if we challenge racism, because to do so seems to threaten our own security. How can we challenge other whites when we may need them in case of an attack?

Sometimes, when I realize the extent of the stereotypes I have learned and act from, I want to disavow fear altogether and convince myself that there is nothing to be afraid of. Or, to counter the stereotype, I try to assume that all men of color are safe and all white men are dangerous. Yet I know that I am foolish if I simply reverse the stereotypes. In a society in which some people are dangerous and violence is a threat, we need to evaluate the danger from each person we're with. Any preconceived notions of danger or safety based on skin color are dysfunctional — they can actually increase our danger and make us less able to protect ourselves. For example, even as white women have moved to the suburbs, put locks on their doors and windows and avoided urban streets at night, they have remained vulnerable to robbery and assault from white male friends, lovers, neighbors and co-workers.

Approximately 73% of sexual violence is committed within the same racial group by heterosexual men who know their victim.[4] If we and our children are beaten or sexually assaulted, it is most likely to be by known heterosexual white men. We justify public policies that disproportionately lock up men of color but these changes do not make it safer for us. To use James Baldwin's phrase, on many levels racism creates an "illusion of safety" for white people.

• Was there ever a time when you heard about violence that a white man committed and said to yourself, "I never would have imagined that so-and-so could have done something like that"?

We are often awarded a presumption of innocence if we are white; other white people assume we are safe until we are proven dangerous. This works to our benefit when we are stopped by the police, shopping in a store, walking down the street or renting equipment such as cars, tools or movies.

• Have you ever been surprised that a Latino or African American man could commit a particular act of violence?

We carry a presumption of guilt for men of color, expecting them to be dangerous. For example, when Susan Smith killed her two children, she claimed that an African American man had kidnapped them. When Charles Stuart killed his pregnant wife in Boston, he stabbed himself and claimed an

African American man had attacked them. In September, 2010, a 15-year-old San Diego girl told her parents and police that she'd been kidnapped and raped by three Latino men. Before she admitted that the entire story was fabricated, the police had conducted an intense manhunt in the community.[5] When the federal building in Oklahoma City was bombed, most people immediately suspected Arab men as the culprits. In each situation, the search for the guilty white man was temporarily diverted toward men of color.

Our personal vigilance is often increased when people of color are present and relaxed when only white people are around. These expectations translate into feeling uneasy whenever we are with significant numbers of people of color. This tendency to fear people of color also leads white people to exaggerate wildly how many there actually are in our society. According to a Gallup Poll, the average US American thinks that 21% of the population are Hispanic, when the real number is 15.1; that 32% are black when the real figure is 12.3 and that a large percent are Jewish when the actual figure is 2.2%. Not even counting Asian Americans, Arab Americans and Native Americans, many people in the US think that people of color constitute a large majority of the population, when the total non-white, non-Christian population is a little more than a third of the population.[6]

All of us who are white need to recognize just how deeply we have been trained to fear and distrust people of color, Jews and Muslims and how much that fear guides our behavior, because that fear is easily manipulated by politicians, the media and corporate leaders. Since the beginning of the civil rights movement, many different individuals have been held up by politicians and the media to represent the "danger" of African Americans to white people. Malcolm X, Huey Newton, Eldridge Cleaver, Martin Luther King, Jr., Angela Davis, "Willie" Horton, Mumia Abu-Jamal, Jesse Jackson, many African American rappers and even President Obama have all been used to symbolize danger and to manipulate white people's fears. As our fears of people of color increase, we are more easily deceived by white leaders who have an aura of trustworthiness simply because they are white.

As white people, we can start by acknowledging the violence we have done to people of color throughout our history. Our fear of violence to ourselves is related to the violence we have done and continue to do to them. We must understand how we have demonized them to justify that violence. Therefore, one way to lower our fear is to acknowledge and reduce our own violence.

Notes

1. Richard Slotkin. *Gunfighter Nation: The Myth of the Frontier in Twentieth-Century America.* Atheneum, 1992, pp. 14-15.
2. Racially motivated government policies exclude Hispanics and African Americans with Native American ancestry from current estimates, so all current demographic figures are highly contested.
3. The life expectancy at birth for United States white males is 74.6 years and for black males is 68.8. Black males have the shortest life span of all racial or ethnic groups in the US with the widest racial gaps in mortality occurring in the prime adult years, ages 25-54. Jiaquan Xu et al. *Deaths: Final Data for 2007.* CDC National Vital Statistics Report Volume 58, Number 19, May 2010. [online], [cited February 13, 2011]. cdc.gov/NCHS/data/nvsr/nvsr58/nvsr58_19. pdf.
4. National Archive of Criminal Justice Data. *National Crime Victimization Survey, 2005.* [online]. [cited February 13, 2011]. icpsr.umich.edu/cocoon/NACJD/STUDY/22746.xml.
5. "False Rape Accusation Furthers Institutionalized Racism." *San Diego Week,* KPBS October 1, 2010. [online]. [cited February 13, 2011]. kpbs.org/videos/2010/oct/01/4906/.
6. US Census estimates in 2008 gave a figure of 34% for people of color and 66% for the white population. *Table 10. Resident Population by Race, Hispanic Origin, and Single Years of Age: 2008.* [online]. [cited February 13, 2011]. census.gov/compendia/statab/2010/tables/10s0010.pdf.

The Geography of Fear

THERE IS ALSO A GEOGRAPHY OF FEAR of being in certain places and certain kinds of spaces. For example, we are all taught to fear violence in the *inner city*, code words for where African Americans and Latino/as live.

There is certainly more street crime in low-income neighborhoods. There is not necessarily more family violence, drugs or economic crime. In any case, most of the crime and violence in low-income areas is not racially motivated. People of color are the most common targets of crime by people of color, and white people are the most common targets of crime by white people. We tend to think that we are particularly vulnerable in inner city neighborhoods because of the racism of people of color. I have found no evidence that this is so.

There are many areas in which straight white males feel fairly safe. They can roam the countryside and the suburbs and generally are not worried they'll be attacked. They can be alone in the woods, at the beach or in the hills and not worry about being assaulted. White women alone are much less safe than white men alone, but white women with other women or with a man are not usually attacked. White lesbians, gay men and bisexuals are less safe than heterosexual white people.

· ·

- In what areas do you routinely feel safe? Why?
- How safe do you think people of color feel in those areas you feel safest in?

· ·

Except in neighborhoods that are predominantly populated by people of their own ethnic group — where they are still vulnerable to higher levels of street crime and the threat of police harassment, false arrest and brutality —

people of color are not safe alone or in groups. In other areas they are verbally attacked; harassed by police; "mistaken" for gardeners, servants or delivery people and shunned or followed by shopkeepers. Their legitimacy is routinely questioned and mistrusted by whites.

The case of Dr. Henry Louis Gates, Jr., a prominent, internationally known professor at Harvard, shows that even educational and class privilege do not protect people of color from white intrusion. Upon returning to his home a couple blocks from Harvard, Gates' attempt to enter his own home through his front door which had a poorly working lock was reported to the police. Although there are many nuances to the events that followed, within a few minutes Gates was arrested in his own house and taken to the police station even though he had a Harvard ID and a driver's license, both showing his picture and the license showing his address.[1]

To sum up, there is nowhere that men and women of color are safe from crime, violence or white racism. Whites, on the other hand, are seldom vulnerable to violence from people of color and can generally avoid high crime areas unless forced by economic circumstances to live or work in one. As white people, we have been trained to see danger in the very presence of people of color. This will not change until we alter the negative images and portrayals of people of color in our society and learn to welcome and value positively their presence and participation.

Notes

1. Tracy Jan. "Harvard Professor Gates Arrested at Cambridge Home." *Boston Globe,* July 20, 2009. [online]. [cited February 13, 2011]. boston.com/news/local/breaking_ news/2009/07/harvard.html.

Exotic and Erotic

- Have you ever imagined it would be exotic, erotic or exciting to have sexual relations with a person of color, a Muslim or Jewish person?
- Have you ever been in a dating or longer-term relationship with someone from one of these groups where these elements were present?

Racism, anti-Muslim and anti-Jewish oppression overlap in the *eroticization of difference*. White people's images of people of color and Muslim and Jewish people make them seem not only dangerous, but also exotic and erotic. Men of color, including Irish men and men from southern and Eastern Europe, at times when they were not considered to be white, as well as Muslim and Jewish men have been portrayed as wild, bestial, aggressive sexual beings with little or no restraint and insatiable appetites for white (Christian) women. White men have been trained to see these men as sexual rivals and to protect white women from them.

Similarly, our dominant culture portrays women of color, Muslim and Jewish women as more passionate and sensual than white Christian women. Through economic systems of exploitation, women of color have been available to white men as slaves, domestic help, factory workers, childcare workers and sex industry workers. White men have been able to sexually exploit these women and then justify their abuse by citing the sexual nature of their victims. In fact, sexual exploitation of women who are vulnerable says more about the sexual nature of white men than of anyone else.

Traditional Christian sexuality permits only a narrow range of sexual behavior within a heterosexual marriage relationship focused on childbearing. Christian concepts of virtue and sin, good and evil are heavily intertwined with these restrictions. Everything that is "immoral" — lust; passion;

non-procreative sex; female assertion, sensuality and pleasure; titillation, homosexuality and non-marital sex — is labeled sinful. White Christian sexuality is portrayed as pure, chaste, procreative and restrained, at least in its ideal form.

White people experience all the varieties of sexual desire that any other group does. However, white women, poor and working-class people, as well as lesbian, gay and bisexual whites, have often been persecuted for sexual trespass even when the real issue was their independence and challenge to authority.

White people have eroticized African Americans more than any other group. African American slaves were seen as sexual commodities, particularly after the slave trade was declared illegal. The ability of African American women to reproduce and increase the slave owner's capital was nearly as important as their ability to work. Many came to be defined by the sexual role that they were forced to play in the plantation economy.

The eroticization of people of color has been used to justify control of entire communities. After the Civil War, when African Americans were no longer protected or valued as slaves, lynching became one form of repression against the African American community. Before that time, there were almost no reports of African American men raping white women. During the first years that lynching was prevalent, rape was not a frequent justification. Lynching was a method to control an unruly, potentially dangerous ex-slave population, a way to terrorize them into not using their newly won freedom.

After the Reconstruction period, African Americans were no longer a credible threat to white people because of the dismantling of post-Civil War rights and the beginning of Jim Crow segregation. Lynching began to be justified by appeals to white people's fear of sexual aggression by African American men. Even then, rape of white women was only alleged in about a third of the situations where men were lynched. It was only after many more years that lynching became primarily justified by claims of African American men's sexual aggression toward white women.[1] However lynchings themselves became forms of eroticized violence as white men castrated and mutilated African American men.

The disproportionate criminalization and punishment of African American men for violence against women continues today. It is evident in media images of African American men as sexual predators and in the disproportionate arrest, sentencing and incarceration of African American men for sexual offences. These patterns are directly tied to attacks on the sexual explicitness of African American musical lyrics, when similarly sexist language from white country and rock groups goes unnoticed.

White women are taught that men of color are highly sexual beings whose very gaze will assault them.[2] They are told that they "need" strong, aggressive and armed white men to protect them from this menace. These beliefs have directed the attention of white women to danger outside of their families, diminishing their ability to defend themselves against rape, domestic violence and incest committed by white men closer to home.

White women are also taught to regard women of color as competitors — temptresses and seducers of white men. This training adds to the general images of danger associated with people of color and makes it difficult for white women to regard women of color as allies. The solidarity between women needed in the struggle against sexism is undermined by racial violence and by white women's fear and mistrust.

At times, white women's groups have supported attacks against the African American community in the name of women's safety. In the late 19th century, the US National American Woman's Suffrage Association refused to take a stand against lynching and mob violence and asked Frederick Douglass, a black man and a staunch NAWSA supporter, not to come to meetings in the South because they did not want to jeopardize white southern support. The association did not support the organizing of chapters by black women for the same reason. Eventually arguments within the organization became more explicitly racist. White women argued that if they could vote, it would buttress the supremacy of the white race against the demands of black people, Indians and newly colonized Spanish-speaking people.[3]

More recently in the 1970s, 80s and 90s, the rape prevention and domestic violence prevention movements have called for stronger police and criminal justice response to violence against women. At times these calls have inadvertently contributed to the targeting of African American men because they have not taken into account racial bias in the legal system and the use of rape and assault charges to physically control men of color.[4] Women of color-led organizations report that this strategy makes it more difficult for women of color because of the danger to them and their families of calling the police for assistance.[5]

At other times white women's groups have been strong, if belated, allies to African American women and men in the fight against lynching, mob violence and false accusations of rape. The Association of Southern Women for the Prevention of Lynching did important and effective work through petition drives, letters and demonstrations. It was formed in 1930, after decades of pioneering work by black women organizers such as Ida B. Wells, Mary Church Terrell and Mary Talbert.[6]

Similarly, there have always been some strong and vocal white women in the rape prevention and domestic violence prevention movements, supporting women of color in leadership positions, reexamining police and criminal justice responses to violence against women and developing an analysis that includes an understanding of race and class.[7]

The issues of race and gender intersect in African American women's lives. This crucial perspective has given them the ability to challenge the limited focus of much political work in the US. For example, in the mid-19th century, Sojourner Truth challenged the suffrage movement to take racism and racial violence seriously with statements such as "If you bait the suffrage-hook with a woman, you will certainly catch a black man."[8] Ida B. Wells continued that tradition in conversations with Susan B. Anthony and statements to suffrage organizations at the end of the century.

African American women have long provided challenges to men and white women in political leadership to sort out the myths and the realities of race- and gender-based violence. Sojourner Truth, Ida B. Wells, Josephine St. Pierre Ruffin, Mary Church Terrell, Lucy Parsons, Claudia Jones and Frances E.W. Harper were some of the African American women leaders in the abolition, anti-lynching and women's suffrage movements who understood the connections between gender and racial violence and provided constant challenges to the exclusive focus of each of these three movements.

Today some of the most nuanced analyses of the intersections of race, gender and class issues are in the writings of women of color and women who are Muslim, Hindu or Jewish. Not only African American women such as Angela Davis, Paula Giddings, Patricia Hill Collins, Beth Richie, Joy James and bell hooks but also women from other cultural backgrounds including Cherrie Moraga, Gloria Anzaldua, Andrea Dworkin, Janice Mirikitani, Andrea Smith, Beth Brant, Chrystos, Trinh T. Minh-ha, Paula Gunn Allen, Melanie Kaye-Kantrowitz, Pat Mora, Winona LaDuke, M. Annette Jaimes and Haunani-Kay Trask provide insightful analysis.

The previous chapter on fear and danger and this chapter on sexuality are even more intertwined than I have discussed. The merging of sex and violence with racism in our society makes people of color, who are seen as dangerous, also seem erotic. Conversely, because of Christian-based prohibitions about sexual expression, erotic projections onto people of color make them seem more dangerous. One way that people can challenge the authority of a society is to violate its sexual taboos. For young white people, the taboos against inter-racial or interfaith sexual relationships, coupled with the eroticized stereotypes of people of color and others, makes having such relationships a gesture of rebellion against white Christian norms. A sexual relationship with a person outside the norm becomes attractive — both arousing and dangerous. Given the stereotypes and the symbolism involved, any person of color — male or female, lesbian, gay or heterosexual — will provide some risk and therefore some excitement and attraction.

Not all interracial relationships are based on projections, stereotypes and symbolic value, but these facets are part of all white people's conceptual bag-gage and do affect our actual relationships with people of color. While some white people have used people of color to make their sexual lives more erotic or thrilling or to defy white (and parental) standards, there are residues of these erotic elements in our relationships with people of color even when we are not sexually involved with them. These residues interfere with our ability to treat them as valued and respected people.

This sense of the erotic and dangerous nature of people of color gets attached not only to their bodies, but also to their music, art and other ele-ments of their culture. Music like rock and roll and rap has been sources of intergenerational conflict in white families. National discussion about gender and family issues such as rape, domestic violence, teenage sexuality, sexual harassment, marital infidelity, interracial dating and miscegenation often have explicit and implicit racial references built into them.

The sexuality we project onto people of color tells us a great deal about white concepts of virtue and immorality but little about white practice and nothing at all about people of color. If we don't examine the sexual ideology of (Christian) whiteness, we will continue to be directed by our sexual fears and fantasies, leading us to commit injustice even as we claim to uphold virtue.

Notes

1. Angela Y. Davis. *Women, Race & Class*. Random House, 1981, pp. 184–187; Elizabeth Pleck. *Rape and the Politics of Race, 1865–1910*. Working Paper No. 213. Wellesley College, Center for Research on Women, 1990.
2. One common crime for which African American men were arrested during the Jim Crow period was "reckless eyeballing."

3. Davis, *Women, Race & Class,* pp. 110–126.

4. Ibid., and bell hooks. *Ain't I a Women: Black Women and Feminism.* South End, 1981.

5. For more about this dynamic, see *INCITE! Women of Color Against Violence.* [online]. [cited February 14, 2011]. incite-national.org/index.php?s=35.

6. Davis, *Women, Race & Class,* p. 195.

7. See "Disloyal to Civilization: Feminism, Racism, Gynephobia" in Adrienne Rich, *On Lies, Secrets and Silence: Selected Prose, 1966–1978.* Norton, 1979; Ann Braden. "A Second Open Letter to Southern White Women." *Southern Exposure,* Vol. 4, #4 (Winter 1977).

8. Davis, *Women, Race & Class,* p. 83.

The Myth of the Happy Family

IN ADDITION TO OUR UNDERSTANDING OF SEXUALITY, we have certain understandings of what a family is and what family relationships should be like. These too are affected by racism.

- What did you learn as a child about what a family was?
- What did your parents convey? What did you learn from TV and movies?

The word *family* probably brings up images of people caring about each other, doing their part to make the whole group work well for everyone. Even when our own family was violent or otherwise dysfunctional, we may have felt that everyone else's was close to the norm. Whether we talk about the human family, our extended family, a network of people or friends who feel like family and our biological/created family, the word *family* conveys good feelings. It is perhaps easier today than in the past to acknowledge the existence of incest, domestic violence, alcoholism, other drug abuse and neglect, but it remains hard to see that many families function because they provide caring, support and nurturing for some members at the expense of others.

Because of violence and unequal power, we are not equally privileged or equally safe within our families. Those of us who are safe, cared for and thriving, or at least not vulnerable to physical or sexual violence (often men and/or adults), can pretend that everything is all right because it is all right for us. Other people may tell us that it looks good from the outside as well, reinforcing our sense of the rightness of things. All too often, what is working for us is not working for other family members. We might have a sense of being part of a happy family, while some members of the family are abusing others.

We believe that if everyone plays their part in a family, then the whole unit works. Each person has a role, with a set of responsibilities and privileges within the family. For most of us, this means a hierarchy where some people — such as parents, men or elders — have more power and authority than others, such as children, women and younger people. The title of an old TV show, *Father Knows Best*, captures this notion: people don't know best for themselves, so they should defer to father/authority. Many of us assume that "father" will take into consideration everyone's needs and interests and benevolently make decisions that are good for all.

People who say they are unhappy in the family or who reject this hierarchy are labeled home wreckers who are breaking up the family, creating divisions and disrupting the smooth functioning of the organization. They are called names such as rabblerouser, complainer, whiner, rebel or teenager and are described as too angry, loud and aggressive. In the 1970s and 1980s, men used these terms to silence or discount women who were challenging incest, domestic violence and inequality in the family. The presumption was that everything was okay until women started to complain.

Racial relations in the US are often described as if people were all a big family.[1] If people of color point out racism in our neighborhoods, workplaces or schools, white people generally react with one of two responses. The first is to defend the family and cast out the troublemaking person of color. "Things were just fine before you got here and made it into a problem. You can just go back to where you came from if you don't like it." (This response also makes it seem like those who are dissatisfied have no right to be here.)

The second response is to reassert white people's role as the benevolent fathers of the family who know what's best. People of color are seen as rebellious or ungrateful children. Our perspective is the overview, the dispassionate consideration of everyone's interests. If the children weren't so angry and rebellious and would just leave decisions to us, we would work it out and take care of their needs too.

Complaints mark issues that need changing. Rather than labeling people complainers or troublemakers, we need to take what they say seriously. Most people do not speak up easily in the face of authority. When people object to what is happening, it is because someone is being exploited, abused or placed in an unsafe situation. Some kind of injustice is occurring.

People and groups bring up problems in different ways. The less powerful and less listened to need to be more forceful when bringing up the fact that the family system is not working for them.[2] The more forcefully people act up or act out, the more defensively, forcefully and repressively authority responds, insisting that they are the problem.

Just as child abuse, domestic violence and marital rape are denied and covered over by the myth of the happy nuclear family, so too racism, poverty and discrimination are covered over by the myth of the happy social community. Our families and family-like groups will always look happy to those with more power and privilege and will always be dangerous for those with less. A happy family can only exist when justice prevails and when everyone in the family has an equal and adequate amount of power, safety and participation.

• •

- Have you ever been in a situation that was formerly all-white and subsequently integrated?
- Did the person (or people) of color raise issues of racism? How did others respond?
- Did the racism they identified exist before they arrived?

• •

I worked at a small non-profit community agency at a time when all the staff was white. After some discussions about racism, we decided that the next person we hired would be a person of color. We subsequently hired a Latina (I'll call her Sylvia) to join our staff. We felt very satisfied with what we had done. After all, our racism led us to believe we were taking a risk in order to do the right thing.

After working with us for a while, Sylvia began to bring to our attention various ways that we were discounting her experience and excluding her from decision making. In addition, she pointed out how we were not serving Latino/a clients well.

Some of us became very upset and felt attacked and discounted. It seemed like we had *more* racism now that Sylvia was on staff. It was easier before she came because we didn't have to watch what we said or did. She was labeled a troublemaker by some and called ungrateful by others. But neither she nor the problems would go away. We were eventually forced to take Sylvia's complaints seriously and decide what to do about them. Even then, we did not include her or other Latino/as in that process.

All of our responses had elements of the happy family syndrome in them. The racism Sylvia identified existed before she arrived, but we blamed her.

Paternalistically, we felt she was unappreciative of all we had done for her. When we acknowledged racial problems, we still felt that we, the white people, should decide how best to fix things. We were the parents and she was the child, and the parents knew what was best.

Sylvia didn't stay long with this organization. However, the group did learn some lessons about how our expectations regarding her and our roles prevented us from acting effectively to identify and solve racial problems.

- Many of us will be in all-white situations that become racially integrated.
- What can you do to support people of color if they are attacked for pointing out racism?

Notes

1. During slavery, most white people in the US viewed the issue as a family affair and viewed white people as parents and enslaved African Americans as children not capable of independence. Public debate was often not over the legitimacy of slavery but whether slave owners were cruel or benevolent masters. In the 20th century, citizens of the Philippines and countries in Central and South America were described as not yet properly raised children toward whom we had a Christian and parental responsibility to *civilize*.
2. In the extreme case where it is completely unsafe, then the problems may be turned inward in self-destructive behavior or acted out. This is true for both individuals and communities.

Beyond Black and White

I GREW UP IN A HOUSE IN WHICH AN AFRICAN AMERICAN WOMAN came once a week to clean. She was the only person of color that I knew personally as a child. Later, when I was in high school, a single African American student transferred to my apparently all-white high school. He was the object of tremendous attention and comment, much of it negative. For years we had talked about the prowess of the African American football and basketball teams in South Central Los Angeles, and now we had a black person among us.

These years were the 1950s and early 1960s, and the civil rights struggle was often in the news. African American athletes were integrating sports, and students were integrating schools, lunch counters, department stores and recreational facilities.

When I became an adult and looked back on my childhood, I thought that these public events and personal experiences defined my exposure to racism. Racism meant black-white relations. When I began to read about racism, I came across books about the civil rights struggle, slavery and the black power movement. Even today, books I can most easily find about racism have titles like *Black Lives, White Lives; Black Children, White Dreams* and *Race: How Blacks and Whites Think and Feel about the American Obsession.*[1]

When I looked more closely at my childhood, I began to notice *other* people of color in my life who were less visible but still present. I played cowboys and Indians with my friends; my food was grown by Latino/a farmworkers; the parks I played in were maintained by Japanese American gardeners; the high school I went to employed African American custodians and used a Native American mascot (the Birmingham Braves) and when my parents sold our house in West Los Angeles to a Japanese American family, they received hate calls because of it.

In the United States, we tend to identify racism with the relationship between African Americans and whites. Even within the Jewish community, black-Jewish discussion groups and questions about black-Jewish relations are the primary racial focus. There are rarely white-Asian American or Jewish-Latino groups although recently there have been Muslim-Jewish dialogue groups.

There are important reasons why the African American struggle for justice and equality is at the forefront of US consciousness. The existence of slavery and Jim Crow segregation and the struggles for justice led by African Americans have been defining historical forces in our development as a nation. African Americans have powerfully and unrelentingly challenged the myths of US democracy and economic opportunity.

However, US society is not just black and white. Dividing anything into black and white makes it seem as if there is one clear line between the two groups: no gray, no fuzziness, no gradations. Many people in this society are bicultural. Many people of color and white people are of racially mixed heritage. Some people of color are so light that they can pass as white.

The black-white division makes it seem as if white people are homogeneous. On the contrary, what counts as white has been contested throughout US history. People from the Middle East have been primarily considered white in our courts and people of color on our streets. There is tremendous complexity, intermingling, struggle for inclusion and resistance to incorporation within European heritages and histories.

Nor has African American culture been homogeneous. Some African Americans have been free for hundreds of years; others remained virtual slaves until just a generation ago. African Americans came from complex and very different African cultures and retained some of those differences for long periods in this country. African Americans have intermarried with Native Americans or with members of other ethnic groups. Ethnic, regional and class differences make most generalizations about African Americans tenuous at best.

The division of racial discussion into black and white is misleading in other ways.

1. It obscures the long and devastating struggle of *Native Americans* for survival, cultural autonomy and sovereignty. Their struggle is largely misunderstood because it is so different from the African American struggle.

2. The struggle of *Spanish-speaking peoples,* which is heavily intertwined with Native American struggles since both include resistance to colonization, is ignored and trivialized.

3. In a similar way, the presence, diversity, and achievements of the many different *Asian, Pacific Islander and Asian American* communities are lumped together as one and are oversimplified. Asian Americans are invisible in much of white culture and are usually excluded from political representation and social power.

Another result of black-white thinking is that we are unable to understand and develop truly multicultural environments. Many of us claim our communities are all-white if there are no African Americans visible. This can make it seem like racism is a problem "over there," in urban areas.

Racism is not only an issue for large cities. Most communities in the United States are multiracial. There are often Native Americans, Latino/as, Asian Americans and Arab Americans in communities where no African Americans are present.

Conversely, we believe we have integrated an event, neighborhood or workplace if there are African Americans present, even though other groups are absent. This belief can foster opportunism. On the one hand, white people can claim that if we are addressing African American concerns we are speaking about the concerns of all people of color. On the other hand, we can avoid dealing with the harsh effects of racism on the African American community by pointing to examples of the integration or progress of other non-white groups such as Asian Americans.

There are other negative results of perceiving racism as a problem of black and white. We maintain the illusion that whites are the majority and therefore deserve a disproportionate share of the national resources. Conversely, we fear that people of color are becoming the majority and that a monolithic group of darker-skinned people will "take over." In addition, racial tension, economic divisions and hate crimes between different communities of color

- Which communities of color are routinely ignored or not seen by white people you know?
- What groups are habitually left out in your thinking?

are misunderstood and ignored because white people are unable to distinguish the complex relationships between these groups.

We must delve into the *complexity*: we cannot be satisfied with what has been achieved. We have to keep asking the questions "Who is still excluded?" "Who remains unseen?" "Who is still being exploited?" When new groups of immigrants arrive, we cannot conveniently forget that long-established communities of color still face racism every day.

Nor can we say that there is more of a certain group so we should put our attention there. Racist actions and policies in the past have determined the numbers of people in particular communities of color living today in the United States. The breeding of slaves, the killing of Native Americans and restrictions on Asian immigration all determined how many people of color from different cultures are currently in this country. More importantly, human dignity and opportunity are not measured in quantities of people. Relatively small population groups such as Native Americans may deserve large amounts of compensatory reparation.

Complexity also exists within the categories we use. "People of color," "Asian American" or even "Korean American" are examples of categories that can confuse and mislead us more than they help. We need to be talking about inclusion within particular communities. If we are talking about the Korean American community or the Lakota community or the Salvadoran community, we need to ask, "Are the women of that community included? Are the young people? Are the elders? Are the poor, those who are queer and trans and the physically challenged included?"

Democracy means the inclusion of all people in the process of making decisions that affect their lives. Our society is undemocratic to the extent that anyone is excluded from the decision-making process. Racism is fundamentally undemocratic and makes a travesty of our democratic ideals. Fighting racism means extending democracy to include all people of color and moving beyond a black-white — or even a simple white-people of color focus.

Notes

1. Bob Blauner. *Black Lives, White Lives: Three Decades of Race Relations in America.* University of California, 1989; Thomas J. Cottle. *Black Children, White Dreams.* Houghton Mifflin, 1974; Studs Terkel. *Race: How Blacks And Whites Think and Feel About the American Obsession.* New Press, 2005.

What's in a Name?

THE WORDS WE USE TO DESCRIBE GROUPS of people have developed historically within the system of racism. These words have changed and
continue to change, partly in response to the struggle to end racism, and partly
in the resistance to and backlash against that struggle. All of our vocabulary is
inadequate and frustrating. However, there is much to learn from attempts to
use accurate and respectful language. It is important that we pay attention to
the words we use because language itself is used to maintain racism.

The phrase *people of color,* which I use in this book, is one such problem-
atic term. Every human being is a person of color. The word *white,* which
has been used to describe European Americans, does not reflect anyone's skin
color so much as a concept of racial purity that has never existed. I use the
phrases *people of color* and *communities of color* to suggest the multitude of
peoples and cultures that have been exploited by European American society
for the last 500 years. However, if we are not careful, this term will also allow
whiteness to stay unmarked and at the center of power, while all other groups
are "colorful" and marked as different. Even the phrase *European American*
as a substitute for white is a problem because there have been communities
of different skin colors, origins and cultures in Europe for centuries. Used as
a racial descriptor, the phrase denies non-white Europeans their history and
presence.)

Other troublesome words used to refer to people of color include:

> *minority* People of color are a majority of the world's population
> and a majority in some of our communities
>
> *third world* This implies people come from somewhere else and
> don't belong in our communities; third also implies less worth than
> first or second

non-white This term equates white as the norm or standard and everything else as different or "non," i.e., negative

The phrase *people of color* itself covers over so much complexity and diversity that it's sometimes more useful to state explicitly the group of people being referred to. However African American, Asian American, Arab American, Native American or Latino/a — each of these terms are also abstractions, engulfing the specific lives of millions of people.

• •

- Who else is excluded from these categories?
- Does African American connote "poor" to white people?
- Does Latino mean heterosexual?
- Does Asian American assume able-bodied?

• •

More specific referents like Japanese American, Hopi or Puerto Rican are still generalizations that hide significant differences while giving a false appearance of inclusiveness. The male bias of our society also gives most racial terms a male identification. I keep the masculine/feminine form of Latino/a precisely to remind us that women and men are included in each of these categories.

Racial referents can be coded for specific meanings relating to class, sexual orientation and physical ability, reflecting broad patterns of inequality within our society.

Language is important not because it should or can be *correct,* but because it should convey respect for and dignity to the people referred to. Everyone should have the choice to name themselves. Many Native Americans, African Americans and immigrants from around the world had their names taken from them and were renamed by missionaries, immigration officials, slave owners, military officers, teachers and representatives of government agencies.[1] Reclaiming lost names, rejecting demeaning names or renaming oneself is a powerful step for an individual or group to take because it challenges the history of subordination in which others have dictated your name.

Sometimes there is not agreement within a community about what people want to be called, often because there is really no coherent community in the first place. Nonetheless, there is always a clear difference between respectful terms and disrespectful ones.

Within the African American community, there are differences over whether to retain use of the word *black*, or to use *African American*. Neither term is without problems, although both terms are respectful. Similarly, in the Native American community there is disagreement over whether *Native American* or *American Indian* is the better term. These discussions reflect concerns about cultural pride, historical roots, the meaning of multiculturalism and strategies for resisting racism. We can learn a lot about the concerns of people of color by listening to their discussions of the issues raised by different terms of self-identity. It is more important that we support those concerns than that we use the most correct words.

• How have different communities of color renamed or redefined themselves during your lifetime?

It can be hard for white people to accept new terms because they challenge long-standing social relationships. Different words call forth different behavior. We may take advantage of changing terminology to try to discredit people of color with comments such as "Why can't they make up their minds about what they want to be called?" Focusing on terminology is a way to divert attention from the underlying challenge to white power and control that the changing vocabulary represents. We may feel less secure that we know the racial rules — what to say and how to act. This alone can cause anxiety for many middle-class people, for whom knowing and following the rules is important.

In the United States, upper-class and successful middle-class people have long prided themselves on using correct language and being well-behaved and respectful. The use of correct racial terminology has been a signifier of class or breeding and has been used to disparage poor and working-class people. In the South, respectable whites, deriving great advantage from segregation, referred to African Americans as *Negroes* and looked down on people who used words like *nigger*.[2] Of course, being overtly polite or respectful in language or personal encounters made these whites no less complicit in systemic racism.

Some of us wonder why people of color want to be called African American, Chinese American or Mexican American. Why can't they just be Americans? Are they holding something back? Do they owe allegiance to another country or continent? Many people from particular ethnic groups want simply to be *American*. However, because white people regularly perceive them to be Latino/a or Asian and therefore not completely 100%-loyal Americans, the force of racism makes it nearly impossible for a Latino/a or Asian American to be just American. Sometimes people of color use hyphenated names to assert inclusion as Americans.

At other times, people use hyphenated names to indicate cultural and social connections that they feel to the countries or continents from which their foreparents emigrated. These names can indicate feelings of connection to distinct cultural communities, especially in response to the strong pressure in this country to give up one's culture in order to be accepted. Such naming can also be a call to a collective political identity. None of these practices has anything to do with one's loyalty to the United States.

We have adopted the word *American* for people who are citizens of the United States. However, there is no single, national culture that defines what it means to be an American, however much some of us wish there were. Literally, anyone born in North, Central or South America is an American. The United States encompasses thousands of distinct cultures, languages and communities: being an American doesn't mean denying one's own culture or fitting into someone else's.

Part of the American myth, the frontier myth, is that the United States was a virgin territory where people could come and discover or create new selves. We conveniently forget that we had to kill off Native Americans to make that frontier empty. We had to chop down the vegetation to make it tillable. We had to deny our own cultural histories, practices and customs to fit in. The traditions of others were lost over time. Today many of us can hardly identify with any specific ethnic identity or culture.

Some of our foreparents resisted assimilation and carried on strong and proud Italian, Greek, Irish, Swedish, German, Russian or Portuguese traditions. But most of us grew to believe that this was a land of newness, separated from the old tired traditions of European countries. This mythology makes it difficult to acknowledge the strengths and contributions of people from various cultures, particularly non-European ones, to the US mix.

There is no reason we can't be proud of being from the United States and of the positive achievements of our fellow citizens. And we can be proud of being New Yorkers or Texans or from the Northwest. We can take pride in our cultural, religious, ethnic and other identities. However, when that pride fosters feelings of superiority, competition or the belittlement of others who are not part of our group, we are breeding intolerance and violence. Further, when we use *American* as a code word for who we, white people, consider good or rich or smart or successful enough to be part of our country, we are maintaining racism in disguise. When we blame our problems on immigrants without papers, Japanese and Chinese capitalists, South American drug cartels or Islamic terrorists, we are refusing to look at our own complicity in political and economic situations and failing to take responsibility for our own problems. It then becomes easy for our leaders to stir up fear and anger against "foreigners," which fuels more militarism and racial violence.

Nationalism can be used to reinforce racism in the opposite direction. If we try to pretend that we have all assimilated into one large melting pot and that differences of culture, tradition and community no longer exist, we can maintain white norms and white racism by pretending to have transcended them. Saying "We're all just Americans and therefore nobody should claim to be Asian American" can be a way to deny the inequality and injustice that still operate in the US. This false inclusion is just as strong a support to racism as exclusionism. In both cases we are using nationalism to reinforce white dominance.

People will always make choices about what traditions to keep or discard and what to name themselves. They deserve respect for the choices they make. Many people in the US have cultural or social ties to other countries — some Irish to Ireland, some Jews to Israel, some Vietnamese to Vietnam, some Filipinos to the Philippines and some African Americans to Ghana or Nigeria. We each live within complex webs of international culture and communication, and no US border limits these kinds of cultural connections. Connecting to traditions and cultures that reach beyond US borders is a source of strength, inspiration and support for many. We need to encourage those connections, not use them to persecute people for having "divided loyalties."

One of the purposes of whiteness is to construct a normative set of values that defines who is entitled to certain resources and privileges. In response, people of color come together to juxtapose their numbers and their social and political influence against that entitlement. They define themselves as people of color against the ultimate dividing line that white racism creates. In small groups, organizations or in institutional settings in which white people are dominant, people of color may band together for similar reasons.

At a different level, because the binary discussion of race relations puts everything in a black-white framework, Asian Americans, Arab Americans,

Latino/as and Native Americans have formed broad coalitions to strengthen their political bargaining power for the distribution of resources, services and political representation. In earlier historical periods, for example, there were no Asian Americans: there were only Japanese Americans, Chinese Americans and Korean Americans. Now these groups sometimes work together, downplaying their differences for strategic reasons, to claim resources and representation against white or African American claims or to counter exclusion and stereotyping.

At the same time as they work in coalition as Asian Americans, however, particular ethnic and national groups are reasserting the uniqueness of their experiences and the importance of their needs for resources, recognition and political representation as Korean Americans, Filipino/as or South Asians. This is a strategic response because white culture denies the importance of cultural identity on the one hand, and on the other hand tends to see all people of color as *other*, without recognizing their specificity.

There is nothing essential about any of these named forms of identity. Resistance to white racism might appear to white people to create clearly delineated, separable groups and thus be racist itself. The terms *people of color, African American, Korean American, Latino/a* — all self-chosen labels in reaction to white racism — reflect real, but not necessarily stable or long-term, cultural or political groupings. They demarcate broad currents within certain groups that are part of their resistance to white domination and racism. They are each historical responses to the politics of white society. That doesn't mean these identities are not real. They are important, serious and significant in the struggle to end racism. They will not go away when racism is eliminated, although they might look very different at that time.

White people cannot forget that communities of color are trying to survive in a white-controlled society. They have constantly to redefine their strategies for survival and resistance. Many of their words are co-opted, commercialized or lose their meaning over time. The slogan "Black is beautiful," originally coined to strengthen pride and self-esteem in the African American community, is now being used by advertisers to market cosmetics, alcohol and clothes.

Individual responses to the fluctuating dynamics of resistance are varied. Particular people of color may herald new forms of resistance, hold on to traditional patterns or emphasize or de-emphasize racial identity at different points in their lives. There is much debate within communities of color about tactics of resistance, including naming practices. Finally, to add one last complicating but crucial factor: race/ethnicity is only one of the factors in the makeup of our identities. At times other factors, such as geographical origin, gender, sexual orientation, parental or work role, may supersede ethnicity as a primary focus. It is important to respect the choices individual people of color make about when and how much to identify with their racial identity, knowing that our society gives a distorted and overemphasized meaning to racial identity.

Notes

1. Renaming was a routine and widespread practice of slave owners and missionaries and sometimes by immigration officials, teachers and government officials. But it was seldom documented except in personal and family histories. For an example of the missionary practice of renaming boarding school children, see Lisa Gitelman and Geoffrey B. Pingree, eds. *New Media: 1740-1915*. Massachusetts Institute of Technology, 2003, p. 79.
2. Of course there is a range of vocabulary and references that whites use according to whether they are in mixed-racial public spaces or in white-only space. It has been well documented that many white people claim a tolerant and colorblind persona when in public and much more freely engage in negative racial talk when they perceive themselves to be in white-only space. See, for example, Picca and Feagin, *Two-Faced Racism*.

Separatism

MANY WHITE PEOPLE BECOME UPSET when people of color get together without us. In our workshops, my colleagues and I sometimes separate people into racial groups. There are always white people who protest by saying, "I want to know what they have to say." "How can we deal with racism without people of color?" "How come they get their own group?" "I think their group will be more fun." "This is reverse racism."

Racism is divisive. Each of these responses reflects some of the pain and confusion of that divisiveness. Although being white — with all the benefits, costs and opportunities that entails — has heavily influenced our lives, it can be difficult to look around and identify with other white people and to recognize that we are in this together. We need to learn how to challenge and support each other.

It is particularly hypocritical for white people to complain about people of color being separatist. For the last 500 years, it is white people who have excluded people of color from our homes, "our" schools, "our" workplaces, "our" neighborhoods and from "our" country. There have been literally thousands of sundown towns throughout the country — cities, towns and neighborhoods in which people of color were prohibited from staying even one night.[1] These ordinances and covenants were usually enforced with violence. Even today people of color are routinely excluded, harassed or told to leave and "go home" by white people.

Most of us don't want to be excluded, but it is only in the last 45 years that people of color have been able to meet in and control their own space without the threat of intrusion by white people of authority. There are strategic reasons why people of color might want to meet together without white people. They may want to be in a safe environment, to enjoy each other's company, to talk about racism, to congregate with people who share certain things and to not have to focus attention on white people and white culture. Some of these are the reasons that any group of people with shared interests or concerns get together. Others are particular to the needs of a minority group in a larger social setting.

Physical and emotional safety is a crucial concern. Women know they aren't necessarily safe with men just because the men say "I'm liberated" or "I'm a feminist." For the same reasons, people of color know that they aren't necessarily safe when white people make similar declarations. At least in terms of racial abuse, it is generally safer for people of color when white people are not around. It is also safer for them to talk about difficult issues, to be vulnerable and to acknowledge conflicts and disagreements within their community without the danger that white people will use these things against them.

Congregating in a group without white people is also less distracting for people of color. Rarely do we whites sit back and listen to people of color without interrupting, without being defensive, without trying to regain attention for ourselves, without criticizing or judging. People of color simply cannot interact with each other with the same amount of attention and respect when white people are present.

Most people of color spend a tremendous amount of time and energy taking care of white people. This has been true historically as people of various ethnic groups cared for our children, took care of our homes, cooked our food and made our clothes. It has also been true emotionally. People of color have often counseled us, nurtured us in our old age, been our nannies or teachers, assuaged our guilt about racism, covered over their pain and anger to protect us, assured us that we were okay even though we were white and, out of economic necessity, put aside the needs of their families and communities to take care of ours. One of the assumptions of whiteness, particularly for people of middle-class economic status or higher, is that people of color will put our needs before theirs.

There are many reasons people congregate. Safety, shared interests and mutual support are primary ones. These are the same reasons white people congregate. If you look around a school cafeteria you might see white students, Latino/a students and Asian American students sitting in separate groups. If you looked closer and knew more about the groups, you might discover that most of the social groupings of white students shared concerns with other groups. Yet many of us who are white might say that the people of color are cliquish or separatist, and we might feel offended. We probably would not question the white students' sitting together. Nor would we necessarily notice the many ways the white students might be discouraging the presence of people of color at their tables.

Since so many public spaces in our society are white in tone, structure and atmosphere, people of different ethnic groups need space to enjoy their own cultural uniqueness, strengths and styles. They are not necessarily rejecting individual white people, plotting revenge or revolution. White society has controlled communities of color while all the time fearing that their members would rebel. Any time we see even a few of "them" together, we become afraid. This fear reflects our own understanding and guilt about the inequalities of the past, as well as the fears we have been taught about people who are different.

Our fear of separation can also lead us to ignore our responsibility for most of the separation. People of color are still routinely and persistently denied access to much public and most private space in the US. There is tremendous and undeniable segregation in housing, schools, jobs and recreational facilities. People of color do not choose to live in barrios, ghettos and reservations any more than white people do. Those who do often do so out of lack of choice. White-controlled institutions and individual discrimination have created this lack of choice. We segregate communities of color and rarely notice or challenge it. But when a group voluntarily congregates, we oppose its right to do so.

It is to our advantage when people of color congregate voluntarily without whites. None of us wants to be racist or to see racism perpetuated. But most of us are not very adept at noticing racism when it occurs or responding vigorously to it. When people of color come together for discussion and support, they become more able to point out and challenge racism.

All too often we let people of color take responsibility for challenging racism. We may describe it as their issue. We may fail to see how seriously and continuously it affects us. In an all-white group, we have a chance to explore our questions, concerns and fears about racism. We have an opportunity gently to challenge other white people about it. We have an opportunity

- How could you bring together white people you know to think about some of the issues raised in this book?
- Who are some white people who can help you do this?

to develop plans for confronting racism and becoming better allies for people of color. Let's take advantage of it!

Seldom do we consciously get together with other whites and talk about racism, about being white and about working for racial justice. We need this time together. Intervening with other white people is an important way that we become allies for people of color.

Notes

1. For hundreds of examples, see James W. Loewen. *Sundown Towns: A Hidden Dimension of American Racism.* Touchstone, 2005.

Part III

Being Allies

What Does an Ally Do?

ACTING AS AN ALLY TO PEOPLE OF COLOR is one of the most important things that white people can do. *Ally* is not an identity, it is a practice. An ally is someone who not only shows up, but one who stays around for the long term. Acting as an ally means living each day in alliance with people of color in the struggle for racial justice because we recognize that we are interdependent.

The lives of all people are intimately intertwined, no matter how invisible those connections may be. The daily benefits I enjoy are directly related to the exploitation and violence directed at people of color both in my neighbourhood and in other countries. We are all in the same boat, and racism is a huge hole in our aspiration to create a democratic, multicultural ship. I may have the benefit of being on a higher deck. People of color may literally drown before me. But ultimately, we will all go down together.[1]

However, there is no simple formula, no one correct way to act as an ally because each of us is different and we have different relationships to social organizations, political processes and economic structures. Acting as an ally to people of color is an ongoing strategic process in which we look at our personal and social resources, evaluate the environment we have helped to create and, working together with people of color and other white allies, decide what needs to be done.

This book is filled with things to do and ways to get involved. These suggestions are not prioritized because they cannot be. What is a priority today may not be tomorrow. What is effective or strategic right now may not be next year. We need to be thinking with others and noticing what is going on around us so we will know how to put our attention, energy and money toward strategic priorities within a long-term vision.

This includes listening to people of color so that we can support the actions they take, the risks they bear in defending their lives and challenging white hegemony. It includes analyzing the struggle of white people to maintain dominance and the struggle of people of color to gain equal opportunity and justice.

We don't need to believe or accept as true everything people of color say. There is no one voice in any community, much less in the complex and diverse communities of color spanning our country. We do need to listen carefully to many voices so we understand and give credence to their experience. We can then evaluate the content of what others are saying by what we know about how racism works and by our own critical thinking and progressive political analysis.

It is important to emphasize this point because often white people become paralyzed when people of color talk about racism. We are afraid to challenge what they say. We will be ineffective as allies if we give up our ability to analyze and think critically.

Listening to people of color and giving critical credence to their experience is not easy because of the training we have received. Most of us were taught that people of color are not as intelligent or as competent as white people and that it is natural that white people be in charge. Nevertheless, it is an important first step. When we hear statements about racism that make us want to react defensively, we can instead keep the following points in mind:

• •

We have seen how racism is a pervasive part of our culture. Therefore we should always assume that racism is at least part of the picture. In light of this assumption, we should look for the *patterns* rather than treating events as isolated occurrences.

Since we know that racism is involved, we know our whiteness is also a factor. We should look for *ways we are acting from assumptions* of white power or privilege. This will help us acknowledge any fear or confusion we may feel. It will allow us to see our tendency to defend ourselves or to assume we should be in control. Then we may want to talk with other white people both to express our feelings and to get support so our tendency towards defensiveness or controlling behavior doesn't get in the way of our acting as effective allies.

• •

People of color will always be on the front lines fighting racism because their lives are at stake. How do we act and support them effectively, both when they are in the room with us and when they are not?

Notes

1. My appreciation to Victor Lewis and Hugh Vasquez for the boat metaphor which is developed more fully in Part V.

Being a Strong White Ally

PEOPLE OF COLOR I have talked with over the years have been remarkably consistent in describing the kinds of support they need from white allies. The following list is compiled from their statements. The focus here is on personal qualities and interpersonal relationships. More active interventions are discussed in the next part of the book.

What People of Color Want from White Allies	
Respect us	Don't take it personally
Listen to us	Honesty
Find out about us	Talk to other white people
Don't take over	Teach your children
Stand by my side	Interrupt jokes and comments
Provide information	about racism
Don't assume you know	Don't ask me to speak for my
what's best for me	people
Money	Don't be scared by my anger
Take risks	Your body on the line
Make mistakes	

Basic Tactics

ALTHOUGH EVERY SITUATION IS DIFFERENT, taking the previous statements into account, I have compiled some general guidelines.

1. *Assume racism is everywhere, every day.* Just as economics influences everything we do, just as our gender and gender politics influence everything we do, assume that racism is affecting whatever is going on. We assume this because it's true and because one of the privileges of being white is not having to see or deal with racism all the time. We have to learn to see the effect that racism has. Notice who speaks, what is said, how things are done and described. Notice who is not present. Notice code words for race and the implications of the policies, patterns and comments that are being expressed. You already notice the skin color of everyone you meet and interact with — now notice what difference it makes.

2. *Notice who is the center of attention and who is the center of power.* Racism works by directing violence and blame toward people of color and consolidating power and privilege for white people.

3. *Notice how racism is denied, minimized and justified.*

4. *Understand and learn from the history of whiteness and racism.* Notice how racism has changed over time and how it has subverted or resisted challenges. Study the tactics that have worked effectively against it.

5. *Understand the connections between racism, economic issues, sexism and other forms of injustice.*

6. *Take a stand against injustice.* Take risks. It is scary, difficult and may bring up feelings of inadequacy, lack of self-confidence, indecision or fear of making mistakes — but ultimately it is the only healthy and moral human thing to do. Intervene in situations where racism is being passed on.

7. *Be strategic.* Decide what is important to challenge and what's not. Think about strategy in particular situations. Attack the source of power.

8. *Don't confuse a battle with the war.* Behind particular incidents and interactions are larger patterns. Racism is flexible and adaptable. There will be gains and losses in the struggle for justice and equality.

9. *Don't call names or be personally abusive.* We usually end up abusing people who have less power than we do because it is less dangerous. Attacking people doesn't address the systemic nature of racism and inequality.

10. *Support the leadership of people of color.*

11. *Learn something about the history of white people who have worked for racial justice.* This is a long history. Their stories can inspire and sustain you.

12. *Don't do it alone.* You will not end racism by yourself. We can do it if we work together. Build support, establish networks and work with already established groups.

13. *Talk with your children and other young people about racism.*

Getting Involved

IT CAN BE DIFFICULT FOR THOSE OF US WHO ARE WHITE to know how to respond when discrimination occurs. In the following interaction, imagine that Roberto is a young Latino student just coming out of a job interview with a white recruiter from a computer company. Roberto is angry, not sure what to do next. He walks down the hall and meets a white teacher who wants to help.[1]

Teacher: Hey, Roberto, how's it going?

Roberto: That son of a bitch! He wasn't going to give me a job. That was really messed up.

Teacher: Hold on there, don't be so angry. It was probably a mistake or something.

Roberto: There was no mistake. The racist bastard. He wants to keep me from getting a good job. Rather have us all on welfare or doing maintenance work.

Teacher: Calm down now or you'll get yourself in more trouble. Don't go digging a hole for yourself. Maybe I could help you if you weren't so angry.

Roberto: That's easy for you to say. This man was discriminating against me. White folks are all the same. They talk about equal opportunity, but it's the same old shit.

Teacher: Wait a minute. I didn't have anything to do with this. Don't blame me, I'm not responsible. If you wouldn't be so angry maybe I could help you. You probably took what he said the wrong way. Maybe you were too sensitive.

Roberto: I could tell. He was racist. That's all. (He storms off.)

The teacher is concerned and is trying to help, but his intervention is not very effective. The teacher is clearly uncomfortable with Roberto's anger. He begins to defend himself, the job recruiter and white people. He ends up feeling attacked for being white. Rather than talking about what happened, he focuses on Roberto's anger and his generalizations about white people. He threatens to get Roberto in trouble himself if Roberto doesn't calm down. As he walks away, he may be thinking "It's no wonder Roberto didn't get hired for the job" or "I tried to help but he was too angry." The teacher leaves having reaffirmed his own innocence and good intentions, withdrawn his compassion and blaming Roberto for his ineffectiveness as an ally.

You probably recognize some of the tactics described in Part I. The teacher denies or minimizes the likelihood of racism, blames Roberto and eventually counterattacks, claiming to be a victim of Roberto's anger and racial generalizations.

This interaction illustrates some of the common feelings that can get in the way of intervening effectively where discrimination is occurring:

1. The feeling that we are being personally attacked. It is difficult to hear the phrases "all white people" or "you white people." We want to defend ourselves and other whites. We don't want to believe that white people could intentionally hurt others. Or we may want to say, "Not me, I'm different."

   Remember these things when you feel attacked. First, this is a question of injustice. You need to focus on what happened and what you can do about it, not on your feelings of being attacked.

2. Someone who has been the victim of *injustice* is legitimately angry and may or may not express that *anger* in ways we like. Criticizing the way people express their anger deflects attention and action away from the injustice that was committed. Often, because white people are complacent about injustice that doesn't affect us directly, it takes a lot of anger and aggressive action to bring attention to a problem. If we were more proactive about identifying and intervening in situations of injustice, people would not have to be so "loud" to get our attention in the first place.

3. Part of the harm of racism is that it forces people of color to be wary and mistrustful of all white people, just as sexism forces women to mistrust all men. People of color face racism every day, often from unexpected quarters. They never know when a white friend, co-worker, teacher, police

officer, doctor or passerby may discriminate, act hostile or say something offensive. They may make statements about all white people based on hurtful previous experiences. We should remind ourself that, although we want to be trusted, trust is not the issue. We are not fighting racism so that people of color will *trust* us. Trust builds over time through our visible efforts to act as allies by fighting racism.

When people are discriminated against, they may feel unseen, stereotyped, attacked — as if a door has been slammed in their face. They may feel frustrated, helpless or angry. They are probably reminded of other similar experiences. They may want to hurt someone in return, or hide their pain or simply forget about the whole experience. Whatever the response, the experience is deeply wounding and painful. It is an act of emotional violence.

It's also an act of economic violence to be denied access to a job, housing, educational program, pay raise or promotion that one deserves. It is a practice that keeps economic resources in the hands of one group and denies them to another.

When a person is discriminated against, it is a serious event and we need to treat it seriously. It is also a common event. For instance, the US government conservatively estimates that there are nearly 1.2 million acts of race-based housing discrimination every year — 12 million every decade.[2] Each year African Americans alone lose more than $120 billion in wages due to discrimination in job markets.[3]

We know that during their lifetime, every person of color will probably have to face many such discriminatory experiences in school, work, housing and community settings.

People of color do not protest discrimination lightly. They know that when they do, white people routinely deny or minimize it, blame them for causing trouble and then counterattack. This is the "happy family" syndrome described earlier.

How could the teacher in the above scenario be a better ally to Roberto? We can go back to the guidelines suggested earlier for help. First, he needs to listen much more carefully to what Roberto is saying. He should assume that Roberto is intelligent, and if he says there was racism involved then there probably was. The teacher should be aware of his own power and position, his tendency to be defensive and his desire to defend other white people or presume their innocence. It would also be worthwhile for him to consider that such occurrences are usually not isolated instances, but a pattern within an organization or institution.

Let's see how these suggestions might operate in a replay of this scene:

Teacher: Hey, Roberto, what's happening?

Roberto: That son of a bitch! He wasn't going to give me a job. He was messin' with me.

Teacher: You're really upset. Tell me what happened.

Roberto: He was discriminating against me. Wasn't going to hire me cause I'm Latino. White folks are all alike. Always playing games.

Teacher: This is serious. Why don't you come into my office and tell me exactly what happened.

Roberto: Okay. This company is advertising for computer programmers, and I'm qualified for the job. But this man tells me there aren't any computer jobs, and then he tries to steer me toward a janitor job. He was a racist bastard.

Teacher: That's tough. I know you would be good in that job. This sounds like a case of job discrimination. Let's write down exactly what happened, and then you can decide what you want to do about it.

Roberto: I want to get that job.

Teacher: If you want to challenge it, I'll help you. Maybe there's something we can do.

This time the teacher was being a strong, supportive ally to Roberto. He did not deny or minimize what happened or defend white people. He did not try to take over, protect or save Roberto. Instead he believed him and offered his support in trying to figure out what to do about the situation.

Notes

1. Adapted from Paul Kivel. *Men's Work: How to Stop the Violence that Tears Our Lives Apart*, rev. ed. Hazelden/Ballantine, 1998.
2. National Fair Housing Alliance. *A Step in the Right Direction: 2010 Fair Housing Trends Report*. May 26, 2010. [online]. [cited February 16, 2011]. nationalfairhousing.org/FairHousingResources/ReportsandResearch/tabid/3917/Default.aspx.
3. Urban Institute Study cited by Tim Wise, *Speaking Treason Fluently*, p. 267.

An Ally Makes a Commitment

NOBODY NEEDS FLY-BY-NIGHT ALLIES. Being an ally takes commitment and perseverance. It is a lifelong struggle to end racism and other forms of injustice. People of color know this well because they have been struggling for generations for recognition of their rights and the opportunity to participate fully in society. The formal struggle to abolish slavery took over 80 years. Women organized for over 60 years to win the right to vote. I was reminded about the long haul recently when my sister sent me a news clipping about my old school in Los Angeles, Birmingham High.

The clipping was about the 17-year struggle to change the "Birmingham Braves" name and caricatured image of an "Indian" used by the school sports teams. I was encouraged to hear that the name and mascot were now being changed, but was upset to read that even still there was an alumni group resisting the change and filing a lawsuit to preserve the old name.

Soon after receiving the article, I had the good fortune to talk with a white woman who had been involved with the struggle over the mascot. The challenge had originated with a group of Native Americans in the San Fernando Valley. The work is part of a national effort by Native Americans and their allies to get sports teams and clubs to relinquish offensive names and mascots. This woman decided to join the group; she was the only white person to do so. She started attending meetings. For the first two or three years, all she did was listen, and the group hardly spoke to her. After a time, members of the group began to acknowledge her presence, talk with her and include her in their activities. This woman learned a tremendous amount about herself, the local Native cultures and the nature of white resistance during the 15 years she was involved with this group. They tried many different strategies, and eventually, because they met with so much intransigence at the high school, they went to the Los Angeles school board.

When the school board finally made its decision to eliminate Native American names and logos in school programs, it affected every school in the Los Angeles area. Subsequently the decision became a model for the Dallas school district's policy and has been adopted by other school districts across the US. This was a long struggle, but much public education was accomplished in the process.[1]

If the woman I talked with had been discouraged or offended because nobody welcomed her or paid her special attention during those first meetings, or if she felt that after a year or two nothing was going to be accomplished, or if she had not listened and learned enough to be able to work with and take leadership from the Native American community, she would have gone home and possibly talked about how she had tried but it hadn't worked. She would not have been transformed by the struggle; she would not have contributed to and been able to celebrate the success of this struggle for Native American dignity and respect. Her work as an ally reminded me of what commitment as an ally really means.

Notes

1. For an overview of the struggle to eliminate Indian mascots, including reference to the Birmingham high school alumni reaction, see *Indian Mascots, Symbols, and Names in Sports: A Brief History of the Controversy*. [online]. [cited February 20, 2011]. users.humboldt.edu/ogayle/kellogg/mascots.html.

I Would Be a Perfect Ally If ...

WE LEARN MANY EXCUSES AND JUSTIFICATIONS FOR RACISM in this society. Our training makes it easy to find reasons not to act as allies to people of color. In order to maintain our commitment to standing up as allies, we must reject the constant temptation to find excuses for inaction.

• •

- What reasons have you used for not taking a stronger stand against racism or for backing away from supporting a person of color?

• •

Following are some of the reasons I've heard white people use. I call them "if only" statements because that's the phrase they usually begin with. We are saying that "if only" people of color do this or that then we will do our part. "If only" lets us blame people of color for our not being reliable allies.

I would be a committed and effective ally

- If only people of color weren't so angry, impatient or demanding.
- If only people of color realized that I am different from other white people. I treat everyone the same.
- If only people of color would realize that we have it hard too.
- If only people of color didn't use phrases like "all white people."
- If only people of color didn't expect the government to do everything for them and wouldn't ask for special treatment.

Another way we justify our withdrawal is to find a person of color who represents, in our minds, the reason why people of color don't really deserve our support. Often these examples have to do with people of color not spending money or time the way we think they should. "I know a person who spends all her money on .... "

This justification sets standards for conduct that we haven't previously applied to white people in the same position. "Look what happened when so-and-so got into office." In most instances, we are criticizing a person of color for not being perfect (by our standards), and then using that person as an example of an entire group.

People of color are not perfect. Within each community of color, people are as diverse as white people, with a full range of human strengths and failings. The question is one of *justice*. No one should have to earn justice. We don't talk about taking away rights or opportunities from all white people because we don't like some of them or because we know some white people who don't make the decisions we think they should. Even when white people break the law, are obviously incompetent for the position they hold, are mean, cruel or inept, it is often difficult to hold them accountable for their actions. Our laws call for equal treatment of everyone. We should apply the same standards and treatments to people of color as we do to white people.

People of color are not representatives of their race. Yet how many times have we said:

> But I know a person of color who ...
> A person of color told me that ...
> So and so is a credit to her race ...
> (Turning to an individual) What do people of color think about
>   that ....?
> Let's ask so and so, he's a person of color.

We would never say that a white person was representative of that race, even if that person were Babe Ruth, Mother Teresa, Hitler, John Lennon or Margaret Thatcher, much less the only white person that happened to be in the room. When was the last time you spoke as a representative for all white people?

••

- Imagine yourself in a room of 50 people where you are the only white person.
- At one point in the middle of a discussion about a major issue, the facilitator turns to you and says, "Could you please tell us what white people think about this issue?"
- How would you feel? What would you say?

- Would it make any difference if the facilitator said, "I know you can't speak for other white people, but could you tell us what the white perspective is on this issue?"
- What support would you want from other people around you in the room?

• •

In that situation would you want a person of color to be your ally by interrupting the racial dynamic and pointing out that there isn't just one white perspective and that you couldn't represent white people? Would you want someone to challenge the other people present and stand up for you? Being a white ally to people of color calls for the same kind of intervention — stepping up when we see any kind of racism being played out.

It's Not Just a Joke

"**D**ID YOU HEAR THE ONE ABOUT THE CHINAMAN WHO ...." What do you do when someone starts to tell a joke that you think is likely to be a racial put-down? What do you do if the racial nature of the joke is only apparent at the punchline? How do you respond to a comment that contains a racial stereotype?

Interrupting racist comments can feel scary because we risk an attack or anger toward us. We are sometimes accused of dampening the mood, being too serious or too sensitive. We may be ridiculed for being friends of the group being attacked. People may think we're arrogant or trying to be politically correct. They may try to get back at us for embarrassing them. If you're in an environment where any of this could happen, remember that, no matter how unsafe it is for you, it's even more unsafe for people of color.

People tell jokes and make comments sometimes out of ignorance, but usually knowing at some level that the comment puts down some group of people and creates collusion between the speaker and the listener. Whether there are people of color present or not, racist joke telling is a form of racial performance. The joke teller is claiming that "we" are normal, intelligent and sane, and others are not. The effect is to exclude someone or some group of people from the group, to make it a little (or a lot) more unsafe for others to be there. Furthermore, by objectifying a group, it makes it that much easier for the next person to tell a joke, make a comment or take stronger action against any member of the objectified group.

The reverse is also true. Interrupting such behavior makes it less safe to harass or discriminate and more safe for the intended targets of the abuse. Doing nothing is tacit approval and collusion with abuse. There is no neutral stance. If someone is being attacked, even by a joke or teasing, there are no innocent bystanders.

As a white person, you can play a powerful role in such a situation. You, as a white person interrupting verbal abuse, may be listened to and heeded because it breaks the collusion from other white people that the abuser expected. If a person of color speaks up first, then you can support that person by stating why you think it is right to challenge the comments. In either case, your intervention as a white person challenging racist comments is important and often effective.

Most white people know that making explicitly racist comments in mixed-racial settings since the civil rights period is considered impolite and frowned upon. However, studies show that such inhibitions are much lower in all-white settings.[1] If you pay attention, you will probably notice many negative racial jokes, comments, put-downs and stereotypes are made in your presence when it appears that only white people are present. People of color, Jews and Muslims who can pass as white often report witnessing such occurrences. In small and intimate family and social networks, a shared white culture is established, maintained and passed on, and the racial order is affirmed. In these situations, white bonding, boundary setting and justification for discrimination and abuse is occurring, and it is important for white allies to interrupt these events.

What can you actually say in the presence of derogatory comments? There are no right or wrong answers. The more you do it the better you get. Even if it doesn't come off as you intended, you will influence others to be more sensitive, and you will model the courage and integrity to interrupt verbal abuse. Following are suggestions for where to start.

If you can tell at the beginning that a joke is likely to be offensive or involves stereotypes and put-downs, you can say something like: "I don't want to hear a joke or story that reinforces stereotypes or puts down a group of people," or "Please stop right there. It sounds like your story is going to make fun of a group of people, and I don't want to hear about it," or "I don't like humor that makes it unsafe for people here" or "I don't want to hear a joke that asks us to laugh at someone else's expense." There are many ways to say something appropriate without attacking or being offensive yourself.

Using "I" statements should be an important part of your strategy. Rather than attacking someone, it is stronger to state how you feel, what you want. Other people may still become defensive, but there is more opportunity for them to hear what you have to say if you word it as an "I" statement.

Often you don't know the story is offensive until the punchline. Or you just are not sure what you're hearing, but it makes you uncomfortable. It is appropriate to say afterwards that "the joke was inappropriate because...," or "the story was offensive because...," or "it made you feel uncomfortable because ...." Trust your feelings about it!

In any of these interactions, you may need to explain further why stories based on stereotypes reinforce abuse, and why jokes and comments that put people down are offensive. Rather than calling someone racist or writing someone off, interrupting abuse is a form of public education. It is a way to put what you know about racial stereotypes and abuse into action to stop them.

Often people telling racial jokes are defensive about being called out; they may argue or defend themselves. You don't have to prove anything, although a good discussion of the issues is a great way to do more education. It's now up to the other person to think about your comments and to decide what to do. Everyone nearby will have heard you make a clear, direct statement challenging verbal abuse. Calling people's attention to something they assumed was innocent makes them more sensitive in the future and encourages them to stop and think about what they say about others.

Some of the other kinds of reactions you can expect, and your potential responses, include the following:

- *It's only a joke.* "It may 'only' be a joke, but it is at someone's expense. It creates an environment that is less safe for the person or group being joked about. Abuse is not a joke."
- *I didn't mean any harm.* "I'm sure you didn't. But you should understand the harm that results even if you didn't mean it, and change what you say."
- *Is this some kind of thought patrol?* "No, people can think whatever they want to. But we are responsible for what we say in public. A verbal attack is like any other kind of attack; it hurts the person attacked. Unless you intentionally want to hurt someone, you should not tell jokes or stories like this."

Sometimes the speaker will try to isolate you by saying that everyone else likes the story, everyone else laughed at the joke. At that point, you might want to turn to the others and ask them if they like hearing jokes that are derogatory, do they like stories that attack people?

Sometimes the joke or derogatory comment will be made by a member of the racial group the comment is about. They may believe negative stereotypes about their racial group, they may want to separate themselves from others like themselves or they may have accepted the racial norms of white peers in order to be accepted. In this situation it is more appropriate and probably more effective to talk to that person separately and express your concerns about how such comments reinforce stereotypes and make the environment unsafe.

Speaking out makes a difference. Even a defensive speaker (and who of us isn't defensive when challenged on our behavior?) will think about what you said and probably speak more carefully in the future. I have found that when I respond to jokes or comments, other people come up to me afterwards and say they are glad I said something because the comments bothered them too but they didn't know what to say. Many of us stand around, uneasy but hesitant to intervene. By speaking out, we model effective intervention and encourage other people to do the same. We set a tone for being active rather than passive, challenging racism rather than colluding with it.

The response to your intervention also lets you know whether the abusive comments are intentional or unintentional, malicious or not. It will give you information about whether the speaker is willing to take responsibility for the effects words have on others. We all have a lot to learn about how racism hurts people. We need to move on from our mistakes, wiser from the process. No one should be trashed.

If the speaker persists in making racially abusive jokes or comments, then further challenge will only result in arguments and fights. People around them need to take the steps necessary to protect themselves from abuse. You may need to think of other tactics to create a safe and respectful environment, including talking with peers to develop a plan for dealing with this person, or talking with a supervisor.

If you are in a climate where people are being put down, teased or made the butt of jokes based on their race, gender, sexual orientation, age or any other factor, you should investigate whether other forms of abuse such as sexual harassment or racial discrimination are occurring as well. Jokes and verbal abuse are obviously not the most important forms that racism takes. However, we all have the right to live, work and socialize in environments free of verbal and emotional harassment. In order to create contexts where white people and people of color can work together to challenge more fundamental forms of racism, we need to be able to talk to each other about the ways that we talk to each other.

Notes

1. For the research and an analysis of what has been labeled *backstage* racism, see Picca and Feagin, *Two-Faced Racism*.

Talking and Working with White People

ONE OF THE RESPONSIBILITIES OF A WHITE ALLY is to work with other white people. But what does this really mean? If we look at Western history, we can see that members of exploited groups have rarely gained political or economic change by converting more and more members of the group in power to their side. Groups in power don't generally make concessions to disenfranchised groups just because they understand that it is the right, moral or just thing to do. Social change comes when people organize to challenge the everyday practices and policies of the organizations and institutions in society. Popular opinion is important at certain times in efforts to create change, but I believe it is unrealistic to think that most white people will become active participants in the struggle for racial justice in the near future. We could spend all of our time talking with other white people, trying to convince them that racism is indeed a problem and that they should do something about it, but I don't think this is an effective or strategic use of our time or energy.

Training, workshops, talks and other forms of popular education are important. I do a lot of each of these things. But to what end? In many of the workshops, I find there are a few white people — often young or adult males — who resist even acknowledging that racism exists. Sometimes loud and vociferous, sometimes soft-spoken, they demand lots of time and attention from the group. They assume that they and their concerns deserve center stage. I know that when white people express such common responses to discussions of white behavior as "White people are under attack," "What I said was misunderstood or misinterpreted" or "I didn't intend to hurt anyone," I want to take care of them by giving them time and attention. It can be difficult for me to set limits with them, to ask them to stop responding and just listen for a bit, to acknowledge their feelings but to juxtapose their perceptions to the greater reality in the room. There are a lot of things I could say:

- I recognize that you don't feel safe, but this is not about safety. Many of us don't feel safe, but we have to keep addressing the structures that put us at risk and that may mean operating out of our comfort level.
- Although it is, of course, personal, it is not personal. The problem under discussion is institutional racism, not their personal behavior, although they have a responsibility for their personal behavior and for addressing racism.
- Rather than defending yourself, I encourage you to just take in what was said, understand the spirit in which it was offered and take some time to reflect upon it before responding.

However, I have never found that it is useful to get into a long discussion with someone who is defensive. It just increases their defensiveness and my frustration. I get caught up in attempting to win them over to the anti-racist side, converting them by the power of my arguments and reasoning.

I've decided that I don't want to be an anti-racist missionary trying to convert white people to a belief in racial justice. This decision has increased my effectiveness as a facilitator because it means I don't get locked into a passionate debate with participants as often, and I no longer try to meet their every defence with a response. I can listen to them and move on to working with other participants and, more importantly, with the group itself.

Make no mistake; my goal is partly to motivate white people to take a stand against racism. But there are plenty of well-intentioned white people who want to move forward in this work. I find it more useful to help them find the understanding and tools to make their work more effective than to spend large quantities of time trying to convert the unconvertible.

I also try to be clear with myself that I am not invested in how many white people I win over. My role as a facilitator is to provide the safety, information and exercises that allow people to understand their role as community members and to figure out how to address injustice. I have no control over what they do with the opportunity, and much as I would like to have the magic dust that would turn everyone I spoke with into anti-racism activists, I know that every individual makes his or her own moral choices. When I work with people, I am trying to send them out the door more connected to each other as part of a community, more aware of injustice in their midst and committed and better equipped to take some specific actions to challenge racism.

When the goal of a group is organizing against racism, then we are not talking about winning people over. We are trying to achieve some concrete changes in the institutional practices we confront, and that requires a combination of social, economic and political pressure. We are not trying to change the minds of government officials, judges and corporate executives; we are trying to change public policy, judicial practice and corporate behavior. Being persuasive by itself is rarely a tactic that works in achieving organizational change.

There were large numbers of African Americans involved at all levels of the civil rights movement, but perhaps not even a majority of African Americans were active participants. There were a substantial number of white allies in the struggle, but certainly they were far from a majority of whites. But those that were active were effective enough in confronting white power that the country could not continue to operate without attending to some of the most glaring aspects of racism at the time.

There are ongoing struggles today to end racism. The question I hope to leave white people with is "Which side are you on?" The side of resistance and backlash, the side that protects white interests and perpetuates injustice? Or the side that is fighting to end racial discrimination, racial violence and racial exploitation? I can challenge others with the question, but I can only answer it for myself.

What about Friends and Family Members?

WE MAY HAVE A LOT MORE AT STAKE PERSONALLY when confronted with friends or family members who are outspokenly racist. Our ability to continue the relationship or to spend time with that person may be at issue. Here again, unfortunately, there is no magic dust that will help them change their minds. In such situations, I have had to decide whether to challenge their opinions, set limits to what they can say around me, end the relationship or agree to disagree. Obviously your decision depends partly on how close and/or important the relationship is to you. Even in those rare times when I have decided to end a relationship, I have tried to make it clear that it is because of my values and because of my commitment to my friends and colleagues of color that I could not continue to spend time with that person's attitude, comments and behavior. I want them to know that it is specifically because of their racism that I can't be around them, not because of personality differences or different interests.

However, in most relationships there are grounds for engagement. All of us who are white have work to do on racism, all of us who are men on sexism, all of us who are straight on heterosexism. Rather than feeling superior or righteous because "I'm not racist," we can gently but seriously challenge each other. I try to engage people in open discussion with questions like:

- Why did you say that?
- Why do you say such stereotyped and negative things about people of color?
- I've known you a long time, and I know you're not as mean-spirited as that comment makes you sound.
- I love you a lot, but I can't let these things that you do around people of color go unchallenged.

- You may know a great deal about ... but when it comes to talking about this issue you're wrong, misinformed, inaccurate, not looking at the whole picture.
- I've been told by Asian Americans that the word you used is very offensive. Did you know that? Are you trying to hurt people?

I find that I can quickly tell if someone is well-intentioned but unaware of the effects of their words, or if they are resistant and not likely to change their behavior.

When relating to friends and family, I speak up because I can no longer remain silent. I refuse to bond or collude with other white people in maintaining racism. I hope my actions make it easier for people of color to be around these particular white people.

But I am also clear that my efforts at this level, as necessary as they are for me, are not going to end racism. This realization keeps me from spending all my time in discussions with Uncle Max and Aunt Jane about how they talk about people of color.

I think it is crucial that as white people we work with other white people. But not every white person, not all of the time, perhaps not even most of the time.

Working with White People

1. Which white people in your personal network of family and friends do you think it makes sense to talk with? And which white people would it not be useful or productive?
2. What long-term anti-racist goals are you trying to achieve in your organization, institution or community?
3. Which white people do you need to work with, influence and organize to achieve those goals?
4. What kind of education will raise white people's awareness and understanding to provide an environment that will support those goals?
5. Which people of color will you talk with to help you answer the previous questions?
6. Which individuals or groups of white people do people of color around you want you to talk or work with?

Allies, Collaborators and Agents

As we have seen, an *ally* takes an active but strategic role in confronting racism. A *collaborator,* on the other hand, is someone who follows the rules (which are set up to benefit white people), doesn't make waves and makes sure that most people of color don't have the information and resources they need to move ahead. Collaborators don't have to be overtly racist (although some are) because the organizations or institutions around them maintain racism without their active contribution. They simply collude with the status quo rather than challenging it. A collaborator says, "I'm just doing my job, just getting by, just raising my family. Racism doesn't affect me." But they continue enjoying the benefits of being white and ignore the costs of racism.

In reality, most of us are *agents* — more actively complicit in perpetuating racism than collaborators. Many of us find ourselves in situations in which, because of racism, we have more status, seniority, experience or inside connections than people of color. This may be in the PTA, in a civic group, in a congregation, in a recreational program, on the job, at school or in a neighborhood. As an ally, we can be welcoming and share information, resources and support. Or as an agent, we can be unwelcoming. We may not share all of the information or resources we have with them. We might set limits on their participation by failing to provide culturally appropriate outreach and opportunities. We may favor other white people with our warmth, information or support. We may give people of color the message that they are not as welcome, not as legitimate, not as acceptable as friends, neighbors, shoppers, members or classmates. In this way most of us, perhaps not consciously or intentionally, act as agents to maintain a white culture of power.

There is an even stronger sense in which I use the word *agent* — to refer to the way that many of us have become agents of the ruling class in maintaining racism through the roles we play in the community.

People in the ruling class — those who are at the top of the economic pyramid — have never wanted to deal directly with people at the bottom of the pyramid, but have wanted to prevent them from organizing for power. Therefore, they have created a space that buffers them from the rest of the population. I call this the *buffer zone*. The buffer zone consists of all the jobs that carry out the agenda of the ruling class without ruling-class presence. The buffer zone has three primary purposes.

The first function is to take care of people at the bottom of the pyramid. If there were a literal free-for-all for the 7% of the wealth that 80% of us have to fight over, there would be chaos and many more people would be dying in the streets (instead of dying invisibly in homes, hospitals, prisons, rest homes and homeless shelters). So there are many occupations to sort out which people get how much of the *seven percent*, and take care of those who aren't really making it. Social welfare workers, nurses, teachers, counselors, case workers of various sorts, advocates for various groups — all these workers (who are mostly women) take care of people at the bottom of the pyramid.

The second function of jobs in the buffer zone is to keep hope alive, to keep alive the myth that anyone can make it in this society, that there is a level playing field and that racism and other forms of discrimination are just minor inconveniences. These jobs, sometimes the same as the caring jobs, determine which people will be the lucky ones to receive jobs and job training, a college education, decent housing or healthcare. The people in these jobs convince people that if they just work hard, follow the rules and don't make waves, they too can get ahead and gain a few benefits from the system. Sometimes getting ahead in this context means getting a job in the buffer zone and becoming one of the people who hands out the benefits.

Before the civil rights movement, there was no need to keep hope alive because most white people did not see racial apartheid as contrary to US ideals. They simply believed that people of color received what they deserved and were naturally inferior. Since racial discrimination is no longer legal, a different system of explanation for racial apartheid is necessary. When a few people of color are allowed to succeed, they can be held of as examples of the end of racism, and all other people of color can be condemned for not being able to take advantage of the wonderful opportunities they have to be successful. Institutionalized racism can then be ignored.

For example, Bill Cosby, Oprah Winfrey, Michael Jordan and most recently President Barack Obama become proof to white people that there are no barriers left. We might say, "What more could they possibly want?" or "Why are they still complaining?" We can pretend to be colorblind and simply ignore persistent discrimination, criminalization, marginalization and everyday racism that people of color experience by keeping our attention on the exceptions.

To some extent, keeping hope alive works to keep some people of color believing that they too can make it. But more importantly, it misleads white people into thinking that the system works, and that those for whom it doesn't have only themselves to blame.[1]

The final function of jobs in the buffer zone is to maintain the system by controlling those who want to make changes. Because people at the bottom keep fighting for change, people at the top need occupations that keep people in their place in our families, schools and neighborhoods, and even overseas in other countries. Police, security guards, prison wardens, soldiers, deans and administrators, immigration officials and fathers in their role as "the discipline in the family" — these are all primarily male buffer zone roles designed to keep people in their place in the hierarchy. (These distinctions are not always so distinct. For instance, many caring roles, such as social worker, also have a strong client control element to them, and the police are now trying to soften their image by including a caring component, using community policing strategies to build trust.)

Some of us are in more powerful positions, where we supervise people of color or allocate benefits to them such as jobs, housing, welfare, educational opportunities. Others of us are in jobs where we monitor or control people of color as police, immigration officials, deans or soldiers. We are paid agents of the ruling class, instructed to use racism to insure that, although a few people of color may advance individually to keep hope alive, people of color as a group don't advance and the racial hierarchy does not change.

Notes

1. For a demonstration of how this reasoning applies to the massive incarceration of African American men, see Michelle Alexander. *The New Jim Crow: Mass Incarceration in the Age of Colorblindness.* New Press, 2010, p. 235.

A Web of Control

EACH SPHERE OF THE BUFFER ZONE CONTRIBUTES to an overall web of control that is devastating to communities of color and serves to keep them out of mainstream institutions. School teachers, counselors and administrators often monitor youth of color closely, isolating them in "special needs" classes, writing them up as behavior and discipline problems, suspending them readily and then blaming their families for not caring and their communities for being dysfunctional.

Social workers monitor and intervene in families of color much more readily than they do in white families. Because of system-wide assumptions that people of color are more likely to scam programs for unneeded benefits and because of limited program funding that requires staff to deny benefits to as many as possible to save money, people of color often face more scrutiny, more paperwork, harsher personal treatment and greater levels of rejection than comparable white people. Limited language proficiency, inadequate educational background, lack of access to public transportation, childcare and other resources prevent many people of low income from access to needed services. Low-income people of color are more likely to face a host of these barriers, and, in addition, to be treated as undeserving and suspect.

Social service providers are also more likely to intervene quickly in the affairs of families of color by calling the police, child welfare and protective services. Children of color are far more likely to be removed from their families by child welfare and protective service workers, and are quicker to be placed into residential programs and foster care.[1]

Police, sheriffs and immigration officials monitor communities of color with great intensity leading to racial profiling, illegal deportations, police brutality, disproportionate citations and arrest rates for petty crimes such as traffic violations, alcohol and marijuana use, prostitution, loitering and being a public nuisance.

Apartment owners, real estate agents, bank loan officers, security guards, Bureau of Indian Affairs staff, youth recreation program staff, public and state parks staff, small business owners, store clerks[2] — there are literally tens of thousands of white people whose jobs have the function of monitoring people of color and limiting where they can be and what they can do.

Although studies show that many exhibit unintentional and unconscious discriminatory behavior, there are many apartment owners, real estate agents and bank loan officers who try to be fair and unbiased in their practices. Overall, however, these professions and the system of housing allocation they are part of do a very efficient job of keeping housing in the United States highly segregated.[3]

The surveillance and punishment of people of color by people in these jobs is enhanced by the many ordinary white people who informally monitor the people of color around them for "suspicious" activity and report their observations to police, immigration officials, housing authorities, school principals, shopping mall security guards and social welfare workers.

These routine white interventions into the lives of people of color are assaults not just on individuals, but on families and communities. The combination of racism in the school, child welfare and criminal/legal and immigration systems devastates children and adults, literally separates and destroys families and makes strong neighborhood, extended family and community networks fragile and unsustainable. Massive societal intervention in the lives of people of color perpetuates intergenerational patterns of disadvantage, vulnerability to violence and economic exploitation.

In African American, Native American, Arab American and in immigrant Asian American and Latino/a communities, the fate of individuals, families and communities are linked. When individuals are harassed, profiled or beaten by the police, when individuals are denied benefits by immigration officials, when children are disproportionately disciplined by school authorities, when children are unnecessarily taken from families and placed in foster care, when people of color are treated unfairly and disproportionately incarcerated by criminal justice authorities, normal human relationships are disrupted, the social capital[4] of the community is seriously diminished and the ability to obtain social services is decreased. No one is unaffected.

When the media use the negative impact of such community attacks to further reinforce negative stereotypes and justify policies by blaming those under attack, such racial mistreatment is seen as normal and acceptable to white people. For example, even though there is much evidence that African American and Latino/a youth are systematically pushed out of schools, the media portray the problem of lack of family support, violence in the community or lack personal effort, reinforcing stereotypes of people of color as uncaring, violent and lazy. Teachers and administrators can then avoid responsibility for their contribution to a school system that operates in a racially discriminatory manner.

White people are almost never subject to reprimand, much less more serious consequences for regular, routine and pervasive patterns of racial discrimination that they personally commit. Even police officers who murder innocent and unarmed black youth rarely receive serious consequences. Whatever level of racism a white person exhibits, we are generally quick to minimize and individualize the damage done, and to attribute their action to inexperience, an accident, a temporary lapse in judgment or extenuating circumstances so we can exonerate and forgive them. This allows us to avoid holding them accountable and avoid examining their role (and ours) in maintaining the web of control over communities of color.

The Buffer Zone

1. Is the work you do part of the buffer zone — either taking care of people at the bottom of the pyramid, keeping hope alive or controlling them?
2. Historically how has your job, career, profession or occupation developed in relationship to communities of color? What impact has it had on different communities of color at different times?
3. How have people in your line of work protected white power and privilege and excluded people of color?
4. Have you noticed individual acts of racism or patterns of racism in the organization or system in which you work?
5. How have individuals and communities of color resisted these actions either from within your work/occupation/profession or from the community?
6. Who are white people who have challenged racism in your work?
7. Who benefits from the work that you do — people at the top of the pyramid, people in the buffer zone or people at the bottom?
8. How can you take into account the impact of the web of control (the entire system of racism) on people of color when you interact with them and when you look at organizational and institutional policies?
9. What will you do to become less of an agent of the wealthy and more of an ally to people of color?

- Am I an agent of the racism that reinforces the racial hierarchy, do I work as an ally to people of color, or are there elements of both roles in my work?
- How can I become more of an ally and less of an agent?

The cumulative impact of the pervasive, everyday web of surveillance, control and enforcement on the lives of people of color should not be underestimated. They always have to operate within white organizations and institutions, are subject to white authority figures and are vulnerable to disrespect or worse from white people around them. Our compassion and our anti-racist action should be guided by our understanding of how this web of control works.

Buffer zone jobs are the largest category of working- and middle-class jobs and are necessary in our society. People go into the helping professions to serve the community and provide needed services. Police officers, nurses, teachers and social workers are routinely honored for their work and dedication. But just because the intent of social service providers and others in buffer zone jobs is well-meaning does not exclude them from accountability for the impact of what they do. Racism is currently built into the structure of the buffer zone, and therefore those white people without an explicit anti-racist commitment and practice, despite their best intent, will be acting as agents of the ruling class in maintaining the racial and economic status quo.

To quote Taiaiake Alfred (substituting the word *racism* for *colonialism*):

> The challenge, and the hope, is for each person to recognize and counteract the effects of [racism] in his or her own life, and thus develop the ability to live in a way that contests [racism]. We are all co-opted to one degree or another, so we can only pity those who are blind or who refuse to open their eyes to the [racial] reality, and who continue to validate, legitimate, and accommodate the interests of that reality in opposition to the goals and values of their own nations.[5]

Notes

1. See Dorothy Roberts. *Shattered Bonds: The Color of Child Welfare*. Basic Books, 2002 for extensive documentation of the impact of racist practices on communities of color.
2. Even white National Basketball Association referees were found in one extensive review of their calls by the NBA to be systematically biased against black players.

3. National Fair Housing Alliance. *Unequal Opportunity: Perpetuating Housing Segregation in America, 2006 Fair Housing Trends Report.* 2006. [online]. [cited February 20, 2011]. mvfairhousing.com/pdfs/2006%20Fair%20Housing%20Trends%20Report.PDF.
4. "Social capital is the intangible good produced by relationships among people, as distinguished from the tangible skills, resources, and knowledge that constitute human capital." James S. Coleman. *Foundations of Social Theory.* Harvard, 1990, p. 98.
5. Taiaiake Alfred. *Peace, Power, Righteousness: An Indigenous Manifesto.* Oxford, 1999, p. 73.

Part IV

The Effects of History

Histories of Racism

THIS PART OF *Uprooting Racism* allows us some insight into how white racism has defined and controlled specific other groups. All of the chapters in this part are about white people and what we have done to people of color, even though they seem to focus on particular groups of people of color. I include this information for several reasons. First, most of us are woefully misinformed about the actual history of interracial relationships, particularly their more devastating aspects. We have been taught lies beginning with the benign story of Columbus's "discovery" of America.

Second, our history affects our current situations and experiences. The effects of slavery, the genocide of Native Americans, the conquest of Mexico and the banning of Chinese and later all Asian immigration continue to influence our lives and the lives of people of color.

Third, we cannot build trust and an honest commitment to creating equality if we ignore the injustices of the past. Our well-intended efforts to change the system will not be taken seriously if we continue to deny or distort the record of white racism.

Fourth, the past, even with all its horror, can give us hope for the future. The United States ended legally sanctioned segregation and broadened its democratic base. We can easily be defeated by the challenges of the present if we don't understand the progress we made in the past.

Finally, we have a long history of white people speaking out for economic and political justice, and we need to reclaim those heroes and continue that commitment.

Unfortunately, when we focus on white racism and its effects on people of color, it can seem as if the lives of people of color are determined by racism, that they are nothing but victims of injustice. Nothing could be further from the truth. They are creators of their own lives and cultures. Racism is one of the social constraints that influence how people of color live, but racism does not determine how they lead their daily lives.

In this book, because the focus is on white racism, there could be the false perception that I am ignoring the cultural, political, economic and personal achievements of people of color. White people do this all the time, even those who are committed to anti-racist work. To counter this tendency, it is important for you to supplement the information in this part with the writing, music, dance, speeches and history of people of color themselves in all the diversity they represent.

If we keep this emphasis in mind, each chapter will help us think more creatively about how to be better allies to Native Americans, African Americans, Asian Americans, Latino/as, Arab Americans, Jews, Muslims, recent immigrants and people of mixed heritage, as well as groups not discussed here, such as South Pacific Islanders and South Asians.

People of Mixed Heritage

NOTHING CHALLENGES WHITE PERCEPTIONS OF RACE more than the millions of people of mixed heritage in the United States. Still largely invisible in our culture, their presence is in sharp contradiction to our expectation that racial difference is binary, clear and simple. People of mixed heritage pose difficult challenges not only for white people, but for people of color as well. Many people of color have been pushed to claim sharply delineated identities in resistance to racism. They have minimized the complexities of their own identities and cultures for strategic reasons. Researchers have found that, on average, African Americans have 22% European ancestry with the range being between 10 and 34%.[1] Virtually all Latino/as and Filipinos are multiracial, as are the majority of American Indians and Native Hawaiians. In the United States, a person is considered a member of the lowest status group from which they have any heritage. Therefore, it is unsafe for most white people to acknowledge having a mixed racial heritage. Although the numbers are substantial, we do not know how many white people fall into this category.

The myth of biological race and the desire to maintain the boundaries (and attendant divisions of wealth) between white people and people of color sustain white people's fear of interracial relationships and mixed heritage children. Often the justification for discrimination and persecution of interracial couples is that the difficulties of living "like that" are so bad because of the racist response of other white people. Present racial prejudice becomes the justification for continued racist practices against people of mixed heritage.

It was only in 1967 that the US Supreme Court ruled remaining miscegenation laws illegal. Even today it is commonly assumed that members of interracial relationships and mixed heritage children lead harder lives, meet more prejudice and have higher rates of divorce, suicide and other personal problems. There is no proof that this is so, and indeed there are indications that such people are more resilient and have higher self-esteem than mono-cultural people.[2]

Racism is also resilient. White people have constantly shifted the vocabu-lary of racism and the ways that we justify our power. The current force of institutional racism in our society may eventually make justifications com-pletely unnecessary. The large numbers of visible people of mixed heritage challenge our present justification of racism, but they do not necessarily chal-lenge the ongoing force of racism itself.

It would be perfectly possible to replace the racial hierarchy of discrete groups in the US with a racially continuous hierarchy, such as is found in Brazil, that still has white people on top. Unless we eliminate white power and privilege, people with lighter skin, regardless of racial heritage, will be more highly valued than people with darker skin.

In reading the chapters which follow, keep in mind that there are people of mixed heritage in all these groups. This shows how inaccurate it is to believe that any group of people is single and coherent.

Notes

1. Fouad Zakharia et al. "Characterizing the Admixed African Ancestry of African Americans." *Genome Biology* 2010:R141 (2009). [online]. [cited February 18, 2011]. genomebiology.com/2009/10/12/R141.
2. Marcia P. Root, ed. *Racially Mixed People in America.* Sage, 1992, pp. 217 and 251.

Native Americans

I GREW UP WATCHING ROY ROGERS, Gene Autry and the Lone Ranger kill Indians. I played cowboys and Indians every chance I had. We fought over who got to be the cowboys because they always won. Native Americans, for me, were reduced to one generic Indian male who was worth about 1/20th of a white cavalry officer. I "knew" what Indians looked like, what they wore, where they lived and how sneaky, brave and clever they were. I knew that part of my responsibility as a white man in the past would have been to protect white women from Indian savages.

Most of all, I knew that the Indians were all dead. It was precisely because they were history that we dressed up as them on Halloween and in Thanksgiving plays. In Cub Scouts I learned to yell and pat my mouth in the Indian war cry, and I was given toy tomahawks so I could pretend to scalp my opponents. I had no understanding that I was recreating a distorted and painful history, and I certainly had no idea that Native Americans were still alive in the United States. For many of us still, Native Americans are largely invisible in our daily lives and are romantic figures in our imaginations. Real people have been replaced by slogans, chants, mascots, historical replicas and new-age imitations.

Today there are over 500 federally recognized Native American nations and numerous unrecognized ones in the United States. At the time that Columbus arrived in the West Indies, there were approximately 15 million indigenous people in North America.[1] Today, after reaching a low point around 1900, 2.4 million people identify as either American Indian or Alaska Native in the United States. When people who claim American Indian/Alaska Native and at least one other race are counted, the number increases to 4.3 million.[2]

The population of the Taino people and other local inhabitants of the West Indies decreased from several million to 22,000 by 1514, only 22 years after Columbus arrived. The population of Native Americans in the continental

United States decreased from 12 million to 237,000 during the first four centuries of US history. During that time, white people expropriated 97.5% of Native American land.[3]

Please read these last two paragraphs again and consider the magnitude of this genocide.

All the land of North America, including the land that you are on at this moment, originally belonged to Native Americans. They did not use the same legal concepts of ownership as we do, but they knew that they had rights to use it in exchange for caring for it.

The Catholic Church officially justified the destruction of Native Americans in papal bulls of 1452 and 1493. The bull of May 4, 1493, *Inter Cetera,* states that "barbarous nations" be "subjugated and over-thrown" as a means of converting them to the Catholic faith and Christian religion.[4] (There is currently an international movement to get this papal bull rescinded.)

But the church did more than sanction the destruction of Native Americans. Priests and other representatives of the church were often the people who carried it out. For example, the missions set up along the California coast were slave labor and death camps for the Indians captured and forced to be there. Between 1779 and 1833, twice as many deaths as births occurred at the missions, often prompting padres to call in Spanish soldiers to raid distant villages for replacements. An early ethnologist, Alfred Kroeber, remarked, "The brute upshot of missionization, in spite of its kindly flavor and humanitarian root, was only one thing: death."[5]

The church was just one of many participants in the process of destroying Native American peoples. Ward Churchill gives a vivid description of this period in US history. Cotton Mather, a noted colonial minister, referred to the burning of Indians as "a barbecue" and to Indians themselves as "wolves — both being beasts of prey, tho' different in shape." In 1783 George Washington ordered that those remaining within the areas of the initial thirteen states be "hunted like beasts" and that a "war of extermination" be waged against Native Americans barring US access to certain desired areas, notably the Ohio River Valley.[6] Washington himself fought for the British against the Indians, and as payment, he received thousands of acres of native peoples' land. He also owned shares in the Mississippi Company, a land speculation group that claimed 2.5 million acres of native land in the Ohio Valley where native people were still living. On May 31, 1779, Washington wrote to General Sullivan, who was leading an expedition against the Iroquois: "The immediate object is their total destruction and devastation and the capture of as many person of every age and sex as possible .... ruin their crops ... and prevent their planting more .... lay waste all settlements around that the country may not be merely overrun, but destroyed."[7]

Or, as Thomas Jefferson put it in 1812, Euro-Americans should drive every Indian in their path "with the beasts of the forests into the stony mountains"; national policy should be to wage war against each native people it encountered "until that tribe is exterminated, or driven beyond the Mississippi." Andrew Jackson characterized Indians as "wild dogs" and supervised the mutilation of about 800 Creek Indian corpses — the bodies of men, women and children that he and his men had massacred. "Scalp bounties paid better than buffalo hides for 'enterprising citizens' in Texas and the Dakotas until the 1880s."[8]

Racism against Native Americans, like all racism, is gendered. White women were said to need protection from rape by Indian men, who were portrayed as sexual animals. Native American women were extolled when they served white men (i.e., Pocahontas, Sacajawea) and were otherwise portrayed as exotic, shy and reserved sexual creatures.

The attempted annihilation of Native Americans in the United States happened. It was systematic, sanctioned by all levels of society and carried out by ordinary citizens as well as by the military and state militias. Most of our predecessors participated, and every single one of them and all of us gained enormously because of this mass murder.

White people have denied the extent of the genocide by minimizing estimates of the number of Native Americans who lived here. Although now discredited by most historical research, there are still attempts to describe North America as an empty wilderness with a few bands of Indians here and there.

Americans have talked about "manifest destiny" as if there were not real white people involved in the process of killing Native Americans and appropriating their land, as if white people were not manifesting and manufacturing that destiny.

White people also justified the genocide by saying that Native Americans died from diseases they were biologically unable to resist. However, we know that at times, white people introduced diseases to Native American populations intentionally and systematically as part of a policy of extermination. For example, "In 1763 Lord Jeffrey Amherst ordered a subordinate to distribute items taken from a smallpox infirmary as 'gifts' during a peace parley with

Pontiac's Confederacy .... Upwards of 100,000 Indians died of smallpox in the ensuing epidemic."[9]

Yet another justification white people have used for their violence is that Native Americans were simple and unsophisticated, and that, by implication, their culture was not really a loss because they were unable to compete in the modern world. In fact, there were long-term, stable, complex and sophisticated cultures in all parts of the US, including the Southwest, Northwest, South, Southern Mississippi Valley, Northeast and the Great Plains. Furthermore, a people's right to exist, control their land and maintain their culture should not be contingent on our judgment of their sophistication.

Native American societies were not primitive and unsophisticated. They were so developed that colonists continually took their ideas and practices and incorporated them into their institutions. White American settlers exploited Native American agricultural, medicinal, hunting and various craft techniques, land use patterns, trade routes and the genetic development of foods and were also heavily influenced by Native American social and political arrangements. Early political leaders, including Thomas Jefferson, Thomas Paine and Benjamin Franklin, acknowledged the Native American origin of many of the ideas they incorporated into the Articles of Confederation and the US Constitution.[10] Early women suffragists such as Elizabeth Cady Stanton, Matilda Joslyn Gage and Lucretia Mott also were inspired by the respectful gender relationships, the lack of violence against women and the strong role that women played in Native American societies to challenge the lack of women's participation in social and political life in US and Canada.[11]

Today our children are not taught, and few adults even know about, the achievements and contributions that Native Americans have made to our lives. Contemporary Native American healing, spiritual, medicinal, agricultural and land use practices continue to be exploited by corporations and individuals with no recognition of their source, no compensation to their originators and even continued attack upon the Native American communities that produced them.

Throughout the United States today, in every state, Native Americans are struggling to regain control of land, end centuries of colonization and stop cultural exploitation. Native American lands are being mined, logged, hunted and developed without permission or adequate compensation. Native Americans are fighting for recognition of their sovereignty, return of appropriated cultural artefacts and the bodies of their ancestors, recognition of their status as Native Americans, protection of sacred religious sites, an end to police and military interference with traditional hunting and fishing rights, culturally appropriate education for their children and the end of stereotyping, inaccuracies and lies about US history and the present realities of Native American life.

At the same time that white people have vilified and annihilated Native Americans, we have constructed a mythologized image of them. We hold them up as natural, ecologically wise, at one with nature, enduring, skillful, brave and in possession of rituals, stories and beliefs that we need to adopt to counter the destructiveness of our modern industrialized lives. Boy Scouts and Campfire Girls, men's lodges and men's movement retreats, new-age spiritual groups — all mimic a generic version of Native American culture. The movie *Avatar* and the exceedingly popular *Twilight* series of books and movies are just two recent examples of this phenomenon.

Our stereotypes are so strong that very often we or our children don't believe that someone who is wearing contemporary clothing is a Native American because he or she "doesn't look like one." These stereotypes allow us to talk about how Native Americans were, without addressing who they are. Such symbolic annihilation is devastating to Native Americans because it renders them invisible and their struggles for sovereignty incomprehensible.

There are many simple and immediate ways that we can counter the continued attacks on Native Americans in our society. The following questions suggest some places to start.

Questions and Actions — Native Americans

1. What people lived on the land you presently inhabit? How were they removed? Where do they live now? Are there any land or tribal recognition claims still pending? Where else in your state are these struggles going on?
2. Do Native Americans have full access to jobs, social services and community resources in your community? For example, what is the unemployment rate for Native American adults and young people?
3. Are Native Americans in your area harassed for exercising or prohibited from exercising traditional hunting and fishing rights?
4. Is there corporate mining, logging or land devastation occurring on Native lands in your region? Are toxic dumps located on Native lands?
5. Is there a climate of hatred toward Native Americans in your area? Is there police harassment or brutality directed toward them?
6. What forms of government, foods, medical treatments, products, names and customs have white people adopted from Native Americans? How much has their contribution been recognized? How has it been exploited?
7. Are local Native American historical sites, relics and burial grounds preserved in ☛

Questions and Actions — Native Americans *cont.*

your community? Are museums being asked to return sacred Native American objects to the people from whom they came? If so, how do they respond?

8. Are you part of a spiritual or growth community that has appropriated Native American rituals, artifacts or customs? How might it feel to Native Americans when people from different religious backgrounds take their sacred rituals and use them as recreational activities or mix them in with traditions from other cultures?

9. Do you hear people refer to Native Americans in derogatory ways or make jokes about Indians? How can you respond when someone does a tomahawk chop or war whoop or otherwise contributes to perpetuating a caricature of Native Americans?

10. Do your children play with toys and video games or watch TV shows or movies where Native Americans are stereotyped, portrayed as the enemy of white people or otherwise degraded? Are there books, pictures or artefacts in your house that degrade, make fun of or stereotype Native Americans?

11. Do textbooks in your local schools accurately and truthfully describe what white settlers and government troops did to Native Americans? Do any romanticize them? Do any speak of a generic Indian? Is the full story of Columbus's and the colonists' practices and policies told?

12. What do you and your children know about Native Americans in the contemporary US?

13. When talking about Native peoples, do you refer to Native Americans generically, assuming there are valid generalizations you can make about all Native Americans, or do you name the nation or culture you are referring to and give specific examples?

14. How could Columbus Day and Thanksgiving activities be changed so they did not disguise the genocide of Native Americans in the West Indies and New England?

Notes

1. M. Annette Jaimes, ed. *The State of Native America: Genocide, Colonization, and Resistance.* South End, 1992, pp. 23–53.
2. Stella U. Ogunwole. *We the People: American Indians and Alaska Natives in the United States.* US Census Bureau, Census 2000 Special Report #CENSR-28, February 2006. [online]. [cited February 18, 2011]. census.gov/prod/2006pubs/censr-28.pdf.
3. Churchill, *Indians Are Us?*, pp. 28–38.
4. Robert A. Williams. *The American Indian in Western Legal Thought: The Discourses of Conquest.* Oxford, 1990, pp. 78-81.
5. John Krist. "The Mission Way of Death." *Oakland Tribune,* January 29, 1998.
6. Churchill, *Indians Are Us?*, pp. 309-316.
7. Bigelow and Peterson, *Rethinking Columbus,* p. 56.
8. Churchill, *Indians Are Us?*, pp. 309–316.
9. Ibid., p. 343; Jaimes, *The State of Native America,* pp. 31–34.
10. Jack Weatherford. *Indian Givers: How the Indians of the Americas Transformed the World.* Fawcett/Columbine, 1988, pp. 133-150.
11. Sally Roesch Wagner. *The Untold Story of the Iroquois Influence on Early Feminists.* Sky Carrier Press, 1996.

African Americans

A S WITH ANY OTHER "RACIAL" IDENTITY, the term *African American* hides tremendous diversity. In the United States, there are Africans, native-born African Americans and immigrants from the West Indies and South America. There are African Americans with hundreds of years of history as free blacks and others whose great-grandparents were slaves. Differences in class, gender, sexual orientation, physical ability and geographically specific cultures are also vitally important in the African American community. There are no biological, economic, cultural or physiological generalizations that hold for them except for the existence of racism itself, which they must all deal with. Even here they are vulnerable in different ways based on their gender, class, age, sexual orientation, location and other factors. Generalizations about the effects of white racism and the modes of African American resistance to it are false and reflect the beliefs of the white people making them.

The first Africans were brought to what is now the United States in 1619. In the earliest days of colonial America, most Africans and 75% of white Europeans were indentured servants and were treated similarly if not equally.[1] Many whites and African Americans fraternized, some intermarried and others worked together to revolt against or escape from servitude.

By and large, in the early days of the colonies, Africans were seen by whites as different, but not innately inferior. Differences in economic status were explained by reasons of class and religion, the result of qualities that related to being poor and non-Christian.

By the early 1700s, there were over a million slaves in the West Indies and South America, as well as a long tradition in Christian Europe of treating non-Christians and darker-skinned people as inferior. These factors, combined with a decrease in the number of indentured servants arriving from Europe, led to the gradual expansion of slavery and increasingly rigid distinctions between white servants and African slaves in the colonies. After the scare of Bacon's Rebellion (in which white and African workers united in arms to challenge the landowning class) in 1676, those in power moved quickly to consolidate slavery in the mid-Atlantic region. The white landowning class systematically codified the separation of African Americans and poor European Americans by legalizing lifetime servitude (slavery) to control the former and by using the latter as a buffer to protect themselves from rebellion by encouraging them to be armed and to serve on slave patrols. Poor whites received the right to own land and indentured servants were given land, tools and often credit when they finished their term of service. These were some of the original forms of white privilege in the US. As historian Ronald Takaki describes the process, "the Virginia elite deliberately pitted white laborers and black slaves against each other. The legislature permitted whites to abuse blacks physically with impunity: in 1680, it prescribed thirty lashes on the bare back 'if any Negro or other slave shall presume to lift up his hand in opposition against any Christian.' Planters used landless whites to help put down slave revolts."[2]

From 1619 until slavery ended officially in 1865, 10 to 15 million Africans were brought to North America, and millions more died en route from their villages to their final destinations. Probably 2 million died while crossing the Atlantic — a journey called the Middle Passage.[3] In all, 30 to 45 million Africans were abducted or killed by our white US and European foreparents.[4]

Please pause a moment and take in the magnitude of these numbers.

Most of the early leaders of what became the United States, including Washington and Jefferson, owned slaves. During the 18th and 19th centuries the slave-based agricultural prosperity of the South fueled the industrial expansion of the North. New waves of immigrants came to a land of opportunity partly supported by the jobs this prosperity generated. For example, jobs in the textile mills and shipbuilding companies of New England and in the clothing sweatshops and trading centers of New York and other large cities were dependent on cheap cotton produced by slave labor in the South. White immigrants prospered not only while African Americans were enslaved, but because they were, benefiting from the many jobs and trades from which African Americans were excluded.

Not all white people supported slavery. There was a longstanding minority tradition of public outcry for the abolition of slavery, particularly among white women in the 19th century. There were also individual white people, such as Robert Carter, who freed their slaves. Carter was the largest landowner and possibly the richest man of his time. Friends with Washington and Jefferson, in mid-life he came to see the immorality of being a slaveholder. At tremendous financial and personal cost, he freed all of his nearly 500 slaves. Others, such as Thomas Paine, were abolitionists or, like Alexander Hamilton, also freed their slaves.

The Civil War and the end of slavery occurred more because of economic tensions between North and South and because of political differences about state's rights and the expansion of slavery than as an outcry against slavery itself. The Civil War was a complicated political, economic and social event, and while the extension of slavery, was a key issue, the abolition of slavery was not a strong concern in the country. As Lincoln wrote in a letter to Horace Greeley:

> Dear Sir: I have not meant to leave any one in doubt.... My paramount object in this struggle is to save the Union, and is not either to save or destroy Slavery. If I could save the Union without freeing any slave, I would do it; and if I could save it by freeing all the slaves, I would do it; and if I could do it by freeing some and leaving others alone, I would also do that. What I do about Slavery and the colored race, I do because it helps to save this Union.[5]

Putting the injustice of slavery behind us is one of the tactics of white resistance we looked at in Part I of this book. We have not yet fully acknowledged as a society the extent of the devastation that white people perpetrated on West African civilization and on African Americans in the US during the period of slavery. We don't talk about the horrors of the Middle Passage, the systematic attempt to eradicate African culture and the everyday participation of common white folks in supporting slavery. We still refer to slavery as something that most people survived. We don't talk about the millions dead, the maimed, the tortured, the broken families, the rape and daily violence. We still talk about good slave owners and pretend that some slaves had it pretty good. One indication of our lack of acknowledgement is that there is still no national or regional museum on slavery and the Middle Passage.

Although slavery was officially abolished by the 13th amendment to the US Constitution in 1865, economic and cultural exploitation; everyday violence including lynching, rape and physical attack; political disenfranchisement; mass incarceration and almost total segregation in the South and the North continue into contemporary times. We have had over 350 years of economic and cultural enrichment of the white community at the expense of African Americans. The effects of that exploitation are in the present.

It is even more of an affront and part of our denial when we hold onto symbols and reenactments that extol white supremacy. The Confederate flag, for example, was the flag of the army that was defending slavery. The Civil War was not just a complex and fascinating military campaign, but a struggle to liberate large numbers of slaves. By continuing to flaunt representations of the defense of slavery, we admit that we are unwilling to acknowledge, and in fact continue to deny or minimize, the pain and horror of those whose families and communities have been scarred by hundreds of years of enslavement.

This minimization of the horrors of the past contributes to our denial of present injustices. A few of us lived through the lynchings of the 1930s and 1940s. Many of us lived through the civil rights struggles of the 1950s and 1960s. All of us are living through the criminalization of African American men, the scapegoating of African American women and the police and state brutality of the last 30 years. Many of us have supported and benefited from segregation in the US during our lifetimes. Many of us and our parents fought against the dismantling of segregation and are still resisting the integration of schools, country clubs, recreation centers, neighborhoods and businesses. Until we have enough integrity to acknowledge our role and the role of our families, friends and neighbors in these injustices, we will continue to stand in the way of progress toward full equality. There is no dividing line between slavery, other forms of white exploitation of African Americans and the present. Until we deal with the past, we will not lessen its overpowering influence on the future.

With the end of slavery and the beginning of large-scale migration to northern cities in significant numbers in the 20th century, the direct assault on African American culture diminished. It was replaced by the exploitation of that culture by white society. The appropriation of music, dance, fashion and various elements of style from African Americans has enriched white culture and individual white people. For example, blues, jazz, rock and roll and rap are all African American musical forms that white people have listened to, copied and profited from.

In recent decades, intergenerational conflict over patterns of socialization and interracial dating often trigger parents' or other adults' fears of the perceived subversive, scary or eroticized elements of African American people and culture. White youth manipulate these fears to create more space for their personal autonomy and individual creativity. Of course, the icons of African

American culture they use — for example, music and clothing styles — have already been bought by white-owned corporations and repackaged for them. These intergenerational disagreements about lifestyles and personal choices tell us more about white racism and about contests of authority within white families than it does about the virtues and values of rock, jazz or rap music.

National discussions about gender roles and male-female relationships, especially their more difficult and troubling aspects, often use the projected fear of African American men as a framework. For example, in the late 19th century, debates about women's independence often referred to the need for white men to protect white women and for white women to depend upon and to be loyal and deserving of such white male protection from sexual predators, who were assumed to be black. More recently, national media attention has focused discussion of contemporary male-female issues on prominent African American men such as Clarence Thomas (sexual harassment), Mike Tyson and Kobe Bryant (rape), Michael Jackson (child sexual assault) and O.J. Simpson (domestic violence). Each of these *issues* is current, volatile and contested. Each strikes deep chords of anger, fear and pain among white people. These African American individuals are presumed to represent naturally male but less civilized or controlled sexuality, and they are perceived to be clearly outside the boundaries of whiteness. If the debate about the larger issues gets hot and we can't reach an understanding, we can write the whole issue off to the perversions of African American individuals.

The focus on fear of African American male sexuality leaves the lives and concerns of African American women unacknowledged. This is despite the fact that African American women have been in the forefront of the fight against racism and the fight for safety and equality for women. This lack of respect for African American women has meant that they have not been acknowledged for the particular needs, concerns, insights, skills and experience they have consistently provided to the struggles to end racism, sexism and other systems of oppression.[6]

White women's roles and relationships have been taken as the norm for all women, and therefore, African American women's lives are often not seen or misunderstood. For example, we have assumed that because large numbers of white women were falling into poverty (the "feminization of poverty"), so were many women of color. In reality, most were already living in poverty and had nowhere to fall from. We have assumed that since white women were primarily domestic workers, taking care of children and the home, slave women were also. In fact, most female slaves were field workers and did the same work as men. Since slavery, African American women have continued to work outside the home, often in the homes of white women.

These patterns have also contributed to the exploitation of white women. The wages paid to African American women as domestics have always put a ceiling on wages paid to white women domestics. The expectations and attitudes of white men toward African American women will always limit the respect and equality accorded white women. This relationship between the exploitation of African American and white women has been particularly damaging to poor and working-class white women.

When white people project personal qualities onto African Americans, it reflects our images of who we think ourselves to be. Statements that African Americans are lazy, promiscuous or stupid are simultaneously statements that white people are hardworking, monogamous and smart. Our stereotyped statements about African American relationships, families and community structure similarly tell us what we want to believe about white social organization. When we describe African American families as matriarchal and violent and their communities as filled with drugs and violence, we are implying that white families are patriarchal and peaceful and that our communities are not filled with drugs and violence. Nothing could be further from the truth. All forms of family violence are endemic in white communities, and use of some drugs is higher among white people than among African Americans.

These characterizations set up a false norm for each community. In fact, there are all kinds of family and community structures in both white and African American communities, with much more overlap than difference. These dichotomies also establish white valuations of what should be accepted as normal. In the examples above, matriarchal family structures are seen as abnormal, needing to be analyzed. Eventually they become an explanation for lack of success in the African American community. Drugs and violence are seen as natural to the African American community — allowing us to be complacent about them — and they only become problems when we find them in the white community or when their effects in the African American community spill over into our white neighborhoods.

The ideological systems we use to justify racism tell us a great deal about the legitimizing structures of different historical periods. Originally white people wanted to see themselves as morally righteous (Christian), then scientifically superior and eventually historically justified. These theories could be used to justify economic arrangements; they enhanced the status of these sciences in particular and the public valuation of science in general. It became persuasive to call upon scientific theory to certify the naturalness of political and economic arrangements.

Now the social sciences have become a stronger legitimizing force for the status quo in US society. Sociological and psychological explanations of the economic disparities between whites and people of color have proliferated. They deal with issues of family structure, community breakdown, individual psychology and the internalized effects of racism itself. They translate into discussions of the black family, the role of women in the black community, the devastation of community infrastructures, ghetto psychology, black rage, issues of self-esteem in African American children and "internalized oppression." What has remained constant is the dominance of white people and the subordination of African Americans.

The resistance and resilience of African Americans in the face of white racism have been defining characteristics of American history and contemporary life. They force us ultimately to see that all our attempts to explain and understand racism fail to change it. These explanatory projects are, in effect, efforts to divert our attention from the practical challenge of creating a society in which African Americans have full political, economic and cultural equality. However critically they analyze the past history of white-African American relationships, each theory reinforces and legitimizes white racism by focusing only on African Americans.

White people are the invisible narrators as well as the only participants in the discussion. We talk to ourselves about African Americans, we describe and then explain their problems — and then we blame them and prescribe solutions that have to do with their changing themselves, their attitudes and their behavior.

Finally we look for people of color to testify to our conclusions. Because communities of color contain people from the full spectrum of moral and political beliefs, it is not hard to find some person of color who says things that validate any theory. These people are paraded as seals of approval for white agendas.

Here again our understanding of white racism should immediately tell us to turn our attention back to white people. What are we saying and doing? How are we implicated in this situation? What privileges, power and moral virtue are we trying to hold on to?

African Americans have been the center of racial attention in the United States, and the struggles of other peoples of color have been defined against theirs. Yet most white people know little about them because layers of whiteness overlay our perceptions, and African Americans have had little opportunity to describe their own experience. Even today we hear the voices of few African Americans. Those we do hear are generally well-educated, successful and professional. A white-controlled news and publishing network is still the gatekeeper, deciding which African American voices are acceptable. For example in 2009, although about ⅓ of the population is now people of color, they accounted for just over 13% of newspaper staff, 9% of news radio staff and 22% of television staff.[7] They are rarely in high-level, decision making positions.

Beyond ending false generalizations about African Americans, there is much white people can do to end racism against them. Below are some questions and activities to use as a starting point.

Questions and Actions — African Americans

1. List ways that at one time you or another member of your family have downplayed, minimized or denied the effects of slavery and post-slavery Jim Crow segregation on the African American community.

2. List ways your family may have colluded with or benefited from the economic exploitation of African Americans.

3. Which contemporary national problems are blamed predominantly on African Americans?

4. Analyze your community. Which parts — neighborhoods, schools, recreational facilities, job sectors, clubs — are presently de facto segregated?
   a. Which of these do you participate in?
   b. Notice specific institutional practices (for example, red-lining, real estate covenants, school district borders, suburban incorporation). List one that you are going to work with others to change.

5. Notice what kinds of individual acts of discrimination keep the segregation in place (decisions by landlords, real estate agents, employers, teachers). What is one thing you can do to support public policies against discrimination and their strong and consistent enforcement?

6. Work to make sure the police are adequately supervised and monitored.

7. Listen to African Americans define their own lives and problems, and push for their involvement at every level in every situation you are involved in. Support their leadership.

8. Find out what you can do to work against the dismantling of affirmative action and other anti-discrimination programs and policies. ☞

Questions and Actions — African Americans *cont.*

9. Notice the sports you watch and the music you listen to. Are there any in which African Americans are major performers?
   a. Who benefits financially and who benefits culturally from the performances of African Americans in these areas?
   b. What are the economic factors that led African Americans to be major participants in those areas?
   c. What are the stereotypes that white people use to justify these concentrations?
   d. Support the efforts of African Americans to become more powerful in these arenas through participation in management, through ownership arrangements, through less exploitive recruitment practices.

10. How can you challenge other white people's stereotypes of African Americans? What information or other preparation do you need to be able to do this well?

11. Introduce your children to the complexities, history and accomplishments of African Americans.

12. Make sure schools and children's programs in your area are multicultural and that African American youth are not singled out for punishment, disproportionately tracked into lower-level academic classes or harassed.

Many of these suggestions apply to being an ally to Latino/as, Asian Americans, Arab Americans and Native Americans as well. Others are specific to African Americans. We cannot focus on African Americans to the exclusion of other people of color, nor avoid dealing with racism against African Americans by focusing on other communities of color.

Notes

1. Ronald Takaki. *A Different Mirror: A History of Multicultural America.* Little Brown, 1993, p. 54.
2. Ibid., p. 67.
3. Howard Zinn. *A People's History of the United States.* Harper, 1980, p. 29.
4. The devastating effects on African societies have been well-documented in such books as Walter Rodney. *How Europe Underdeveloped Africa.* Howard University Press, 1982.
5. Zinn, *A People's History.* p. 186.
6. Angela Y. Davis. *Women, Race & Class.* Paula Giddings. *When and Where I Enter: The Impact of Black Women on Race and Sex in America.* Bantam, 1985.
7. Farai Chideya. "American Journalism Must Embrace Diversity as well as Digital Technology." *Huffington Post,* April 15, 2010. [online]. [cited February 20, 2011]. huffingtonpost.com/farai-chideya/american-journalism-must_b_539574.html.

Asian Americans

ASIAN AMERICANS HAVE EMIGRATED from over 20 countries and an even greater number of distinct cultures. Like every other referent for a racial group, the term *Asian American* lumps together vastly different cultural groups and subsumes the class, gender and diversity of millions of people.

The role of Asian Americans has always been ambiguous in a country that sees race as a polarity between black and white. Although we have viewed Asian Americans as inferior for much of our history, at times we have accorded honorary white status to those who have assimilated most completely. For example, white ambiguity about the racial status of Chinese immigrants (the majority of Asians in the West and South in the late 19th century) was reflected in constant shifts in how they were officially categorized. Historian Gary Okihiro describes Louisiana's census:

> In 1860, Chinese were classified as whites; in 1870, they were listed as Chinese; in 1880, children of Chinese men and non-Chinese women were classed as Chinese; but in 1900, all of these children were reclassified as blacks or whites and only those born in China or with two Chinese parents were listed as Chinese.[1]

White people's relationship to Asian Americans is deeply anchored in Eurocentric beliefs. The West has a nearly 3,000-year-old history of relations with Asia. Early Greeks such as Hippocrates, Herodotus and Aristotle had negative things to say about Asians, and these were commonly accepted stereotypes in their time.[2]

White people have seldom been able to step far enough out of a Eurocentric focus to understand Asian Americans as part of Asian history and culture. In the European and American invasions of Asia in the 19th and early 20th centuries, we met peoples who had 3,000 to 5,000 years of highly sophisticated and continuously recorded history. Despite this history, or perhaps in response to it, we only acknowledge Asians from the time they arrived in North America; we only accept them once they give up, renounce or betray their broader historical culture.

Our current anti-Asian rhetoric claims that we are under attack or being besieged. We cite Japanese or Chinese imperialism to feed our fears that Asian Americans have come to overrun the United States and take away our jobs and industries. Asians, it must be remembered, did not come to North America; the United States went to Asia. It is best to remind ourselves that it was we who forcefully opened up Japan and China to US trade in the 19th century after they refused to have anything to do with us. Asians did not come to take the wealth of America; in the last two decades, industries from the United States have gone to Asia. And we might add that, more recently, Vietnamese, Cambodians and Laotians did not come to invade the United States, but to escape the invasion and disruption of their countries by US military and economic forces.

Business interests in the mid-19th century encouraged substantial numbers of Chinese to immigrate to the US to replace African Americans after slavery was abolished and African Americans began to gain power during Reconstruction. When Reconstruction ended and African Americans were forced back to the fields, Asians became less desirable as field hands. Chinese workers were used to compete with African American labor, and this use of Asian workers against African Americans continued for decades. For instance, soon after African Americans organized the Brotherhood of Sleeping Car Porters in 1925, Filipino men were brought in and were given the jobs African Americans had formerly held. The struggles of African American and Chinese workers intertwined, and white business leaders played one group against the other, employing Chinese and other Asian workers when they needed them and excluding them from work when they didn't.[3]

Beginning in 1882 with the Chinese Exclusion Act and only ending with the 1965 Immigration Act, Asian immigration to the US was either illegal or so sharply limited as to be virtually nonexistent. During periods in which immigration was allowed, often only men were permitted to come. The government did not permit Asians who were living in the United States to become naturalized citizens for most of that time. In the late 19th and early 20th centuries, whites passed more than 600 separate pieces of anti-Asian legislation limiting or excluding persons of Asian ancestry from citizenship.[4]

Non-citizens had no legal rights. Whites could kill Asians with impunity because Asians could not testify against them. It was only in 1952 that the last bars to Asians becoming citizens were lifted.

All white immigrants benefited tremendously from the restriction of Asian immigration, even those who were only subsequently accepted as "white." In addition, they benefited from the expanding industrial economy in the Northeast and Midwest based on tin, rubber and other raw materials arriving from European and US colonies in Asia such as Malaysia, the Philippines, China and India.

We allowed few Asian women into the US in the 19th and early 20th centuries. Those women who did settle here have been nearly invisible to us. We tend to see Asian Americans as men, while portraying Asian women as passive, dependent, sensual and obedient — sexual objects for the use of white men. Through our limited focus on Asian American men and Asian women, we have tried to understand Asian American history without connecting it to the home countries from which people came. This perspective has distorted our understanding of Asian family structure, male life here and the lives of women who remained in Asia.

We like to think that white people are modern and forward-looking. We often describe Asian cultures as tradition-bound. We think that innovations and "progress" come from us, and resistance to change comes from Asians. When Asian Americans propose different ways of approaching problems, we reject their ideas and describe their communities as more traditional than ours. Thus we reinforce our stereotypes that Asian Americans are conservative and that we are modern, progressive and forward-looking.

We have also done the opposite, taking these same stereotypes of other cultures and turned them into virtues. We may say that Asians are hardworking, patient, industrious, meditative and steady. US business leaders have held up the Japanese as innovative and hardworking and used them as examples to pressure US workers to work harder and be more adaptable to the needs of business. These stereotypes have also been used to justify quotas on Japanese products and "Buy American" campaigns.

Different groups of Asian Americans have often been held up to prove that the US is a country where even recent immigrants can get ahead. Koreans are one of the more recent groups to be used in this way.

In media portrayals of the 1992 uprising in Los Angeles, Koreans and African Americans were pitted against each other. This opposition distorted the reality of what took place in the uprising. It also shifted attention away from the huge role that white society has had in creating the conditions that sparked the uprising. The biggest immediate obstacles to success in both the African American and Korean communities are the exploitation and oppression experienced as a result of white social practices such as housing and job discrimination, and the restructuring of the economy by large corporations, not the actions or personal prejudices of blacks and Koreans toward each other's communities.

These practices set up Koreans and other Asian Americans (as well as some Jews and Arab Americans) to be buffers between white neighborhoods and African American ones. For example, structural discrimination and anti-immigrant bias force well-educated Koreans to become small shop owners in African American and Latino/a communities, where they faced small profits and vulnerability to violence. Deteriorating economic conditions, coupled with media attention to their "success," directed people's anger toward them rather than toward economic policymakers. Koreans were clearly set up to be sacrificed to rioters. Their calls to the Los Angeles Police Department and to state and local officials for protection were unanswered.[5]

White people, on the other hand, could sit back and watch the show, perhaps temporarily uneasy about things getting out of hand, but nevertheless buffered from the direct effects of the violence and assured of protection. When rioters attacked major shopping malls in white Culver City, however, they were quickly stopped by police.[6]

A good illustration of how white people's lack of acceptance, suspicion and fear of Asian Americans lead to violence and discrimination is the death of Vincent Chin in 1982. Chin was a Chinese American living in Detroit who was killed by two white unemployed auto workers who believed he was Japanese. He had lived in the United States all his life. His killers had been led to believe that they couldn't get work because of the import of Japanese cars. They believed that Japanese corporations were responsible for their unemployment and that any Japanese American was complicit with the Japanese government. And they couldn't tell a Japanese American from a Chinese American. The sentence they each eventually received for killing Chin was barely a reprimand — three years' probation and a $3,000 fine.[7]

Wen Ho Lee is a Taiwanese American nuclear scientist who, while working at Los Alamos, was accused of releasing classified nuclear documents in 1999. He was held in solitary confinement for nine months by the government and then released, without having been charged for espionage. In 2006 he won a settlement from the government of nearly $900,000.

Wen Ho Lee was vindicated, but Vincent Chin is dead — both among many Asian Americans blamed for economic problems, targeted for being dangerous immigrants and then attacked. We must ask ourselves how many decades, generations, centuries even people must live here before they are accepted as "all-American" if they are not white.

White people have used the "success" of some Asian Americans[8] to demonstrate the lack of racism in the US and the opportunity that African Americans have supposedly had and not used. Some white people label Asians a "model minority," a code phrase (see Part I) implying Asian Americans are hardworking, industrious, thrifty, future oriented and law-abiding, as all good white Christians are (or at least should be). However, this is just another example of projecting our own stereotypes onto Asian Americans.

Racism keeps some people the targets of violence (physical, emotional or economic) regardless of their financial success, and it keeps other (white) people safe and protected. Many Japanese Americans were highly "successful" in the western United States, but were still attacked, locked up in concentration camps and subjected to mob violence during World War II. Economic success may offer some protection against the worst effects of racism, but many white Americans still consider Asian Americans (and other people of color) as different and inferior. Without the dismantling of white control and domination, no amount of economic success will protect people from continued attack and injustice. Vincent Chin could have been rich or poor, a citizen or non-citizen — what mattered to the two men who killed him was that he was Asian American.

White people need to be considerably better informed about the particular histories and complexity of Asian American communities in the US. We need to break down our simplified stereotypes by going beyond an awareness of the Chinese New Year and the Japanese internment. We have to analyze critically any information we are given and counter it with a better understanding of the actual dynamics both within and between different communities.

Within particular Asian American communities, there have been accomplishments and much resistance to racism. There have been many kinds of cross-influences and effects — a constant exchange and mutual influence between many different Asian American cultures. The complexity of these dynamics defies simple generalizations about economic success or model minorities.

Questions and Actions — Asian Americans

1. What specific Asian American cultural communities live in your area? How can you find out more about the uniqueness of each particular community?
2. List four key Asian American concerns.
3. Are different Asian American groups represented in your city and county governments, school boards and other local political institutions?
4. What are some of the "positive" stereotypes that you hear about Asian Americans? What complexities and problems do these stereotypes cover up? What can you learn about white self-images from these stereotypes?
5. How have different Asian American groups been scapegoated for economic problems in your community? How have non-American Asians been blamed?
6. What do white people expect of Asian Americans for acceptance into the white community? Are there hidden reservations or conditions for that acceptance?
7. How are Asian American and Asian culture and history represented in the schools in your community?
8. Do you and your children have accurate knowledge about the struggles for independence from colonialism of the Filipinos, Chinese, Koreans, Vietnamese and Indians?
9. How has the relationship of the US with particular Asian countries affected the immigration of Asians and their treatment once here?

Notes

1. Gary Y. Okihiro. *Margins and Mainstreams: Asians in American History and Culture.* University of Washington, 1994, p. 53.
2. Ibid., pp. 8–9.
3. Ibid., Chapter 2; Takaki, *A Different Mirror,* pp. 202–204.
4. Yen Le Espiritu. *Asian American Panethnicity: Bridging Institutions and Identities,* Temple University, 1992, p. 135.
5. Robert Gooding-Williams, ed. *Reading Rodney King, Reading Urban Uprising.* Routledge, 1993, p. 201.
6. Ibid., pp. 196–211.
7. Espiritu, *Asian American Panethnicity,* pp. 141–143.
8. Average family income figures for Asian Americans hide large disparities in the distribution of wealth. Substantial groups of Asian Americans live in poverty. Generalizations about average income lump together different communities, some long established and some very recent, as well as covering over gender and class differences in income and opportunity. Meizhu Lui et. al. *The Color of Wealth: The Story Behind the US Racial Wealth Divide.* New Press, 2006, pp. 209-215.

Latino/as

I N ITS 2009 UPDATE, THE US CENSUS BUREAU estimates that Hispanics made up 16% of the population in the United States, over 48 million people. They comprised 37% of the populations of California and Texas, 15% of New York's population, nearly 22% of Florida's, 31% of Arizona's, 47% of New Mexico's and 20% of Colorado's.[1]

The variations of Spanish spoken are many, and the differences between communities of Latino/as are large. Some groups, such as Cuban Americans or Puerto Ricans, have kept strong national identities. Others are from families that have lived in the US for hundreds of years and have Spanish-derived cultures but no connection with another country.

The very terminology used to describe Latino/as has been in great dispute over the years. I use *Latino/a* because, when speaking in very general terms, it is broadly inclusive and tends to be preferred by Spanish-speaking people. I use the masculine/feminine ending to remind us to recognize women in other cultures. However *Hispanic* and *Latino/a* derive their meaning from Spain, and these words conceal the connections to North and South American land struggles and the intermingling of Spanish-derived culture with Native American cultures.

I also use the term *Spanish-speaking* because most Latino/as in the US are connected to longstanding and complex Spanish language cultures that span the hemisphere, even if they don't personally speak the language. This term also emphasizes that many issues we should consider are cultural as well as economic or political.

There is no national identity or set of interests uniting Latino/as except their concern for the end of white racism toward Spanish-speaking people. Many Latino/as prefer to be called Cubano/as, Mexicano/as or Puertoriqueño/as/Boricuans. These are the three largest groups of Spanish-speaking people in the United States; many Latino/a identities are formed primarily within these communities.

Part of the white *creation story* which we tell on Thanksgiving relates how white roots are deep, how we were the original European settlers. Contrary to our story, descendants of Spanish colonists have lived in the Southeast, Southwest and West for considerably longer than most English-speaking people. The first permanent European settlement within the current United States borders was established at St. Augustine, in what is now Florida, in 1565. From settlements in Florida, Mexico and the West Indies, approximately ⅓ of the present territory of the continental United States was invaded by Spanish soldiers and missionaries and conquered in the most brutal way. A combination of Spanish (male) administrators, conquistadors, ranchers and missionaries killed, tortured and enslaved most of the Native American men and killed, raped and intermarried with the Native American women in what are now the states of California, Utah, Nevada, Arizona, New Mexico, Texas and parts of Colorado and Wyoming.[2]

When anyone's ancestors arrived in the United States — whether 400 years ago or last week — should not be important. But the white creation story fuels anti-immigrant violence because it lets us conveniently forget that many of us were immigrants ourselves not so long ago, and many of the people we target as unwelcome have roots far back in US history. Ironically, this is most true in states with strong anti-immigrant organizing like Arizona where the majority of white people have family histories of less than 60 years in the area. Cracking down on immigrants without papers promotes police harassment, job and housing discrimination and denial of health and educational services to anyone whom a white person "mistakes" for an undocumented immigrant.

The Monroe Doctrine, written in 1823, was the first attempt to articulate the US perception that all of the Western Hemisphere was "our backyard," and that we could control what happened there in order to protect ourselves from outsiders. Since then the US has initiated hundreds of invasions and interventions in Central and South American countries, leading to the deaths of tens of thousands of people and creating havoc in the lives and economies of local populations.

For example, in 1830, when the Mexican government outlawed slavery and prohibited further American immigration into Texas, whites were outraged and thousands continued to move into Texas as illegal aliens. They rose against Mexican rule in 1836 and, although initially defeated, were eventually victorious, claiming independence as the Lone Star State. Texas was annexed by the United States in 1845. Then the US instigated border skirmishes in order to justify a brutal invasion of Mexico in 1846, resulting in the Treaty of Guadalupe Hidalgo in 1848 in which Mexico was forced to hand over all of California, New Mexico, Nevada and parts of Colorado, Arizona and Utah. As one congressman wrote at the time about our "manifest destiny" to rule the hemisphere, "This continent was intended by Providence as a vast theatre on which to work out the grand experiment of Republican government, under the auspices of the Anglo-Saxon race."[3]

In 1898, the US declared war on Spain and took over a war of independence that Cubans had started in 1895. Within three months, the US defeated the Spanish forces and required them to turn over control of Cuba to us, completely ignoring the Cubans who had been fighting for their freedom. We also took over Puerto Rico, annexed Hawaii, occupied Wake Island and Guam in the Pacific and claimed the Philippines. Filipinos had been engaged in a long-term war of independence with Spain, and in 1899, they rose up against US rule. President McKinley sent in 70,000 troops. Three years later, 1/6 of the Philippine population was dead and the war was over.[4]

More recently, many Spanish-speaking people have arrived from Cuba, the Dominican Republic and many Central and South American countries. These immigrations have been connected with US foreign policy and economic expansion. Groups of refugees came to the United States seeking asylum and economic opportunity. US government and corporate policy also directly encouraged migration through the Bracero program, which brought more than 5 million Mexican workers to the United States between 1942 and 1964 as cheap agricultural labor.[5]

We are clearly hypocritical when we blame recent Spanish-speaking immigrants for our economic problems and when we try to enforce a rigid border separation between Mexico (or Cuba or Haiti) and the United States. Corporate interests demand cheap labor and free movement of capital and resources throughout the Americas and have pushed through the North American Free Trade Agreement (NAFTA), the General Agreement on Tariffs and Trade (GATT) and other policies conducive to their ends. And they encourage us to blame low-wage Mexican and Central American workers for the lack of jobs and economic dislocation that result from those policies.

White elites in the US have long been concerned with both expanding and maintaining our national borders. Expansion is seen as economic opportunity, while the maintenance consists of keeping Spanish-speaking people on the fringes of society and not allowing them into centers of power and control. The struggles of many Latino/a people in the US have therefore been focused on the borderlands, both physical and figurative, between Anglo and Spanish land and culture.

Latino/as have occupied various positions in the racial hierarchy of the United States depending upon economic and cultural factors. After the annexation of the Southwest in 1848, Mexican people had enough economic clout and "civilized" habits that they were accepted as white and given the rights of citizenship in California.[6] This was in contrast to the few blacks there, who were ranked far below Mexicans; to the Chinese, who were ranked slightly above Native Americans and had no rights and to the Native Americans, who were considered barely human and were killed indiscriminately.[7] California's racial hierarchy still has white people on top, but today Spanish-speaking people are considered, along with African Americans, to be at the bottom, and most Asian Americans are held up as closer to white and treated far better.

Latino/as are under-represented, undercounted and underestimated. Their lives, culture and the deprivations they have suffered are invisible to us. For example, in the Los Angeles uprising in 1992, the greatest number of people killed from any ethnic group were Latino/as. The greatest damage done was to property owned by Latino/as. Immediately following the uprising, there was an immigration crackdown and hundreds of Spanish-speaking Los Angeles residents were deported, most without trials or legal recourse.[8] Similarly in the aftermath of hurricane Katrina, the media barely mentioned the impact on the significant immigrant Latino/a (and Native American) communities in the hardest hit southern states.

Spanish-speaking people can participate in literary, musical, dramatic, political and popular developments throughout the Spanish-speaking world. They have access to a major international culture that is largely invisible to monolingual white people. The Spanish-speaking people of the US could bring these dynamic, cosmopolitan and creative currents into mainstream US culture. Some of them obviously have been introduced, yet most of the time they are resisted. White people have fought against the use of Spanish in schools and workplaces and have ignored, made fun of and attacked Spanish language culture as being inferior, uncivilized, rural, traditional, monolithic, subversive and dangerous. What are white people trying to maintain, and what do we fear, when we attack a vital, international culture of which we are ignorant?

We are saying that English is the language of culture and achievement, and European-based civilization is the source of all beneficial contributions to the world. We are, in addition, demonstrating that white racism is not only about economic and political domination, but is also about cultural hegemony. It is about white people and white institutions being able to define what culture is, who gets to participate in it and what language, literature, art and music are included.

It is crucial for us to understand the importance of racism as a system of cultural domination. White people have long denied or minimized the importance of culture to people's everyday lives. We have appealed to universal, international and human standards and values in our politics, science and philosophy. This makes it very difficult for us to recognize the value of culture in our own lives, much less in other people's. We fail to see the inspirational role that culture plays in resistance to domination by people of color. Using music as an example, when we are unfamiliar with the contributions of Reuben Blades, Lila Downs, Mercedes Sosa, Tito Puente, Carlos Santana, Flaco Jimenez, Los Lobos, Selena and Villa-Lobos, we deny ourselves access to the richness, creativity and inspiration that their culture could provide us. Instead of maintaining cultural borders, we need to become much better at crossing them.

We cannot eliminate racism without understanding its cultural dimensions. White racism is supported by economic, political and cultural practices that operate partly by marketing sanitized versions of other people's cultures to us and packaging them as exotic, natural and authentic. Their cultures are distorted by this marketing and packaging and by the separation of cultures from the people actually living them. At the same time, white cultural practices are rendered invisible by our focus on other people's practices. In this sense, the border keeping Spanish-speaking people out of the mainstream of US society is maintained by economic and cultural domination, language barriers and geographic segregation.

Use the questions and the suggestions in the chapters on Native Americans, African Americans and Asian Americans to guide your work as an ally to Latino/as.

Questions and Actions — Latino/as

1. Which groups of Latino/a people live in your town, city or rural area?
2. Which groups of Latino/a people provide labor or services on which you personally or the economy are dependent (farm workers, low-wage manufacturing workers or workers in factories near the Mexican border)?
3. What do you gain and what do you lose when workers are poorly paid, work in unsanitary conditions, are exposed to dangerous chemicals and have unsafe working conditions?
4. How well are Latino/a communities represented in your local governments?
5. Are there adequate support services for Spanish-speaking families and Spanish-speaking youth in your area? How could you find out?
6. How has the history of US involvement with Mexico, Cuba, Puerto Rico and El Salvador influenced the status and position of the immigrant communities that arrived here from those countries?
7. How have stereotypes of Latino/as helped prepare for or justify invasions and control of South and Central American countries?
8. Have you been involved with solidarity work with Spanish-speaking countries? How might that work have been connected to the exploitation of Latino/a communities closer to home?
9. Did your foreparents speak a native language that has been lost in your family or community? What other losses accompanied the pressure to be a monolingual community?
10. How has the emergence of English as the language used in international communication affected people whose primary language is not English?
11. Do you speak Spanish? If not, what might be reasons for learning to do so? Why haven't you learned it in the past?

Notes

1. US Census Bureau. *Hispanic Americans by the Numbers.* Infoplease website. [online]. [cited September 5, 2010]. infoplease.com/spot/hhmcensus1.html#axzz0yhKjCmJB.
2. This is the area originally colonized by the Spanish and transferred to the US after the Mexican American war in 1848.
3. Takaki, *A Different Mirror,* p. 176.
4. Zinn, *A People's History,* pp. 306–310.
5. Denis Lynn Daly Heyck. *Barrios and Borderlands: Cultures of Latinos and Latinas in the United States.* Routledge, 1994, p. 6.
6. Almaguer, *Racial Fault Lines,* pp. 54–56.
7. Ibid., pp. 7–9.
8. Gooding-Williams, ed. *Reading Rodney King,* p. 122.

Arab Americans

O N MAY 24, 2001, months before the bombings of the World Trade Center and the Pentagon, I came across the following sentences in two different articles on the front page of the *New York Times*:

> Like most Afghan men he wore a turban coiled around his head like a holy bandage.

> Afghanistan, known these days as a womb for global jihad ...

Our images of Arabs and our images of Islam are primarily filtered through a Western media lens filled with stereotypes, disrespect, misinformation and emotionally laden descriptions. Images of Arabs and of Islam are conflated, producing a confusing and distorted picture of both, and tainting Arab Americans with misrepresentations. For example, despite the common perception that Arab Americans are Muslims, the majority are Christian.[1]

The stereotypes of Arab and Arab American men as untrustworthy and deceptive businessmen, terrorists, fanatics, sheiks and traders riding camels — and of women as seductive or submissive — are still so pervasive that sometimes I find it difficult to imagine other images. Have you seen images recently of:

- an Arab American father playing catch with his son or daughter?
- an Arab American woman in a business suit?
- Arab American youth doing community service?
- an Arab American community celebrating a birth or marriage?

In one panoramic survey of Arab characters and images in 900 films, 12 were positive, 50 were balanced and all the rest negative.[2] How can we treat Arabs respectfully and inclusively when they are portrayed as exotic or erotic, sinister and threatening, totally alien and dangerous to white Christians?

As with other communities of color, Arab Americans are very diverse, coming from such countries as Algeria, Egypt, Iraq, Jordan, Kuwait, Lebanon, Libya, Palestine, Mauritania, Morocco, Qatar, Saudi Arabia, Yemen, Sudan, Syria, Tunisia and the United Arab Emirates. (Iran and Turkey are not Arabic-speaking countries, and their citizens are not considered Arabs.) There are probably between 4 to 6 million Arab Americans in the United States today, living in communities throughout the country.

The first wave of Arab American immigrants came to the Western Hemisphere during the late 19th century (beginning around 1880 through the end of World War I). They were mostly from what was called the Greater Syria area, which included Lebanon, homeland to many among the early immigrants. These immigrants were primarily Christian, and substantial numbers of this first generation became peddlers, shopkeepers and traders. Later waves of immigrants came from a variety of Arabic-speaking countries and were mostly Sunni Muslims.

Early Arab American immigrants were yet another group that the legal system attempted to place within its rigid racial classification system. In the early 20th century, they were denied citizenship in the US and Canada because they were labeled Asian and therefore were not considered white. For example, in 1914, George Dow was denied permission to become a US citizen because he was a Syrian of Asiatic birth, and the law (a 1790 US Statute) stated that only free white persons could become citizens. The following year a different court ruled that 19th-century laws allowed Syrians, because they were so closely related to "white persons," to become citizens.[3]

In 1942, the difficulty with arbitrary racial classifications was again apparent in divergent court rulings based on race and religion. One court decision ruled that Yemenis were not eligible for citizenship "especially because of their dark skin and the fact that they are 'part of the Mohammedan world,' separated from Christian Europe by a wide gulf."[4] Two years later, another Arab was granted citizenship because the judge considered Arabs to share an Aryan culture with whites. Generally they have been seen by white Americans as not quite white and not quite colored.

The result of hundreds of years of stereotypes, dating back to the demonization of Muslims during the European crusades, is extreme hostility towards Arab Americans today. George McGovern in 1972, Jimmy Carter in 1976, Ronald Reagan in 1980, Walter Mondale in 1984 and Hillary Clinton in 2000 all rejected political and financial support from Arab Americans and even returned contributions that had been previously received, denying them the opportunity as citizens to support the candidates of their choice.[5] The demonization continues, represented in books with titles such as *Sacred Rage* or *In the Name of God,* in Hollywood movies such as *Delta Force* and *True Lies* and in the PBS documentary *Jihad in America.* Political statements and media portrayals contribute directly to a social climate that fosters violence against Arab Americans.

Such a climate of anti-Arab racism was much in evidence during the first Gulf War against Iraq. For example, in a nationally televised news briefing on NBC, February 27, 1991, General Norman Schwarzkopf, head of our military operations, stated that the Iraqis "are not part of the same human race we are."[6] *Time* magazine, the *New York Times* and many other media carried editorials, articles and cartoons describing Arabs as less than human. During this period, Islamic mosques in the United States were broken into or bombed; shots were fired into the homes of known Arabs; a taxi driver in Fort Worth, Texas, was attacked and killed; some Muslim schools and Islamic societies were vandalized and Arab Americans received hate calls.

This harassment and violence only increased after 9/11. Anti-Arab hate crimes rose dramatically, including beatings and murder. Racial profiling and surveillance by law enforcement became routine practice. Housing, job and others forms of discrimination no longer even needed to be justified. And the negative portrayal of Arabs on TV, in the movies and in video games constantly reinforces anti-Arab American hatred and violence.

Arab Americans have reached the highest levels of professional achievement throughout the United States and Canada, have been political and social leaders and have contributed to the arts and sciences. However, they continue to be vilified in the media, left out of mainstream political and social affairs, misrepresented in textbooks and excluded from multicultural curricula. They are also readily blamed for the actions of Arabs or Muslims in any part of the world and are vulnerable to verbal and physical attack simply for being of Arab descent.

The targeting of Arab Americans for violence makes us all less safe in two ways. First, we do not respond to the extreme violence of white men as quickly or as thoroughly as we should be because our attention is on "Arab terrorists." For example, since the Oklahoma City bombing by white men, white extremist groups have hatched conspiracies to bomb buildings, banks, refineries, utilities, clinics and bridges; to assassinate politicians, judges, civil rights figures, and others; to attack Army bases, National Guard armories and a train; to rob banks and armored cars and to amass illegal machine guns, missiles and explosives.[7]

The United States has a long history of home-grown white male terrorists including the Ku Klux Klan, the assassins of John Kennedy and Martin Luther King, the Symbionese Liberation Army, Timothy McVeigh, the anti-abortionist murderers of Dr. Bernard Slepian, Dr. George Tiller and others, the bombing of the Olympics in Centennial Park by anti-abortionist Eric Rudolph, the Columbine High School massacre, the 2001 anthrax letter attacks and the Hutaree Militia.

Our main danger is from within, from white male terrorists such as Joseph Stack who drove his airplane into a building in Austin, Texas, that housed the FBI and CIA as well as the IRS in February of 2010. He was a US citizen who plotted and committed an act of terrorism resulting in the death of at least one person and property damage in the millions of dollars.[8]

In a similar vein, racist policies that have led to the deployment of thousands of immigration officials and the militarization of the US-Mexican border have not stopped a single terrorist. Not one of the known terrorists involved in the September 11, 2001, attacks is alleged to have arrived illegally via the Mexican-US border.

We are also put at risk because, in the name of combating terrorism against Arabs, our civil liberties are compromised through such legislation as the Illegal Immigration Reform and Immigrant Responsibility Act, the Anti-Terrorism and Effective Death Penalty Act and the Patriot Act. This latter legislation creates a new class of persons who are vulnerable to being deported simply because of their association with a list of "terrorist" groups. The creation of a set of removal courts, free from judicial review, also threatens legal protections of all people in the US. This bill harks back to the McCarthy-era witch hunts of the early 1950s, during which thousands of people were penalized merely for association with groups proscribed by the US government.

A final issue to consider is how American anti-Arab racism allows us to be manipulated around foreign policy issues. In the last few years, the US has invaded Iraq, Afghanistan, Pakistan and Somalia, bombed Yemen and provided arms and other supplies to Israel, which has invaded Syria, Lebanon and Palestine. At the same time, our government has supported dictatorships and ruling elites in Saudi Arabia, Egypt, Jordan, Kuwait and the United Arab Emirates. Without a high level of anti-Arab feeling in the United States, popular support would be lacking for such military aggression — all in clear breach of international law. We will continue to be manipulated by government and military propaganda until we understand the complexities of Arab societies, understand the distinctions between Islamic cultures and Arabic ones and overcome our anti-Arab racism so that we can see Arab peoples and Arab Americans as distinct, fully human members of our communities.

Questions and Actions — Arab Americans

1. What are some of the cultural traditions, community organizations and political issues of the Arab American communities in your local area?

2. Who are some of the national Arab American leaders, and what organizations are prominent nationally?

3. How can you respond when people around you make anti-Arab comments?

4. Have there been anti-Arab harassment, racial profiling or hate crimes in your area? How can you join efforts to combat such harassment and hate crimes?

5. How can you join with others to challenge media stereotypes, misinformation and lack of positive coverage of Arab Americans?

6. Western nations contribute billions of dollars a year in arms and other resources to Saudi Arabia, Egypt, Israel, Pakistan and other countries supporting war and repression and, ultimately, fueling anti-Western feeling and terrorism. How can you work to insure that money is directed to build a foundation for peace in the Middle East?

Notes

1. Saud Joseph. "Against the Grain of the Nation: The Arab" in Michael W. Suleiman, ed. *Arabs in America: Building a New Future.* Temple, 1999, p. 260.
2. "Doing Race: An Introduction." in Markus and Moya, *Doing Race,* p. 75.
3. Tehranian, *White Washed,* pp. 57-59.
4. Suleiman, *Arabs in America,* p. 7.
5. For more on the political disenfranchisement of Arab Americans, see Alia Malek's *A Country Called Amreeka: Arab Roots, American Stories.* Free Press, 2009.
6. Quoted from the *Globe and Mail* and cited in Karim H. Karim. *Islamic Peril: Media and Global Violence,* rev. ed. Black Rose, 2003, p. 152.
7. This information is culled from various issues of the Southern Poverty Law Center's "Intelligence Report." For more information on the over 1,000 hate groups in the US, consult their website and magazine: [online]. [cited February 25, 2011]. splcenter.org/get-informed/intelligence-report.
8. Ryan Owens, Sarah Netter and Pierre Thomas. "Texas Plane Crash: Wife of Joe Stack Calls Attack 'Unimaginable Tragedy' Authorities Investigating Whether Explosives on Plane When It Crashed." *abcnews.com,* February 19, 2010. [online], [cited February 21, 2011]. abcnews. go.com/GMA/texas-plane-crash-authorities-investigating-suicidal-pilot-joe/story?id=9885576.

Muslims

O N AUGUST 25, 2010, Ahmed H. Sharif, a taxi driver in New York City, was attacked with a knife and slashed on the neck and face by Michael Enright. The attack occurred immediately after he had replied yes to his young white Christian passenger's question about whether he was a Muslim. After fleeing the taxi cab, Enright was quickly caught by the police and charged with attempted murder.[1] The attack on Ahmed Sharif is, like all hate crimes, a reminder to the Muslim community that they are under siege, seen by many white Americans as outsiders and vulnerable to violence.

Anti-Muslim oppression — often referred to as Islamophobia — is a combination of religious, racial and cultural oppression targeting the presence, dress, behavior, job and educational opportunities, and institutions of anyone perceived to be not only Muslim but Arab or generally from the Middle East. Muslims are racially profiled in airports and in urban settings, routinely discriminated against in job and housing situations and portrayed as dangerous fanatics in the popular media — particularly in books, movies and video games. Islamic organizations are under intense surveillance by the government, are denied access to some of the funding and other opportunities that Christian and Jewish groups have access to, have their charitable activities challenged, are routinely denied building permits and have their mosques and cultural centers attacked.

What popular culture does not reflect is that most Muslims are neither Arab nor from the Middle East. Of the over 1.57 billion Muslims in the world (about 23% of the world's population), the majority live in countries as diverse as Indonesia, Malaysia, Pakistan, Sudan, China, Nigeria, Kenya, India and the Philippines.[2] The countries with the largest Muslim populations are (not in order) Indonesia, Pakistan, Bangladesh, India, Turkey, Iran, Egypt, Nigeria and China. Each of these countries has between 50 and 100 million Muslim citizens. Despite the dramatic religious and cultural variety of the Muslim world, Islam is often portrayed in the US as a monolithic, militaristic religion, unchanged since the seventh century, hostile to Christianity and inimical to all things modern and Western. Muslims themselves are often assumed to be mindless adherents, devoid of any individuality: fanatical, blind followers of extremist clerics.

Muslims have been treated as the prototypical enemy of Western Christendom since the first crusade was announced by the Pope in 1095. The crusade was conceived as an expedition to unite the fighting rulers and people of southern Europe under a new common identity as Christian. In his proclamation, the Pope denounced Islam as an abomination and enemy of God and declared that every Christian had a moral obligation to march to the Holy Land and claim it from "the Moors." The subsequent war to claim the areas of Spain and Portugal for Christendom was also labeled a crusade.[3] Over the following centuries, Christian secular and religious leaders forged a common European identity whose defining characteristic was defense against spiritual and physical threat from Islam.

During the 15th century, in the first process of racial (as opposed to ethnic) cleansing, Spanish rulers began persecuting the Moors as well as Jews in their attempt to create a racially and religiously pure country, expelling the Moors entirely from Spain in 1609.

The Spanish Inquisition was established to hunt down *conversos* (Moors and Jews who were suspected of falsely converting to Christianity) so they would not pollute the blood of a new national and eventually European identity. During this period, the religious identity "Christian" began to take on a racial component, signifying *white Christian,* and the word *European* began to be equated with both *white* and *Christian.*[4] Emerging nation-states such as Spain claimed legitimacy from a unity of faith and a common pseudo-scientific racial heritage encapsulated in the Spanish phrases *sangre puro* and *limpieza de sangre.*[5]

During this period of nation building and emerging national identities, the word *Moor* was used as both a religious and a racial signifier and a general term to describe the Other — the perennial enemy of Christendom anywhere in the world who, by rejecting Christianity, "remains outside the Western economic, cultural, and political consensus."[6] As one commentator has written "the term 'Moor' was used interchangeably with such similarly ambiguous terms as 'African,' 'Ethiopian,' 'Negro,' and even 'Indian' to designate a figure from different parts or the whole of African (or beyond) who was either black or Moslem, neither, or both ... characterized alternately and sometimes simultaneously in contradictory extremes, as noble or monstrous, civil or savage."[7]

In contrast, there have been periods in US political history when Islam was not treated as an enemy of Christendom and relations between the US and Muslim nations were friendly. Washington, Franklin and Jefferson respected and had generally positive things to say about the religion. In 1777, Morocco was the first country in the world to recognize the new United States government, with Tunisia following suit the next year. Even in the period of the Barbary War against pirates off the coast of North Africa, Islam was referred to with respect and a political alternative to war was sought to the conflict. At the same time, however, stereotypes about Muslims as infidels were promulgated by Christian priests and ministers and expressed in popular culture, often through the negative portrayal of Native Americans as Moors.[8]

Islam was first brought to the United States by slaves from Africa. It has been estimated that 20-30% of the men and 12-15% of the women enslaved were Muslim.[9] However, practicing Islam was difficult for slaves, and many were forced to convert to Christianity. There were also some Muslim immigrants from Arab countries in the early days of the Republic.

Throughout the 19th and 20th centuries in the United States, various immigration laws favored Arab Christian communities and worked to restrict the arrival of Muslims.[10] With the collapse of the Ottoman Empire after World War I, the US began to play a larger role in West Asia. However, it was only after the collapse of the British Empire and the creation of the state of Israel that the US began seriously intervening in Middle East countries and heavily funding right-wing regimes such as that of the Shah in Iran and the Saudi royal family in Saudi Arabia.

After World War II, immigration from Muslim countries increased. At the same time, the African American Muslim community continued to grow, now about 25% of the Muslim population in the US. Besides the 4% who are Hispanic, the rest of the Muslim population is primarily first- or second-generation immigrants from South Asia (India and Pakistan), various West Asian countries such as Iraq and Afghanistan, Turkey and Iran, and Indonesia, Bosnia, Kenya, Somalia and Malaysia. Estimates of the total Muslim American population in the US range widely, but there are probably somewhere between four to five million. As a Pew Research Survey title suggests, most Muslims in the US are well-educated and middle-class. The report concludes that Muslim Americans are "largely assimilated, happy with their lives, and moderate with respect to many of the issues that have divided Muslims and Westerners around the world."[11]

The target of present-day Islamophobia is Muslims not as they are, but as they have been imagined for centuries in the Western imagination. They are the dark, menacing, non-Christian Other, intent on destroying Western civilization. They are interchangeable with Jews, African Americans, Native Americans or undocumented immigrants. And this danger becomes the justification for public policy that targets individual Muslims and Muslims as a group for systematic marginalization, discrimination, harassment, hate crimes and continual vilification.

Recent controversies over the siting of Mosques and Islamic cultural centers are indicative of deep-seated Islamophobia and racism. While some Christians claim that their concern is the location of an Islamic cultural center so close to Ground Zero, in fact, there are protests against the building of mosques in such diverse places as Murfreesboro, TN, Sheboygan, MI, and Temecula, CA, as well as in Brooklyn and Staten Island, NY. In Columbia, TN a mosque has been burned down and in Cedar Rapids, Jacksonville, Detroit and Seattle mosques have been smeared with animal feces, defaced with graffiti, vandalized, attacked with pipe bombs and set afire by arsonists.[12] Just the day before the attack on Ahmed Sharif, a mosque in Madera, CA, was attacked for the third time within a week.[13] In Columbia, in a powerful act of solidarity with the Muslim community, the local pastor of the Presbyterian Church gave the Muslim community the keys to the church and said that they could use it as their house of worship.

The protest against the Park51 Islamic cultural center proposed for a site two blocks from the location of the 9/11 bombings is indicative of Islamophobia. Protesters assume that because Al-Qaeda is a Muslim organization, all Muslims are terrorists, that there were no Muslims who died in the 9/11 attacks or who played roles in the rescue of people caught in the buildings and that an old Burlington Coat Store is suddenly "hallowed ground." They also assume that Muslims should not enjoy the same religious freedom as Christians or Jews, even while many Muslims are risking their lives fighting as US soldiers in Afghanistan and Iraq.

The continuing controversy over whether President Obama is a Muslim is another example of racism and Islamophobia. Underlying the disbelief that Obama is a Christian is an assumption that African Americans cannot be true

Christians and will always be outsiders. This disbelief is based on an assumption that Muslims and people of color are dangerous, and neither can be the equal of law-abiding, white Christian Americans.

These issues are obviously stirred up by conservative political leaders and mainstream corporate media. But they tap into widespread underlying beliefs that must be taken seriously. In August 2010, a Pew poll showed that 18% of the population believes Obama is a Muslim, only 34% believe he is a Christian, 43% claim not to know his religion (even after all the furor over the statements of his pastor Reverend Jeremiah Wright two years earlier).[14] A more general USA Today/Gallup poll conducted in July 2006 found that 39% of respondents said they felt at least some prejudice against Muslims. The same percentage favored requiring Muslims, including US citizens, to carry a special ID "as a means of preventing terrorist attacks in the United States." About ⅓ said US Muslims were sympathetic to Al-Qaeda, and over ⅕ said they wouldn't want Muslims as neighbors.[15] Those numbers would likely be much higher today as conservative leaders stir up latent anti-Muslim sentiment.

Just as with racial profiling and discrimination directed against other groups, Islamophobia threatens our collective safety when resources are selectively and inappropriately directed at entire communities rather than at criminal behavior which is prevalent in all communities. It threatens our civil and religious

---

Questions and Actions — Muslims

1. What are some of the cultural traditions, community organizations and political issues of the Muslims communities in your local area?
2. Who are some of the national Muslim leaders and what organizations are prominent nationally?
3. Do you know some of the fundamental beliefs of Islam and something about the major organizational branches? Where can you find out more about Islam?
4. How can you respond when people around you make anti- Muslim comments?
5. Have there been anti-Muslim harassment, racial profiling or hate crimes in your area? How can you join efforts to combat such harassment and hate crimes?
6. How can you join with others to challenge media stereotypes, misinformation and lack of positive coverage of Muslims?
7. Western nations spend billions of dollars a year supporting war and repression and, ultimately, fueling anti-Western feeling and terrorism in such Muslim countries as Indonesia, Sudan, Yemen, Pakistan, Afghanistan and Iraq. How can you work to insure that money is directed to build a foundation for peace in those countries?

liberties when one group is singled out as not entitled to constitutionally guaranteed rights. It also curtails our freedom when surveillance and harassment are legally sanctioned and we must limit civil rights in order to "prevent attack." When we speak out and stand strong as allies to the Muslim community, we challenge violence and injustice, increase our safety and freedom, challenge age-old Christian stereotypes and myths and uphold the legal rights to freedom of religion, freedom of assembly and freedom from discrimination and attack. Now is the time to work with Muslims to challenge Islamophobia.

Notes

1. Tom Hays. "Ahmed H. Sharif, slashed Muslim taxi driver to visit NYC mayor." *Associated Press*, August 26, 2010. [online]. [cited February 22, 2011]. csmonitor.com/From-the-news-wires/2010/0826/Ahmed-H.-Sharif-slashed-Muslim-taxi-driver-to-visit-NYC-mayor.

2. Pew Research Center. *Mapping the Global Muslim Population: A Report on the Size and Distribution of the World's Muslim Population.* October 7, 2009. [online], [cited February 22, 2011]. pewforum.org/Mapping-the-Global-Muslim-Population.aspx.

3. I use the word *claim* rather than the more common *reclaim* intentionally because Christians had no more historical right to control these areas than Muslims did. There were crusades waged by Christians against Moors, Slavs, dissident Christian groups such as the Cathars and even against individual secular Christian leaders over a period of 600 years.

4. As part of this whitening process, Western Christianity transformed God and Jesus into light-skinned Europeans.

5. The limpieza de sangre statute was passed in 1449.

6. Anouar Majid. *We Are All Moors: Ending Centuries of Crusades Against Muslims and Other Minorities.* University of Minnesota, 2009, p. 62.

7. Ibid., p. 63.

8. Ibid., p. 71.

9. Samuel S. Hill et. al. *Encyclopedia of Religion in the South.* Mercer University, 2005, p. 394.

10. See the previous chapter on Arab Americans. Many Arab Christians claimed immigration rights as white people. Although not all these claims were upheld by the courts, a significant number of Lebanese, Palestinians and Syrians successfully entered the US.

11. Pew Research Center. *Muslim Americans: Middle Class and Mostly Mainstream.* May 22, 2007. [online]. [cited August 10, 2010]. http://pewresearch.org/assets/pdf/muslim-americans.pdf.

12. Responsible for Equality and Liberty (R.E.A.L.) Organization. *Coast-to-coast Anti-Islam Movement Results in Protests, Attacks on Mosques.* July 22, 2010. [online]. [cited February 22, 2011]. realcourage.org/2010/07/coast-to-coast/.

13. Joseph Picard. "Mosque Attack in California Refers to Ground Zero." *International Business Times*, August 26, 2010. [online]. [cited February 22, 2011]. ibtimes.com/articles/46449/20100826/mosque-islam-hate.htm.

14. The Pew Research Center for the People & the Press. *Growing Number of Americans Say Obama is a Muslim: Religion, Politics and the President.* August 19, 2010. [online]. [cited February 23, 2011]. pewresearch.org/pubs/1701/poll-obama-muslim-christian-church-out-of-politics-political-leaders-religious.

15. Marilyn Elias. "USA's Muslims Under a Cloud." *USA Today,* August 10, 2006. [online]. [cited February 23, 2011]. usatoday.com/news/nation/2006-08-09-muslim-american-cover_x.htm.

Jewish People

WHEN I'M IN A WORKSHOP ON RACISM, and the facilitators tell everyone to break up into a white group and a people of color group, I immediately want to say, "Wait a minute. I'm not white." There are many white people in the United States and throughout Europe who would immediately agree. "Of course you're not white. Jewish people are part of the contamination of the white Christian race, along with people of color, Roma, the mentally challenged and lesbian, gay and bisexual people." These attitudes are based on the conjunction of whiteness with Christianity.

Jews were considered inferior and a threat to Christians because they rejected Jesus as the son of God. In addition, they were falsely accused of killing Jesus because of stories in the New Testament. Various anti-Jewish stereotypes were disseminated by early church leaders such as St. John Chrysostom, who wrote:

> The Jews are full of hatred for the rest of mankind and are the enemies of all gentiles: they are parasites on the gentile societies that harbor them; they are addicted to money, and through the power of money, they aspire to be rulers of the world.[1]

Early Christian church leaders continually attacked Jews on theological grounds and condoned the actions of Christians who vandalized synagogues and killed Jews. When Christianity became the official religion of the Roman Empire in the 4th century, Jews became even more vulnerable to violence from Christians. They were banned from public office and from many occupations, and some were forced to become tax collectors. They were subject to special taxes, prohibited from practicing their religion and building or repairing synagogues, not allowed to intermarry with Christians and prohibited from holding any civil or economic position higher than any Christian. They were subject to forced conversions and commonly referred to as a source of religious pollution, contagion and disease, setting the stage for later racially based anti-Jewish oppression.[2]

Large-scale attacks on Jews by Christians occurred during the crusades, when Jews were seen as the European agents of the Muslim/Arab "infidels" who controlled the Holy Lands. Although the goal of the church was to attack Arabs and reclaim Jerusalem, most crusaders never left Europe. As they pillaged their way toward Jerusalem, they rounded up and killed thousands of Jews and destroyed their communities.

In subsequent centuries, Jews were forced to convert or were banished from such regions as England (1290), France (1306, 1322, 1394), Hungary (1367), Strasbourg (1381), Austria (1421) and Cologne (1426). Jews fought to defend themselves, fled, converted or looked for protection from secular rulers, but were generally not powerful enough to protect themselves from Christian violence.[3]

On July 1, 1492, the Spanish monarchs, pressed by the Inquisition, gave all Jews 90 days either to convert or to pack up whatever they could and leave the country they had lived in for centuries.[4] Even after the Spanish expulsion, the Inquisition continued to persecute those suspected of "idolatry." Under the laws of purity of blood, any person with even one drop of Jewish blood was condemned. To prove their innocence, suspects had to display genealogical charts proving they had no Jewish ancestry. The Inquisition, drawing on anti-Jewish stereotypes from early church teachings, combined religious and biological justifications for persecution, setting the stage for the later development of biologically based theories of racism.

Many Jews fled from Spain to Portugal, but within a few years were forced to flee again after being given the choice of forced baptism or death. Subsequently they faced persecution and expulsion from the Italian peninsula and from many German cities and principalities in the 16th century, as well as pogroms in the Ukraine in the mid-17th century.[5]

Anti-Jewish hatred became rooted in Protestant Christianity during the *Enlightenment* through the writings of such key figures as Martin Luther. In 1543, Luther wrote "Against the Jews and Their Lies" in which he accused the Jews of being not only the bloodthirsty murderers of Christianity, but also of the German people. He wrote:

> We are at fault in not avenging all this innocent blood of our Lord and Churches and the blood of the children which they have shed

since then, and which still shines forth from their Jewish eyes and skin. We are at fault in not slaying them.[6]

Luther went on to suggest that Germans burn the houses and synagogues of the Jews, ban their rabbis under pain of death, withdraw Jewish safe-conduct on the highways, prohibit usury, institute manual labor for young Jews and, finally, confiscate their wealth and expel them from Germany.

Jews were held to be a nation of outcasts who had killed Christ, rejected Christianity, used the blood of Christian children in Passover rituals and prevented the Second Coming by their failure to convert. Even before biological theories of race, they were believed automatically to pass on these traits to each succeeding generation regardless of where they lived, what they practiced and even, in many cases, whether or not they converted to Christianity.

These were official policies of the Catholic Church and many Protestant denominations and the common beliefs of many Christians. It was only in 1965, for instance, that the bishops of Vatican Council II voted to absolve contemporary Jews of any guilt for the crucifixion of Jesus and to repudiate the belief that God rejected the Jews because they refused to accept Jesus as the savior.[7]

Jewish people were originally Arabs. Whatever their original distinguishable Arab or "Semitic" characteristics, through rape, intermarriage, forced exile, conversion and assimilation, Jews today are part of many cultural groups on several continents. Jewish people are not only not a race — we have seen how this is not a meaningful concept — but they also come in many shades and colors, from nearly black Ethiopian Jews, to dark brown Jews from the Cochin coast of India, to light brown Jews from Argentina and Morocco, to blond and light-skinned Jews in Denmark and England. While this diversity is a refutation of racial stereotypes, it can make Jews more vulnerable when another group of people is claiming some kind of national identity, religious unity or genetic purity. The membership application of the Invisible Empire of the Knights of the Ku Klux Klan requires one to "swear that I am a White Person of Non-Jewish ancestry."[8]

When Jews walk down the street, their skin color is immediately visible, while their cultural practices and religious beliefs are not. If they *pass* for white and don't voluntarily give away the fact that they're Jewish, they enjoy the same respect and privilege that other white people are given in our society. Their presence is accepted, their words are listened to and they have more police and judicial protection. If their name is recognizably Jewish, if they are wearing traditional clothes or religious objects or if their appearance or mannerisms fit certain stereotypes of what it means to be or look or act Jewish, then passing is not an option. If they can't or don't want to pass, they are vulnerable to the same jokes, harassment, discrimination and violence that target other non-white, non-Christian people. That in itself is a strong incentive to try to pass.

In order to pass, they have to give up, minimize or downplay any aspects of their life and appearance that are visibly Jewish. They can't say or do anything that will mark them as different. Since being Jewish, at its core, is inherently a range of ways of being, talking and doing things that are not Christian, the more they pass the less they are who they are. At any time, they might be found out and face mistrust, ignorance, discrimination or outright abuse.

In the United States, besides the threat of violence and the constant pressure to assimilate, one of the prices people pay to be accepted as white is to collude in perpetuating racism. This is a price that many southern and eastern Europeans as well as assimilated Jews have paid. They come to believe that economic improvement for themselves is different than economic justice for everyone. Some Jewish people, probably no fewer or no more than in other groups, have paid that price. Today in US society, there is some privilege attached to being white, or, we might say, conditionally white. We will accept you as white on the condition that you support the racial hierarchy which keeps people of color on the bottom. Jewish people who are "white" (like Irish, Polish, Finnish or Spanish people) are safer, have greater educational and economic opportunity and are generally more accepted than African Americans, Latino/as, Asian Americans, Arab Americans and Native Americans. That is what being accepted as white is all about.

Many Jewish people have accepted this racial hierarchy in exchange for feelings of safety and acceptance. Consequently, they have established, in this country and in Israel, race-based systems within the Jewish community. Jewish people of color are the majority of Jews in the world and constitute 20% of the US Jewish population.[9] Despite this fact, European-descended Jews dominate culture and politics in the Jewish communities of both Israel and the United States. This has rendered non-white Jewish people invisible and made it seem that racism is an issue that Jewish people are separate from. Yet we carry the pain, violence and confusion of racism within our own bodies and in the distribution of economic and cultural power within our Jewish communities.

One way white people retain power is by attacking strong and powerful individuals of color (such as Louis Farrakhan or Jesse Jackson) who are mobilizing people. We should all understand that white people will try to set up Jewish people to attack African American leaders and vice versa. Then they don't have to take the heat directly. If we are challenging Louis Farrakhan's anti-Jewish statements but not Glen Beck's or Bill O'Reilly's, then we are contributing to racism and being strategically ineffective. White Christian leaders like nothing better than to see groups taking potshots at each other.

Ruling classes have always used cultural differences to exploit people and to determine the roles that outside groups would play in the economic system. Ruling classes use systems of oppression such as these:

- to divide people, exploiting some groups more heavily than others
- to strengthen white cultural solidarity and chauvinism
- to make white workers feel lucky they have some privilege or status no matter how heavily exploited they are
- to divert working- and middle-class attention from the wealthy by focusing on scapegoats "above" them (Jewish bankers) and "below" them (African American women on welfare).

Whenever the stereotypes of Jewish money or power go unchallenged, the injustice of our economic system is strengthened and racism continues.

There are other complex strands in anti-Jewish oppression. People of color who are Christian have adopted and passed on anti-Jewish lies about the role of the Jewish people in Western history. Many Christians of color are capable of condoning violence against Jews even while they are themselves the targets of racism. This leads many people who are fighting racism, whether they are people of color or white people, to downplay the importance of anti-Jewish oppression and not respond vigorously when Jews are attacked. Colluding with anti-Jewish oppression, even through silence, contributes to inequality and racial injustice.

Muslims also have a long history of anti-Jewish practices and justifications. At the same time, in Europe and America, Jews and Moors have been categorized together as infidels and as threats to Christianity and to Western civilization. Although it is beyond the scope of this book, we have much to learn about how racism operates by analyzing the ways anti-Arab racism is part of anti-Jewish oppression, how Arab societies have contributed to anti-Jewish violence, how European-based parts of Jewish American and Israeli society have contributed to anti-Arab racism, and how white Christian-dominated Western societies have set up Jews and Arabs to fight each other in the eastern Mediterranean region.

Looking in detail at how anti-Jewish oppression operates gives us further insight into the dynamics of racism. It helps us see that racism is not simply a religious, biological or cultural persecution. It rests, instead, on a hierarchy and on institutionalization of power and violence. Ruling classes and dominant groups who benefit most from that power use economic, religious, cultural, biological, historical or sociological justifications as needed to maintain their control. They can offer safe haven, economic success, voting rights, tolerance and even status as honorary whites to various groups when their support is needed. Just as quickly, they can withdraw those favors and set the wrath of the rest of the populace against selected scapegoats when a diversion is called for. The only long-term corrective to this dynamic is the democratic dispersion of political, economic and social power to all people within a society and the creation of a democratic, anti-racist, anti-sexist and secular multicultural state.

Bringing up anti-Jewish oppression does not distract from the struggle to end racism; it enhances it, making it clearer how Christian values are a cornerstone of racism. My greatest effectiveness as an ally to people of color comes when I draw on Jewish experience of Christian dominance, racism, institutionalized violence and economic injustice. For now, consider the following questions as they apply to you.

Questions and Actions — Jewish People

If you are Christian or of Christian background

1. What did you learn in religious school or church or from the Bible about Jewish people? What did you learn about people of color?
2. What non-explicit messages did you receive about both groups from your Christian heritage?
3. In what ways is it true and in what ways is it not true to say "The United States is a Christian country?" How would you respond if someone said this in your presence?
4. What are some of the ways that Jews are blamed for social problems?
5. Beginning with the fact that Jesus and Mary were Arab Jews, in what ways has Christianity whitewashed its origins?
6. How can you challenge anti-Jewish oppression expressed by other Christians and within your church? ☛

Questions and Actions — Jewish People *cont.*

If you are Jewish

1. Are you generally treated as white or as non-white in Jewish society? In gentile society?
2. What forms does racism take within the US Jewish community?
3. What kind of support do you need from Christian allies when anti-Jewish statements or actions are being committed?
4. How can you draw on your Jewish identity, history and experience to be an ally to (other) people of color?
5. When you or other Jewish people raise issues of racism, do you find yourselves attacked? What support do you need from Christians when this happens? What support do you need from other Jewish people?
6. How could you challenge racism within the Jewish community?

Notes

1. Paul Lawrence Rose. *German Question/Jewish Question: Revolutionary Antisemitism from Kant to Wagner.* Princeton, 1990, p. 3.
2. Rosemary Radford Ruether. *Faith and Fratricide: The Theological Roots of Anti-Semitism.* Seabury, 1974, pp. 184–204.
3. There is a good map of Jewish Expulsions and Resettlement areas (1100-1500) at: Florida Center for Instructional Technology. "Map of Jewish expulsions and resettlement areas in Europe." *A Teacher's Guide to the Holocaust,* 2005. [online]. [cited February 24, 2011]. fcit.usf.edu/HOLOCAUST/gallery/expuls.htm.
4. Carroll, *Constantine's Sword,* pp. 361-362.
5. Evyatar Friesel. *Atlas of Modern Jewish History.* Oxford, 1990; Martin Gilbert. *Atlas of Jewish History.* Morrow, 1992.
6. Rose, *German Question/Jewish Question,* p. 7.
7. David G. Singer. "From St. Paul's Abrogation of the Old Covenant to Hitler's War Against the Jews: The Response of American Catholic Thinkers to the Holocaust, 1945-76." In David A. Gerber, ed. *Anti-Semitism in American History.* University of Illinois, 1987, p. 386.
8. Elly Bulkin, Minnie Bruce Pratt and Barbara Smith. *Yours in Struggle: Three Feminist Perspective on Anti-Semitism and Racism.* Firebrand, 1988, p. 104.
9. Diane Tobin et. al. *In Every Tongue: The Racial & Ethnic Diversity of the Jewish People.* Institute for Jewish and Community Research, 2005, p. 24. For more on diversity in the Jewish community, see also Melanie Kaye/Kantrowitz. *The Colors of Jews: Racial Politics and Radical Diasporism.* Indiana, 2007.

Recent Immigrants

IMMIGRATION IS A RACIAL ISSUE. US Immigration and Naturalization Service (INS) officials do not stop white people or conduct raids to stem the flow of large numbers of illegal Canadian, British and eastern European immigrants. There are not hundreds of miles of barbed-wire fencing between Canada and the US. And vigilante groups do not patrol that border.

Obviously, one of the great strengths of Canada, the United States, New Zealand and Australia as nations has been their ability to welcome the presence and contributions of new immigrants. But not all immigrants and not all the time. Recent immigrants have always been both feared and disdained by older residents. And immigrants of color, during periods when they were allowed to enter these countries, have always been treated differently than lighter-skinned arrivals.

As mentioned in earlier chapters in this part, throughout most of US history the immigration of Asians, Africans (except those enslaved), South and Central Americans and people from the Middle East has been restricted if not totally forbidden. Citizenship, and therefore voting rights, was explicitly limited to white people. Not all Europeans were welcomed either, and many returned to their countries of origin because of the harsh treatment they received. But over the last 400 years, there has been almost continuous opportunity for white Europeans to arrive and settle in the US, find jobs, establish families and build communities.

Many of us in the West like to think of our countries as magnets for immigration because of the opportunity to be found here. Many of us believe that our countries are the most civilized in the world, with coveted resources that everyone else is desperate to gain access to. This misperception has allowed us to construct a fantasy about alien invasion — hordes of people massed at our borders, frantically trying to sneak across only to overrun our communities, take our jobs and use up our social services. To complement this image we have constructed metaphors of immigrants as carriers of disease, infection, plague, varmints, infestation — or simply as invaders. Nothing could be further from the truth.

Most immigrants from less developed countries migrate to other less developed countries, not to industrialized ones. Less than 2% of the world's migration ends in the United States.[1] Many factors fuel immigration including war, natural disaster, famine and lack of work. The United States is a major cause of migration around the world because its foreign policies have disrupted stable social and economic systems in many countries. There are many Southeast Asians in the US because we engaged in war in Southeast Asia and then welcomed those who supported our cause. There are immigrants from Cuba and Haiti here because we have supported dictatorships in those countries in the past, and corporate exploitation and trade embargos led to these countries' impoverishment. There are Mexicans and Central Americans here because corporate agribusiness, manufacturing and extraction industries have invaded and severely disrupted both rural and urban economies, concentrated wealth among an elite and forced people to migrate to urban areas or out of the country in search of work to support themselves and their families.[2]

In addition, the United States has been a major promoter of International Monetary Fund (IMF) structural adjustment policies, World Bank loans for large-scale agricultural modernization projects and "free trade" agreements that have forced millions of people to move from rural areas into cities and from one nation to another in search of food, work and safety. Women in developing countries have been particularly hard hit by these practices. When women are displaced from their land or unable to continue farming because of policies emphasizing export agriculture, they end up migrating to cities to work in textile, manufacturing or electronic industries, or traveling to other countries to do nursing, domestic, textile or sex work.[3]

The United States has generally not been against immigration as much as it has been against the long-term development of non-white immigrant communities. English and Irish immigrants were brought over to clear and settle the East Coast, Chinese laborers were brought over to build the railroads and Mexican labor was brought in to work the fields of the Southwest in the Bracero program. The labor of all groups was exploited, but there was still a color line at the border. People of color were not expected or encouraged to stay. During the limited period when Chinese men were given permission to immigrate, no Chinese women were allowed into the country, and even during great labor shortages, Mexicans were only given short-term visas. No such restrictions applied to English and Irish immigrants.

Once they arrived in the US, why did white immigrants fare better than immigrants of color? Immigrants from Ireland, Italy, Spain, Greece and various regions of Eastern Europe faced violence, discrimination and social prejudice and limited access to jobs, housing and education, just like immigrants from other regions of the world. However immigrants from Southern and Eastern Europe, both men and women, were able to come in significant numbers. Although they faced discrimination, these immigrants were not driven out of trades, professions and other occupations the way African Americans and immigrants of color were. White immigrants were able to become citizens, could vote and therefore were able to develop political strength. There were few laws preventing them from participating in civil society or from owning land and businesses. The government established public schools, hospitals and other services specifically to help them assimilate into US society. And while they did occasionally face violent attack, it was nowhere near as brutal and sustained, nor was it supported by the government as was the violence experienced by immigrants of color. Immigrants of color had as little status and government protection as African Americans and Native Americans, and therefore were subject to discrimination, hate crimes and mob violence. They were often killed with impunity, oftentimes with state or national government collusion or active participation.[4]

One thing that is similar between white immigrants then and immigrants of color today is the pattern of learning English and general cultural assimilation. The first generation has difficulty learning English, and many speak only their native language and live in fairly homogeneous communities. The second generation is often bilingual, moving into nearby, more affluent and mixed areas. The third generation not only is fluent in English but has lost their foreparents' native language and much of their culture, although, as we have seen, there are still many barriers to people of color, immigrants or those not living in white-designated areas.[5]

Today the selective control of immigration to serve economic needs continues, as technology workers from South and East Asia enter the US on special visas to serve the interests of the computer industry, and women of color are imported from economically exploited countries as nurses under the Nursing Relief Act of 1989. Large communities of Mexican, Central American and

Asian immigrants provide the labor force for the textile, computer, food harvesting and service sectors of the US economy. Businesses are not interested in eliminating illegal immigration — heavily exploited immigrant labor is a source of great profit to them. They are interested in controlling immigration, using the system to undermine immigrants' ability to organize against their exploitation and keeping citizen workers alienated from and unable to unite with immigrant workers. As writer and historian Grace Chang notes, "immigration from the Third World into the United States doesn't just happen to a set of factors but is carefully orchestrated — that is, desired, planned, compelled, managed, accelerated, slowed, and periodically stopped — by the direct actions of US interests, including the government as state and as employer, private employers, and corporations."[6]

Studies show that high levels of immigration do not increase joblessness even among the lowest-paid workers, and there is little correlation between immigration and wage level. While immigrant labor does bring down wages in low-wage sectors by about 5%, this impact is more than offset by the increased demand for goods and services they create which creates more jobs and a subsequent increase in wages.[7] Nor do immigrants bring disease or reduce health standards. Even though most immigrants come from countries poorer than the United States, recent immigrants are healthier than the US-born population in general, and babies born to immigrant mothers are healthier than those born to US-born mothers.[8]

Immigrants do not drain our social services. In fact, just the opposite is true. In general, children, the elderly, the infirm and those with disabilities do not emigrate. Immigrants come as adult workers, having been raised and educated at the expense of their country of origin. In addition, language barriers, fears of deportation and the generally poor level of social services offered in the United States mean that immigrants use fewer public services than comparable groups of citizens. One study has shown that even legal immigrants use less than their share of medical care, unemployment insurance, food and educational programs, aid programs for families with dependent children and retirement programs.[9] About 75% of undocumented workers work on the books and pay payroll taxes including Medicaid and Social Security, contributing, for example, $8.7 billion to Social Security which they can never use.[10] The US Internal Revenue Service has determined that undocumented immigrants paid almost $50 billion in federal taxes from 1996 to 2003.[11] Forcing them to use false social security numbers means that currently they are taxed without representation and without return. Undocumented immigrants also pay sales taxes, gasoline taxes and all the taxes that everyone else pays. The reality is that US citizens of all races benefit significantly from the economic and cultural contributions of recent immigrants, including those that are undocumented.

Despite the presence of over 20,000 Immigration and Customs Enforcement (ICE) officials with a budget in 2010 of $5.7 billion, many employers do not generally comply with immigration laws or report illegal workers unless those workers are demanding higher wages, safer working conditions, basic benefits or the right to form a union and bargain collectively. ICE is used as the threat and enforcement tool to deport workers who are asserting workers' rights. If immigration laws were vigorously and consistently enforced, much of the dirtiest and poorest-paid agricultural fieldwork, manufacturing, textile, meat packing and maintenance work throughout the US would immediately come to a halt. The intent of immigration laws is not to stop the work, but to maintain the highly exploitive conditions under which it is done.[12]

Many white people say that they are in favor of legal immigration and only against undocumented immigration. Today's immigration laws favor those who have family who are US citizens or permanent residents. This translates into the reality that most people of color in the world are permanently excluded. Those who arrive here without documents are no more "illegal" than people of color were who could not vote or use public facilities before the civil rights movement. Racially discriminatory laws deem the actions of people of color illegal when they try to access the same rights and opportunities as white people.

US Immigration and Customs Enforcement has been placed under the Department of Homeland Security which leads more and more people to confuse the regulation of immigration with protecting ourselves against terrorism. Because ICE is part of Homeland Security, under the Secure Communities program, 287(g) program, the Border Enforcement Security Task Force, the Criminal Alien Program, Intergovernmental Service Agreements and the State Criminal Alien Assistance Program, local law enforcement agencies are being pressured to enforce immigration laws, something they are ill-prepared to do and which diverts much-needed resources from routine law enforcement activities. In addition, when local police become ICE agents, it seriously compromises their relationships with immigrant communities and makes normal crime prevention and criminal investigations much more difficult. Under these programs, tens of thousands of immigrants who have no criminal record and pose no identifiable threat to anybody have been detailed and deported.[13] Deporting busboys, gardeners and car wash workers for not having legal papers with them when they are stopped by officials leads to broken families, separation of parents and children and fearful and devastated immigrant communities. It does nothing to protect us from terrorism. Recent laws like Arizona's SB1070 go even further, mandating local law enforcement officials to stop anyone who they have reasonable suspicion might be an unlawful immigrant. Although parts of this bill were declared unconstitutional by the courts, other states are considering similar legislation.[14]

Like all attempts to monitor, control and punish communities of color, current immigration policies target individuals and communities and throw up further racial barriers to full participation in US society. These policies lead to insecure communities, disrupted lives and families and further hardship to already stressed communities. They provide convenient scapegoats for economic problems that leave the real causes and culprits unnoticed. They make a mockery out of our claims that all people are treated equally.

The only way fully to incorporate immigrants into our communities is to normalize their status and provide them with full rights and benefits. Until this occurs, employers' ability to exploit them will continue to depress wages and set working people against each other, contributing to the further exploitation of all workers and the continuing harassment of Latino/a and Asian American communities under the guise of immigration enforcement.

We are heavily indebted to immigrants, both those with and those without legal documents, for our daily well-being. At the same time, these workers are some of the most highly exploited people in our society. To change this, we can begin to work for full rights and protections for immigrants and refugees. All immigrants and refugees should enjoy:

- Full legal rights regardless of status
- Access to education and healthcare programs regardless of status
- Access to permanent residency
- Clear and uniform standards for the granting of refugee status regardless of country of origin
- Standards that include vulnerability to domestic violence, femicide and female genital mutilation as criteria for refugee status

204 | Uprooting Racism

Questions and Actions — Recent Immigrants

1. Were your foreparents legal immigrants to the US when people of color were excluded?
2. In what ways do you benefit from the work of immigrants, including those who are undocumented, for clothes, meat, vegetables, fruit, electronic goods and other household items?
3. In what ways do you benefit from the work of immigrants for services such as domestic work, gardening, childcare, elder care, nursing, transportation (taxi, bus and van services), hotel room services and restaurant work?
4. How can you challenge those who argue that immigrants are dangerous to our communities and deserve to be racially profiled, criminalized and punished?
5. In what ways can you support just, non-racist immigration reform?

- Elimination of employer sanctions and an end to visas tied to employment
- Release if they have been held without charges or denied legal rights

We should also work for:

- Resolution of the backlogs of visa applicants
- Demilitarization of the US-Mexico border
- Non-governmental oversight of Immigration and Customs Enforcement

---

Notes

1. Grace Chang. *Disposable Domestics: Immigrant Women Workers in the Global Economy.* South End, 2000, p. 2.
2. Aviva Chomsky. *"They Take Our Jobs!": And 20 Other Myths About Immigration.* Beacon, 2007, pp. 5-7.
3. For a detailed description of how this process works over several job sectors, see Chang, *Disposable Domestics.*
4. For detailed accounts of how immigrants of color were treated, see Takaki, *A Different Mirror,* especially Chapters 10 on Asian Americans and 12 on Latino/as.
5. Rinku Sen with Fekkak Mamdouh. *The Accidental American: Immigration and Citizenship in the Age of Globalization.* Berrett-Koehler, 2008, p. 153.
6. Chang. *Disposable Domestics,* pp. 3-4.
7. Sen with Mamdouh. *The Accidental American,* p. 160.
8. Southern Poverty Law Center. "Intelligence Report: The Immigrants: Myths and Reality." Issue 101 (Spring 2001), p. 12.
9. Randolph Capps et al. *A Profile of Low-Income Working Immigrant Families.* Urban Institute, June, 2005. [online]. [cited February 24, 2011]. urban.org/publications/311206.html.
10. Eduardo Porter. "Illegal Immigrants Are Bolstering Social Security with Billions." *New York Times,* April 5, 2005. [online]. [cited February 24, 2011]. nytimes.com/2005/04/05/business/05immigration.html?_r=1.

11. Statement of The Honorable Mark W. Everson, Commissioner, Internal Revenue Service, Testimony Before the House Committee on Ways and Means, July 26, 2006.

12. Sen with Mamdouh. *The Accidental American,* pp. 58-59, 140-141.

13. Nina Bernstein. "Target of Immigrant Raids Shifted." *New York Times,* February 3, 2009. [online]. [cited February 24, 2011]. nytimes.com/2009/02/04/us/04raids.html?_r=3& pagewanted=1&emc=eta1.

14. For more on Arizona SB1070, see Randal C. Archibold. "Arizona Enacts Stringent Law on Immigration." *New York Times,* April 23, 2010. [online]. [cited February 24, 2011]. nytimes.com/2010/04/24/us/politics/24immig.html.

We All Stand to Gain

I N ALL OF THESE CHAPTERS, we have seen that racism has been established and maintained to exploit the land and labor of people of color and to preserve white dominance. Theft of Native American land, genocide, slavery, sundown towns, anti-miscegenation, immigration restrictions, eugenics, limitations on reproductive options, mass criminalization, residential boarding schools, child protection, welfare and foster care systems, racial profiling and police brutality, internment — these are just some of the forms that the surveillance, control and punishment of communities of color takes to protect white power, wealth and privilege.

Yet people of color are not just the result of what white people have done to them or even of how they have resisted racism. The lives and cultures of people of color can only be conveyed through their own voices, and I encourage you to listen to those voices. Your life will be changed as a result.

To broaden the narrow thinking which constrains white people's worldview and understanding, we need to promote the thinking, creative expression and leadership of people of color. We should do this not because the result will be better-than-white thinking, but because we have systematically controlled, exploited and stymied such expression for hundreds of years. We have a historic responsibility to work for the end of white cultural, political and economic exploitation.

In return, the burden of guilt, blame, shame and sadness will be lifted from our shoulders. We will no longer be standing on the backs of other people with all the precariousness that position entails. We will have an active role to play in ending injustice. We will gain immeasurably from the contributions that people of color make to the world without exploiting them for it. And we will have a more accurate assessment of the contributions of white people. We will better see that leadership, wisdom and creative expression have nothing to do with racial groupings, but result from the rich interplay between individual creativity, culture, circumstances, politics and history — and defy any categorization.

Part V

Fighting Institutional Racism

Institutional Racism

RACISM IS NOT JUST THE SUM TOTAL of all the individual acts in which white people discriminate, harass, stereotype or otherwise mistreat people of color. The accumulated effects of centuries of white racism have given it an institutional nature that is more entrenched than racial prejudice. In fact, institutional racism is barely touched by changes in individual white consciousness. We often find it difficult to see or to know how to challenge it because we are so used to focusing on individual actions and attitudes.

One example of institutional racism is that professors of color (and white women) make considerably less money than their white (and male) counterparts. Prejudice and acts of discrimination by individual white faculty and administrators contribute to this disparity. But even if all white people were completely racially neutral, the disparities would persist.

Some of the reasons for these systemic disparities are that past discrimination excluded students of color from academic programs. Segregated and inferior schools have forced students of color to play catch up in college, taking longer to complete their studies. Established networks of white academics have made it easier for white students, particularly males, to get into the best universities, thereby getting better training, credentials and research opportunities. These networks help them to find out about scholarship opportunities and to find postdoctoral positions, thus advancing their careers faster.

People of color have only recently been allowed into many academic professions. The factors mentioned above result in white professors being hired at higher starting salary levels than corresponding professors of color. Lack of peers of color for support, racism from white colleagues and pressure on the limited number of professors of color to advise students of color contribute to higher workloads and less support for academics of color than for their white peers. In addition, recent cutbacks and salary and hiring freezes in many universities have prevented faculty of color from catching up with white faculty who have already reached high salary levels.

The result of these patterns is that faculty of color earn approximately 75% of what white faculty with comparable qualifications earn. A faculty member of color, working in the same department, who was equally qualified, the same age and with the same years of experience as white colleagues could be making $15,000 to $25,000 less a year and have considerably less job security and fewer other benefits.[1] This could be true without a single overt act of discrimination in the department or the university.

Nor can this pattern of institutional racism be eliminated in one generation, as some of us might hope. There are few professors of color in most disciplines, and therefore, few role models, mentors and advisors for current students of color, discouraging some and making it harder for others. None of the factors mentioned above have improved in the last three decades, and some have even deteriorated.

Differences in public school funding by race are another example of institutional racism. Although in most states there is a standard reimbursement per student to school districts, the actual amount spent on students' education depends on many factors including local property taxes, contributions from parents, volunteer hours from community members, business and foundation contributions. The average spent per pupil can vary by thousands of dollars even in the same metropolitan area.

Most students in the United States go to schools that are highly segregated by race because of discriminatory housing and lending practices and estate tax laws which promote the transfer of wealth through generations. Predominantly white schools spend much more per student than schools in which the majority are students of color. The average difference in spending is probably about 2 to 1, although in many areas the greatest differences can run 8 to 1 or 10 to 1.[2] An additional $1,500 per year per student gives a class of 30 children $45,000 more a year. Without a single overt act of discrimination, the educational opportunities of most children of color in the US are greatly deficient when compared to those of white children. Today we have an educational system that is nearly as racially segregated and unequal as it was before the US Supreme Court's *Brown v. Board of Education* ruling outlawed intentional school segregation in 1954. This is institutional racism.

As you read the chapters in this part, recall the web of control described in Part III. Each institution mentioned here reinforces others and contributes to the web of surveillance, control and punishment under which people of color live. Each institution denies them the rights and benefits of being full participants in US society and, at the same time, demeans, harasses and attacks them, their families and communities and puts them at further disadvantage. Each institution is a pillar of societal racism just as individual racist acts and longstanding racist policies are pillars of these institutions.

Notes

1. I have just summarized some of the factors putting professors of color at economic and emotional disadvantage. Women of color face additional barriers. They all face racism in other, non-academic areas of their lives. There have been no specific studies of professors, but Joe Feagin and Melvin P. Sikes's *Living with Racism: The Black Middle-Class Experience,* Beacon, 1994, contains detailed descriptions of the kinds of disadvantages I have referred to.
2. Linda Darling-Hammond. "Structured for Failure: Race, Resources, and Student Achievement." In Markus and Moya, *Doing Race,* pp. 295-321.

Land and Housing

L AND IS WEALTH. It is the foundation for housing, the source of food, the producer of wood, minerals, oil, gas and other resources, the location of industry. The history of racism in the United States can be traced to people's possession of and dispossession from land. Racism today is still inscribed with those practices and patterns of dispossession.

The accumulation of white wealth began with the theft of land. When settlers arrived on the continent, Native Americans used all of the land to sustain themselves and their communities. Steadily, using extreme force, white people pushed Native Americans off their land. The church had ruled before Columbus even set sail that any land, anywhere in the world, not ruled by Christian leaders could be legitimately claimed by Christians. In other words, those who set out to "discover" land were acting under a god-given mandate to steal it from its non-Christian residents. This legal "Doctrine of Discovery" is still cited in contemporary land use cases involving Native Americans.[1]

Early settlers stole vast tracts of land, contradictorily claiming it was both uninhabited and that its inhabitants were not using it productively. Speculators such as George Washington became rich from selling land to which they had no title or right. Native Americans were routinely forced to move from area to area to land that white people did not want — until they decided they wanted it. Nor could Native Americans claim title to land in court because they had no legal standing. By the end of the colonial period, most land had been accumulated into vast farms and estates by the US ruling class, enshrining their power in the Constitution by granting voting rights only to white Christian men of property, i.e, those who owned land.

In 1862, the first section of what eventually amounted to 270,000,000 acres of land was opened up to homesteading by primarily white Christian men (you had to be a citizen or intended citizen to qualify). Over 10% of the land area of the United States was ultimately given away for free after the US army had violently driven Native Americans off and white settlers "made improvements" to the land. Today, 46 million white people or 20% of the white population are direct beneficiaries of the Homestead Act.[2]

In 1887, the Dawes Act broke up tribal holdings into small individual properties and allowed the US government to claim the "surplus," thus facilitating white people acquiring even more Native American land. At the same time, the federal government took responsibility for collecting fees from anyone who used tribal land, with the money to be held in a trust fund. Although the fees were consistently undervalued by the government, over the decades billions were paid by mining, oil and gas companies, ranchers and others who degraded the land through extraction and pollution; even now over $350 million is collected annually by the Bureau of Indian Affairs, part of the Interior Department. The money was supposed to be given to the descendants of the original Indian land owners, but every audit since 1928 has found billions missing from the trust fund.[3] It is certainly the biggest and longest-standing financial scandal in the history of the United States.

In 1996, in the largest-ever class action lawsuit against the US government, more than 300,000 Native Americans asked for $27.5 billion in settlement. The government delayed, often claiming that vital records couldn't be found. It was later discovered that boxes of documents were being destroyed even as lawyers from the government said they were searching for them. The director of the Bureau of Indian Affairs and the Secretary of the Interior were eventually held in contempt and fined, but no restitution was made and the amount owed continued to accumulate. After some time, the total amount owed Native Americans was calculated to be close to $50 billion, but despite repeated audits reporting massive government fraud and incompetence and several court rulings in favor of the plaintiffs, the government delayed payments and refused a settlement.

Finally, in December 2009, Attorney General Eric Holder reached an agreement with Native American groups to pay plaintiffs $3.4 billion, $2 billion of which would be set aside for a land consolidation scholarship program to benefit Native American investments. The settlement is currently scheduled to be finalized and implemented in 2011.[4]

Many white people are resentful of Native Americans being able to run casinos on their land (only about 5% of Native nations do so), but every year the federal government deprives Native peoples of billions of dollars in legitimate land use fees, keeping Native communities in poverty.

In general, African Americans could not own land until after the Civil War in most of the US. After the war, blacks could buy land if they had the money, and a few were able to purchase farms and urban home sites. Some were even able to become prosperous from land, work and businesses. However eventually, no matter how long established or successful, whites found ways to dispossess them of their land and possessions, usually forcing them to vacate their homes in what can be called a process of ethnic cleansing that no part of the country was immune to.

White people used a variety of means to carry out black ethnic cleansing. There were large-scale race riots that destroyed entire city sections of prosperous black communities such as Tulsa, Oklahoma, and Rosewood, Florida. There were smaller-scale murders, threats and intimidation that pushed blacks out of towns and counties in fear of their lives. In hundreds, probably thousands of places across the country, black populations declined precipitously, often within days or weeks because African Americans were murdered, warned to leave or burned out. They lost their land, homes and possessions, anything they could not carry with them.

Most of those towns and counties have stayed white. For example, Forsyth County, Georgia, is now a white commuter area in the Atlanta metropolitan area. In 1912, there was a racial cleansing in which its white residents drove out the 1000 black residents. Forced to flee within days, most blacks lost everything and whites quickly took over their land and possessions. Nearly a century later in 2000, out of a population of 98,000, there were only 684 blacks, most living on the county's border.[5]

In other towns, counties, neighborhoods and suburbs, cleansing wasn't necessary because white people never allowed people of color to settle in the first place. Sometimes a county's reputation was enough to keep people away or too afraid to return and claim their land and possessions. Sometimes threats and intimidation was used, including explicit warning signs such as "Nigger, Don't Let the Sun Go Down On You in ...." Two towns in Nevada sounded a whistle at 6 PM to warn Native Americans to leave.

Today, when a cross is burned in a yard or graffiti is written on a doorway, wall or fence, people of color understand it as a warning that they are not wanted and if they do not leave, more serious violence will follow. They have a century and a half of evidence that white people will burn out or kill them if they ignore or are ignorant of these warnings. They also know that few whites will try to protect them and that they will have little legal redress, can hope for little more than an apology decades, or even a hundred years, later.

The support of farming in the US is another land use issue that demonstrates massive racial disparities. The government has systematically supported white farmers by providing subsidized loans, agricultural colleges, extensive networks of rural agricultural support, crop supports and subsidies. Recently it was revealed that access to credit and other government support was systematically denied to black and Native farmers in the 1960s, 70s and 80s, leading thousands to lose their farms. In a massive settlement in 1999, the government admitted longstanding policies and practices of racial discrimination. In 2011, President Obama signed the bill that would settle the claims.[6]

The result of these and many other land policies is that white people own 98% of all privately owned agricultural land in the US.[7]

Although main targets of exclusion and discrimination have been Native Americans and African Americans, other groups such as Jews, Asian Americans (primarily Chinese and Japanese) and Latino/as (primarily Mexicans) have also been subject to racial cleansing and exclusion in both urban and rural areas. Most infamously, 110,000 Japanese Americans were rounded up and sent to concentration camps at the beginning of World War II, losing their land, homes and almost everything they owned. But there are many other less publicized examples of white people using intimidation, arson and physical violence to expel or keep people of color and Jews out of neighborhoods and towns. Historian James Loewen estimates that there may have been 10,000 of these white-only areas at their height in 1970, and that millions of people live in or grew up in sundown towns and suburbs.[8]

When civil rights laws made formal segregation illegal in the 1960s, white people began moving out of urban areas to the suburbs to recreate whites-only areas. This was facilitated by federal housing policies and subsidies for building roads, schools and other infrastructure in new areas. Whites-only communities were maintained as gated communities through the use of redlining, steering and implicit agreements. White real estate agents might steer white clients and people of color into different neighborhoods, quote higher rents or house prices to people of color or use selective advertising to fill vacancies or promote properties.

As historian Loewen emphasizes, very few white towns or suburbs are that way by accident. Although today the means of enforcement are usually more subtle (and clearly illegal), white people in the US continue to flock to and segregate themselves within all-white enclaves. Threats, intimidation, past reputation, tacit agreements and subtle pressure can all maintain white segregation. White people, when deciding where to live, may not even be consciously aware that they are being steered or that they themselves favor white only areas, camouflaging their interests with such racially coded phrases as *safety, good schools* or *nicer neighborhoods.* As sociologist Bonilla-Silva observes, "although a variety of data suggest racial considerations are central to whites' residential choices, more than 90 percent of whites state in surveys that they have no problem with the idea of blacks moving into their neighborhoods."[9]

Meanwhile, the prosperous communities of color that had flourished in the postwar era were again demolished. Funded by the federal government and cleared through the use of eminent domain laws, large public projects such as ports, post offices, airports, convention centers and sports stadiums, as well as freeways and rapid transit systems designed to service suburban areas, destroyed the housing, communal networks, small businesses, cultural centers and generally thriving communities that people of color had created in urban centers. Those communities that remained had no economic infrastructure left as corporations moved manufacturing facilities overseas and local businesses located their offices and stores in the suburbs. White city governments often located garbage dumps and toxic waste facilities in communities of color.[10]

The current cycle of white displacement of people of color from the land continues as older white people decide that the suburbs don't meet their needs and younger white people look for inexpensive housing in culturally diverse

Questions and Actions — Land and Housing

1. If you find yourself in a city, neighborhood, suburb or school that is predominantly white, ask yourself whose land you are on and how did white people gain control of it?
2. How was white ownership maintained?
3. What means have white people used to keep people of color out? How do they still maintain control?
4. How is where you live different, in environmental quality, safety, infrastructure or beauty, than where people of color live?
5. Even if where you live is currently integrated, it might have racial discrimination or violence as part of its history. Find out about the history of the community you live in. What impact does that history continue to have on land use or land accessibility today?

urban areas. Labeled *gentrification,* this process is fueled by local development policies that emphasize high-end condos, boutique businesses, high-tech jobs and the advantages of "environmentally friendly" living. The overall effect is to destroy intact, if vulnerable, communities of color by raising rents and housing prices, pushing out local ethnic businesses and diminishing job opportunities as small-scale manufacturing is replaced by more favored land uses.[11]

The land you live on was surely stolen from Native Americans, but it is also likely to have been either subsequently stolen from African Americans or other people of color, or just maintained as white-only space by systematic racial policies and practices.

Notes

1. For a detailed history and current legal examples of the use of this doctrine, see Steven T. Newcomb. *Pagans in the Promised Land: Decoding the Doctrine of Christian Discovery.* Fulcrum, 2008.

2. Trina Williams. *The Homestead Act: A Major Asset-building Policy in American History.* Center for Social Development, Washington University, 2000.

3. This information is drawn from Michael Riley. "Feds Settle Suit over Mismanagement of Indian Trust Lands." *Denver Post,* February 26, 2011. [online]. [cited February 26, 2011]. denverpost.com/ci_13956753; Joel Dyer. "Billions Missing from US Indian Trust Fund." *Albion Monitor,* August 15, 1996. [online]. [cited February 26, 2011]. albionmonitor.com/free/biatrustfund.html.

4. Ibid.

5. For a full description of several racial cleansings, see Elliot Jaspin. *Buried in the Bitter Waters: The Hidden History of Racial Cleansing in America.* Basic, 2007. For information on Forsyth County, see pp. 6-7 and 125-151.

6. Steve Baragona. "U.S. Government Settles Claims with Black, Native American Farmers." *Voice of America News.com,* December 6, 2010. [online]. [cited February 26, 2011]. voanews.com/english/news/usa/US-Government-Settles-with--111394004.html.

7. Jess Gilbert et al. *Who Owns the Land? Agricultural Land Ownership by Race/Ethnicity in Rural America.* Economic Research Service/USDA Newsletter, Vol. 17, #4 (Winter, 2002).

8. Loewen, *Sundown Towns,* p. 12.

9. Eduardo Bonilla-Silva. *Racism Without Racists: Color-Blind Racism and the Persistence of Racial Inequality in the United States,* 2nd ed. Rowman & Littlefield, 2006, p. 11.

10. For a detailed account of the dumping of garbage and toxic and environmentally damaging waste in poor communities of color, see Robert D. Bullard. *Dumping in Dixie: Race, Class, and Environmental Quality,* 3rd ed. Westview, 2000; Robert D. Bullard and Benjamin Chavis Jr. *Confronting Environmental Racism: Voices from the Grassroots.* South End, 1999.

11. For a detailed analysis of gentrification, see Maureen Kennedy and Paul Leonard. *Dealing with Neighborhood Change: A Primer on Gentrification and Policy Choices.* The Brookings Institution Center on Urban and Metropolitan Policy and PolicyLink, April 2001. [online. [cited February 26, 2011]. policylink.org/atf/cf/%7B97C6D565-BB43-406D-A6D5-ECA3BBF35AF0%7D/DealingWithGentrification_final.pdf.

Public Policy

PUBLIC POLICY REFERS TO government planning, decision making and allocation of public resources. Government officials are constantly confronted by an array of issues affecting our communities. Which issues are addressed, how they are addressed, who gets to participate in the discussion and what solutions are considered viable are all influenced by racism. Any informed, active citizen can influence the nature of public policy discussion and decisions, although here again, white people, particularly those with money and connections, have long had greater political influence.

People can influence public policy at several levels. We are most powerful when we organize around particular issues or programs and create pressure that public officials must respond to. The civil rights, women's liberation, disability rights and other movements are examples of large-scale organizing that led to new laws, executive orders, funding appropriations, federal guidelines and other specific results.

Another way to influence public policy is by electing officials who represent our interests. This is always complex because candidates run on a platform of interests, some of which may be progressive and others of which may not be. They also make promises during elections and then do not or cannot follow through. Unless there is public pressure and support while elected officials are in office, they alone don't have the leverage to fight entrenched interests.

People are also able to respond to proposed legislation, state initiatives, nominations of public officials and public planning documents. Concerted mobilization of people dramatically increases our effectiveness in responding to issues. Unless we analyze issues carefully and critically, keeping a focus on how they affect racism and race relations, we will not be able to marshal our forces effectively.

We will not get very far in the struggle for racial justice unless we have significant national public support and leadership to address racial injustice directly and forcefully. This calls for no less than massive *reinvestment* in communities of color to redress the long-term effects of racism. Some might call it reinvestment for what was taken out of communities of color by white people. Others might call it restorative justice. The concept is often referred to as reparation.

In the 20th century, we have seen national and international examples of reparations. The German government paid reparations both to individual Jews who suffered losses during the Holocaust and to the state of Israel. The US government paid reparations to Japanese Americans for the losses they suffered from the confiscation of their property and their forced relocation during World War II. We also saw investment in devastated European communities through the Marshall Plan; the US government gave an additional $13 billion in aid (about 10 times that amount in today's dollars) to 16 war-torn countries.[1]

Particularly within the African American community, the demand for reparations for slavery and its aftermath has been gaining momentum in recent years. Senator Bill Owens introduced the first reparations bill in the Massachusetts state senate. Over the years, John Conyers, a Democrat from Michigan, has introduced several bills to put the issue of reparations on the table in the US House of Representatives. These bills would establish a commission to examine the institution of slavery and economic discrimination against African Americans and recommend appropriate remedies. There have also been public conferences, books, talks and lawsuits. These are relatively new developments, but the idea of reparations for African Americans has a long history.

On January 16, 1865, General William T. Sherman issued Special Field Order No.15, which awarded all the Sea Islands south of Charleston, South Carolina, and a significant portion of coastal lands to newly freed slaves to homestead. Each freedman was eligible for 40 acres of tillable ground. The order became a proposed law that was passed by both houses but ultimately vetoed by President Andrew Johnson.[2]

The principle under which Germany paid reparations was stated in the 1952 Luxembourg Agreement, which said that a state that victimized inhabitants on the basis of group membership has an obligation to compensate that group on the same basis. Slavery was a system legitimized in the US

Constitution and enforced through local, state and federal statutes. The genocide of Native Americans, the destruction of their cultures and the establishment and failure of the treaty system were acts of the US government. In both cases, individuals were targeted simply because of their membership in a particular group, and the damage from those systems continues to this day.[3]

One form that reparations for Native Americans could take would be the return of land. For example, there is much federal land that is no longer being used as military bases. The government has promised to give priority to the claims of Native Americans for such land, but in practice this policy has not been carried out. Cleaning up and returning unused land would be a first step in restoring an economic base to Native communities.[4]

Whether we call it reinvestment, restoration, redistribution or reparations, it is a process by which US society, through public policy, takes responsibility for killing millions of people, stealing land and exploiting the labor and culture of Native Americans, African Americans, Latino/as and Asian Americans during the last 500 years of European settlement in North America. Public reinvestment needs to be focused and accountable.

People of color do not want handouts. They say they want an end to racial exploitation; they want the same opportunities white people have. These opportunities include meaningful and effective education for themselves and their children, decent jobs, adequate healthcare, safe streets, quality childcare, adequate social services and the chance to be represented by people who truly share their interests. These are opportunities that all people deserve and that, according to our founding documents, we are honor bound to provide equally for all. We can certainly afford to do so, and we cannot afford not to.

How do we pay for reinvestment? It is no secret, but still little discussed among us, that wealth is concentrated among a relatively few in the United States. In 2007, the top 20% of the population owned 93% of the financial wealth of the entire country.[5] The wealth of the top 1 percent of the population of the United States averages over $18 million per household.[6] The astoundingly high concentration of wealth is the direct result of hundreds of years of exploitation of poor, working- and middle-class people by the rich, and of people of color by white people.

In the last two decades, the concentration of wealth has increased. Income, capital gains and inheritance taxes have been significantly cut allowing those with the most wealth to pass on even greater amounts to their children. We have corporate welfare policies, such as unlimited deduction for interest on corporate debt, intangible asset write-offs, foreign tax credits and write-offs for the banks' foreign debt losses.

Such government policy favors the rich over the rest of us, and white people over people of color. We need to tax the income and accumulated wealth of the small percentage of individuals, families and corporations that control our economy and communities. Then we need to reinvest that money in community-controlled and racially just development. Poor, working- and middle-class people of all races, women and men, young and old, people with disabilities, rural, urban and suburban dwellers would benefit if we did so.

The tax structure of the United States is complex, at least partly to protect the tremendous accumulation and concentration of wealth. A detailed analysis of it is beyond the scope of this book. We could make the entire system simpler and substantially more just with a few major changes. Here are some suggestions that are adapted from Barlett and Steele's *America: Who Really Pays the Taxes?:* [7]

- Eliminate all tax credits and exemptions except the personal exemption.
- Eliminate all itemized deductions.
- Lower the lowest rates and raise the highest rates in a simple scale.
- Eliminate special treatment for capital gains.
- Impose the income tax on the increase in value of all holdings at death.
- Withhold taxes on all income, regardless of source.
- Have a means test for all individual government benefits such as social security.
- Impose a 1% excise tax on all securities and options trading.
- Eliminate corporate tax preferences and increase corporate taxes to generate about 31% of total income tax collections.
- Tax income earned in the United States regardless of the filer's country of residence.
- Eliminate write-offs for taxes paid to foreign governments.
- Raise taxes on overseas investors.
- Raise taxes on foreign companies earning money in the United States.

Public policy issues change over time, but every public policy issue in the United States is at least partly an issue of race. We must always pay attention to the racial consequences of any issue that is being considered, even economically "progressive" ones, so it doesn't have racist effects.

We can do three things to take strategic action on public policy issues:

1. Assume that there are substantial racial implications for every issue before us.

2. Understand the ways that issues are framed in racial terms, in code or openly, to build support for a ruling-class agenda.

3. Keep revisiting issues that we thought were once settled, because our gains are subject to erosion and counterattack.

Public action through educational and organizing efforts is what influences and shapes public policy debate. During the first 2/3 of the 19th century, African Americans and white people worked to make abolition an issue that could not be avoided. Civil and voting rights for African Americans became public policy issues as a result of grassroots organizing that occurred during the civil rights movement. Japanese Americans organized, lobbied and advocated for many years until making reparations for the internment of Japanese American citizens during World War II became an issue the government had to address. These are the kinds of campaigns we can support. This is the kind of public action we need to take.

Any public policy issue can be analyzed using these and other questions. They stimulate our critical thinking so we do not mistakenly collude with an agenda that benefits a few and keeps the class, racial and gender status quo in place.

Questions and Actions — Public Policy

1. How is the problem being defined? Who is defining the problem? Who is not part of the discussion?
2. Who is being blamed for the problem? What racial or other fears are being appealed to?
3. What is the core issue?
4. What is the historical context for this issue?
5. What is being proposed as a solution? What would be the actual results of such a proposal?
6. How would this proposal affect people of color? How would it affect white people?
7. How would this proposal affect the rich?
8. How would it affect women? Young people? Poor and working people?
9. What are other options?
10. How are people organizing to address this problem in a more progressive way? How are people organizing to resist any racial backlash this issue might represent?
11. What is one thing you could do to address this problem?

Notes

1. For detailed information about these and many other reparations processes, consult Pablo De Greif, ed. *The Handbook of Reparations*. Oxford, 2008.
2. Zinn, *A People's History of the United States,* p. 197.
3. Some of this information comes from Salim Muwakkil. "Why American Blacks Deserve Reparations." *Chicago Tribune,* February 5, 2001. [online]. [cited February 25, 2011]. commondreams.org/views01/0205-04.htm.
4. Ibid.
5. Edward N. Wolff. *Recent Trends in Household Wealth in the United States: Rising Debt and the Middle-Class Squeeze — An Update to 2007.* Levy Economics Institute of Bard College, Working Paper No. 589, March 2010. [online]. [cited February 25, 2011]. levyinstitute.org/scholars/?auth=286.
6. Ibid.
7. Donald L. Barlett and James B. Steele. *America: Who Really Pays the Taxes?* Simon & Schuster, 1994, pp. 338–341.

Sample Analysis — Immigration Policy

T HROUGHOUT THIS BOOK we have seen how people of color are routinely scapegoated for social problems over which they have little influence. Recent immigrants make up one of the most vulnerable groups of people of color (see the chapter on "Recent Immigrants" in Part IV). Although some immigrants are highly skilled, highly trained or have family and economic resources, most are poor, isolated by language and culture and disoriented by a new society. Many are fleeing war, poverty or political repression. Many of our own foreparents faced similar conditions when they arrived one, five or ten generations ago.

Who has legal documents and who doesn't is not a question of impartial legal standards. Immigration policy is an arm of foreign policy as well as an instrument of white racism. Cubans fleeing Castro have been preferred over Haitians fleeing Duvalier; Vietnamese fleeing communism have been preferred over Salvadorano/as fleeing US-supported dictators and Europeans have been preferred over people of color. These are recent examples of how political factors influence immigration policy, which in turn determines who is "legal" or undocumented.

Current debate over immigration by people without legal documentation provides a good case study of how to look at public policy issues.

Here are answers, concerning immigration policy, to the questions posed at the end of previous chapter.

1. The problem is defined as: "illegal" immigration places a disproportionate burden on the states that have to pay for the services provided to these immigrants. State politicians say this produces state budget deficits when the federal government mandates services but doesn't pay for them. White political leaders, the media and states' rights advocates are primarily

defining the problem while poor and working people, people of color and immigrants are excluded from the discussion.

2. Only recent immigrants without papers from Central America and Asia are being blamed for these problems. This becomes a way to blame the entire Latino/a and Asian American immigrant communities, allowing the government to keep them under tight control and surveillance and to further cut back social services to the poor. Defining immigrants without documents and the Latino/a and Asian American immigrant communities as the problem appeals to white people's fear of people of color and immigrants, our fear of losing jobs and our fear of budget deficits and further cutbacks.

3. The stated issues are: the federal government is not funding federally mandated services; politicians want to reduce federal and state budget deficits; corporations are moving jobs overseas causing loss of jobs in the United States. The primary issue, however, is that our political leaders are stirring up a white backlash against communities of color by blaming them for economic and social problems. This backlash uses *illegal alien* as a racially coded word for immigrant of color, playing into the economic and racial fears of working- and middle-class whites.

4. Historically, white people have used issues of states' rights to fight against relinquishing white power. The Civil War was fought over whether the states or the federal government had the right to set policy on slavery, not on whether slavery per se was right or wrong. Much of the resistance to the civil rights movement was based on similar arguments about states' rights and the role of the federal government in enforcing desegregation, voting rights and access to education. Once again white people are trying to roll back gains in government policy that benefit the poorest and most vulnerable members of our society.

5. The specific proposals being advanced, such as Arizona's State Bill 1070, would turn local law enforcement personnel into immigration officials, encourage racial profiling, cut off all services to immigrants lacking legal papers and would deport as many as possible. The intended result is a net savings from not providing services to them and the opening up their jobs to legal residents. Most studies indicate that immigrants actually contribute more to the community in taxes, job creation and the revitalization of neighborhoods than they require from it in economic support.[1] Over

time their contributions increase, and costs decrease further. They do take jobs — usually those that whites don't want or won't do — but their need for services creates jobs as well.

6. In the long term, this proposed "solution" furthers impoverishes the Latino/a and Asian American immigrant communities. It cuts them off from schooling, healthcare and other essential public services, disrupts families, promotes racial profiling and targets them for further police and immigration harassment and intimidation as well as violence from individuals.

7. Anti-immigrant bills further segregate white people from people of color, reinforce our racial stereotypes and contribute to further racial injustice. They focus our attention on the immigrant community rather than on the true source of the economic dislocation we are currently experiencing. These bills benefit businesses which exploit immigrant workers.

8. Under these proposals, certain groups would be hit particularly hard. Bearing primary responsibility for the health and welfare of the family, immigrant women would have less access to work, education, safety and healthcare and fewer resources for raising children. These proposals make all Asian American and Latina women more vulnerable to sexual and racial harassment at work, and to physical and sexual violence within the family. Such laws keep children of immigrants without papers out of school and healthcare systems, and intensify a two-tier system in which some children have opportunities and others are without future prospects of decent work.

9. There are other options for balancing state budgets, creating jobs and paying for social services. We could increase taxation of rich individuals and corporate wealth. We could divert money from the exorbitant expenses on surveillance and enforcement in immigrant communities. We could use that money to create jobs, job training, school programs and social services to integrate immigrants more quickly into the economy.

10. A great deal of organizing against anti-immigrant policies has already occurred. Some programs provide services and legal assistance to immigrants without documents. Some are organizing immigrant workers so they will have a stronger voice in the political system. There are organizations addressing economic dislocation and redevelopment, while others are organizing and doing educational work against ballot initiatives and

legislative proposals that attack immigrants. There are also campaigns of non-compliance with initiatives already passed, coordinated by teachers and healthcare workers.

11. There are many ways to become involved. You can join an organization supporting immigrant rights, and you can make a financial contribution to an organization working with immigrants and refugees. You can write letters, phone or send faxes and e-mail to policymakers, and you can work with others to protest the enforcement of policies that discriminate against immigrants. You can challenge other people when you hear racially prejudiced or misinformed statements about this issue. You can help others think critically about how racism operates in an issue like this.

Using this chapter as an example of critical analysis of social issues, take another current public policy debate and scrutinize it using the same questions.

Notes

1. Sen with Mamdouh. *The Accidental American,* p. 160.

Voting

M ANY OF US HAVE COME TO TAKE OUR RIGHT TO VOTE for granted, forget-
ting our foreparents' long struggles to achieve it. Originally only white
men with property could vote, less than 10% of the colonial population.
People fought for hundreds of years to extend the right to vote, first to poor
and working-class white men, then to men of color and finally to women.

In this chapter, I will deal primarily with the situation in the United States
because of the widespread and well-documented practice of disenfranchising voters of color. However, all white-dominated countries have histories of
denying people of color the right to vote.

In the 2000 presidential election in the United States, whites constituted
almost 95% of George W. Bush's total vote. People of color accounted for
almost 30% of Al Gore's total, although they were only 19% of the total voters.[1] But were people of color adequately represented? Did their votes count?

On election day, African American and Haitian voters were harassed by
police; their names were removed from the rolls; they were turned away from
the polls even when they had valid ID; they were asked to show more ID
than white voters had to show; they were threatened with deportation; they
had the polls close early on them (some as early as 4:30) and they saw their
ballots left uncounted by outdated machinery. These "irregularities" and ille-
galities affected the votes of tens of thousands of voters in Florida, which
turned out to be the pivotal state in determining the final presidential election results. But Florida was not the only state to report voting irregularities,
nor were African Americans and Haitians the only voters kept from voting.
Reports indicate that there were incidents of voter intimidation, voter turn-
backs and other illegal practices in several other states, including Michigan,
Georgia, Missouri, New York, Arkansas and Illinois.[2] In Texas, and possibly
in other states, Latino/as were asked to show extra identification that whites

were not required to show, and they reported being intimidated by men hanging around the voting booths dressed in green, the color of the uniform of immigration officials. Older Mexicans who requested absentee ballots were visited by sheriffs and other law-enforcement officials in what appeared to be attempts at intimidation. There were also many cases where polls had an inadequate supply of bilingual ballots and poll watchers.[3]

Denying people of color the right to vote is a practice deeply embedded in the US political system, and we need to understand that history so we don't consider the present practices anomalous. Our Founding Fathers, in a compromise to ensure that southern states would participate in the union, agreed that slaves, although they could not vote, would count as $3/5$ of a person for the purpose of calculating the Electoral College representatives that a state was allotted. Then the number of representatives was used to calculate the number of electoral votes that each state would have. This compromise gave the southern states a political advantage so powerful that southern slave owners controlled the presidency for 50 of the first 72 years of the country's history.[4]

African Americans received the right to vote with the passage of the 15th Amendment to the US Constitution in 1870. But the two-party, winner-take-all Electoral College system continues to discriminate against and marginalize people of color. In the 2000 election, Bush won the electoral votes of every southern state and every border state except Maryland, despite the fact that 53% of all blacks (over 90% of whom voted for the Democrats) live in the southern states. There are more white Republicans than black votes in each of those states, so the votes of almost half of the people of color in the entire country were discounted. Millions of Native American and Latino/a voters who live in overwhelmingly white, Republican states like Arizona, Nevada, Oklahoma, Utah, Montana and Texas were equally unrepresented by Electoral College voting.

A further dilution of the votes of people of color occurs because of the way electoral votes are unequally distributed between rural and urban states. For example, in Wyoming in 2004, one Electoral College vote corresponded to 165,000 voters, while in more populated states, with more voters of color, the ratio was one Electoral College vote to over 600,000 voters. A voter in Wyoming had 68 times as much representation in the Senate for the same reasons. This gap in representation is widening and has major racial implications. By 2025, the four states of New York, California, Texas and Florida will have non-white majorities and 25% of the nation's population but will have the same representation as the four states of Wyoming, Montana, Idaho and North Dakota.[5]

The Electoral College system is not the only way that people of color lose voting representation. After emancipation and the passage of the 14th and 15th Amendments, the southern states worked to exclude newly enfranchised black voters. The white ruling class of the South was very explicit about what it was doing. For example, in Virginia, US Senator Carter Glass worked to expand disenfranchisement laws along with poll taxes and literacy tests. He described the state's 1901 convention this way:

> Discrimination! Why that is precisely what we propose. That, exactly, is what this Convention was elected for — to discriminate to the very extremity of permissible action under the limits of the Federal Constitution, with a view to the elimination of every Negro voter who can be gotten rid of legally, without materially impairing the numerical strength of the white electorate.[6]

In Alabama, the criminal code in the constitution of 1901 was, according to the chair of the convention John Knox, designed to "ensure white supremacy," and crimes worthy of disenfranchisement were classified depending in large part by whether delegates thought blacks were likely to commit them.[7] The state was also focused on excluding poor whites. Delegates "wished to disfranchise most of the Negroes and the uneducated and propertyless whites in order to legally create a conservative electorate," wrote historian Malcolm McMillan.[8]

Historically, another way white people disenfranchised voters of color was by disenfranchising felons — but not just any felons.[9] Many states disenfranchised criminals even before the Civil War. But after the Civil War and Reconstruction in the South, legal codes were created to limit the effects of the 14th and 15th Amendments which gave blacks equal protection under the law and gave black men the right to vote. In Mississippi, the convention of 1890 replaced laws disenfranchising all convicts, with laws disenfranchising only people convicted of the crimes blacks were supposedly more likely to commit. For almost a century thereafter, you couldn't lose your right to vote in Mississippi if you committed murder or rape, but you could if you married someone of another race. In Florida, the constitution drafted in 1868 disenfranchised ex-felons as well as anyone convicted of larceny, again a crime that whites considered ex-slaves were most likely to commit.

The provisions that came out of those post-Reconstruction conventions, from poll taxes to grandfather clauses[10] to literacy tests, were almost all struck down by the Civil Rights Act of 1965. The only one still standing is the felony provision, which means that 1.8 million black men (13% of all black men in America — approximately one out of seven) are currently denied the right to vote because of incarceration or past felony convictions.[11] Although rules vary state by state, the United States is the only industrialized country that denies former prisoners the vote, even though they have completed their sentences and are fully integrated into the community.

In an extensive study of two poor and mostly black communities in Tallahassee, Florida, criminal justice professor Todd Clear was unable to find a single family without at least one disenfranchised man — he concluded that this made it unlikely the community would be able to band together when, for example, a state senator proposes locating a toxic waste dump nearby.

As journalist Nicholas Thompson of the *Washington Monthly* noted, "Felons, of course, aren't just murderers and muggers. Three out of every five felony convictions don't lead to jail time, and there's no clear line you have to cross to earn one…. Stopping payment on a check of more than $150 with intent to defraud makes you a felon in Florida. Being caught with one-fifth of an ounce of crack earns you a federal felony, but being caught with one-fifth of an ounce of cocaine only earns a misdemeanor."

Besides being arbitrary, racially biased and a continuation of historic patterns of discrimination, Thompson wrote, "Denying felons the right to vote after they have served their sentences and done their time runs against both the idea that people can redeem themselves and one of the nation's most important principles, the right to choose who governs you." As prominent neoconservative social theorist James Q. Wilson said, "A perpetual loss of the right to vote serves no practical or philosophical purpose."[12]

Even those people of color who can vote are marginalized due to our two-party political system. I think Bob Wing, editor of *Colorlines* magazine, has described this most clearly.

> To win elections, both parties must take their most loyal voters for granted and focus their message and money to win over the so-called undecided voters who will actually decide which party wins each election. The undecideds are mostly white affluent suburban-ites; both parties try to position their politics, rhetoric and policies

to woo them. The interests of people of color are ignored or even attacked by both parties as they pander to the "center."[13]

There are, of course, other strategies white people use to keep people of color from voting or to keep their votes from counting: at-large elections, gerrymandering, failure to redistrict when called for, packing (drawing electoral districts so that the majority of a group is packed into one area, which therefore gives it only a single representative) and its opposite cracking (spreading out voters of color over several districts so that their votes are diluted). Finally, because the Electoral College vote distribution is tied to the census and we know that the census undercounts communities of color, those communities lose political representation through this mechanism as well. The Census Bureau has refused to adjust the 2000 census results to account for a known undercount that leaves our 3.3 million people, all of whom are poor and many of whom are people of color. It also has serious repercussions in the distribution of federal and state funds for social programs and community development grants.

White people often complain that people of color don't vote in large enough numbers. I've heard it said that "They must not care enough." But how many white people would vote if we were harassed on the way to the poll and, when we got there, told we weren't listed or that we needed to show extra identification? How many would vote if, when we tried to make a complaint, there was no one who spoke our language to help us, and all the complaint lines were busy and understaffed? How many would vote if we discovered later that many of our votes were thrown out because of "irregularities" in the ballots and voting machines? What if this had been going on for over a hundred years?

Our system of voting needs a drastic overhaul. There are some simple places to begin:

- Eliminate the Electoral College system
- Develop a system of proportional representation for elections (This type of system is already in place in many municipal and county elections, and various forms are used throughout the world)
- Institute federal monitoring of elections
- Allow for district voting in local elections
- Develop a multi-party system of government
- Redistrict by population, supervised by widely representative bodies of citizens from each community

- Remove restrictions on ex-felons' voting and set up programs to help them register, as Canada does
- Install modern, easy-to-use, transparent voting machinery, keep the polls open 24 hours or more and declare voting day a national holiday
- Institute election-day registration

There are already community groups working on many of these issues. By becoming active on this issue you are strengthening democracy and making sure that *all* votes count.

Notes

1. Gore received the votes of 90% of the African Americans, 63% percent of Latino/as, 55% of Asians and 81% of Jews who voted. No data is available for Native Americans. These voting statistics are from Voter News Service and were quoted in Bob Wing. "White Power in Election 2000." *Colorlines* magazine (Spring 2001), p. 6.
2. Testimony of Hilary Shelton, director, Washington bureau of the NAACP before the Senate Governmental Affairs Committee, May 9, 2001.
3. Elizabeth Martinez. "The Next Four Years: Ally or Die." *Shades of Power* (Winter 2000-01), pp. 1, 20.
4. David Brion Davis. "The Central Fact of American History." *AmericanHeritage.com*, 2008. [online]. [cited February 28, 2011]. americanheritage.com/articles/magazine/ah/2005/1/2005_1_65.shtml; David R. Roediger. *How Race Survived US History: From Settlement and Slavery to the Obama Phenomenon. Verso*, 2008, pp. 50-51.
5. Steven Hill. *Why Progressives Lose: Affirmative Action for Conservatives.* Center for Voting and Democracy, 2003. [online]. [cited February 28, 2011]. archive.fairvote.org/articles/progressivepopulis.htm.
6. Nicholas Thompson. "Locking Up the Vote: Disenfranchisement of Former Felons Was the Real Crime in Florida." *Washington Monthly* (January/February 2001). [online]. [cited February 26, 2011]. washingtonmonthly.com/features/2001/0101.thompson.html.
7. Laura Conaway and James Ridgeway. "Democracy in Chains." *Village Voice*, November 28, 2000. [online]. [cited February 26, 2011]. villagevoice.com/2000-11-28/news/democracy-in-chains/.
8. Quoted in Thompson, "Locking Up the Vote." It is important to note that states where people of color are disenfranchised or where they receive the lowest wages are often the same states in which poor and working-class whites are disenfranchised and paid the lowest wages as well.
9. The following information is adapted from Manning Marable. "Stealing the Election: The Compromises of 1876 and 2000." *Standards*, Vol. 7, no. 2 (Spring-Summer 2001). [online]. [cited February 26, 2011]. colorado.edu/journals/standards/V7N2/FIRST/marable.html.
10. A provision introduced in the South after the Reconstruction period that only those whose grandfathers could vote could themselves vote, eliminating almost all Blacks from voting rolls.
11. Prison Policy Initiative. *Felon Disenfranchisement: Jim Crow Redux.* December 6, 2005. [online]. [cited February 26, 2011]. prisonpolicy.org/articles/prisonindex_jimcrow.pdf.
12. Thompson, "Locking Up the Vote."
13. Bob Wing. *The Structure of White Power and the Color of Election 2000.* December 7, 2000. [online]. [cited February 26, 2011]. africa.upenn.edu/Urgent_Action/apic121300b.html.

Affirmative Action

THERE ARE MANY WAYS TO ATTACK RACISM — affirmative action is one particular legal remedy to address and redress systematic economic and political discrimination against any group that is under-represented or has a history of being discriminated against in particular institutions. It is designed to eliminate institutional discrimination in situations where decisions, policies and procedures that may not be *explicitly* discriminatory have had a negative impact on a specific group of people. Yet today we have a vocal minority saying we should stop affirmative action not only as a legal remedy, but also as a social commitment. These people are saying we have gone too far in correcting racial injustice, but of course they are not challenging traditional forms of preference and discrimination that favor the rich, the educated, white people and men.

Affirmative action is practiced in many areas of our society. We have hiring and recruiting preferences for veterans, women and the children of alumni of many universities; special economic incentives for purchase of US-made products; import quotas against foreign goods and agricultural and textile subsidies. These practices have led to a huge over-representation of white people, men and people of middle-, upper-middle- and ruling-class backgrounds in our universities, in well-paid jobs and in the professions. One indication that attacks on affirmative action are part of a white backlash against equality is that affirmative action that primarily benefits white people is not being questioned.

Many forms of discrimination in our society are illegal. The federal government put in place affirmative action programs to redress racial inequality and injustice in a series of steps, beginning with an executive order issued by President John F. Kennedy in 1961. The Civil Rights Act of 1964 made discrimination illegal and established equal employment opportunity for all Americans regardless of race, cultural background, color or religion. Subsequent executive orders, in particular Executive Order 11246 issued by President Lyndon B. Johnson in September 1965, made affirmative action goals mandatory for all federally funded programs and moved monitoring and enforcement of affirmative action programs out of the White House and into the Labor Department. These policies and the government action that followed were a response to the tremendous mobilization of African Americans and white allies pushing for integration and racial justice during the late 1950s and early 1960s.[1]

However, racism, rather than being self-correcting, is self-perpetuating. The disadvantages to people of color and the benefits to white people are passed on to each succeeding generation unless remedial action is taken. The disadvantages to people of color coalesce into institutional practices that adversely affect people of color even though their intent may be race neutral. We have to take positive steps to eliminate and compensate for these institutional effects of racism, even when there is no discernible discriminatory intent.

For example, most people hear about job opportunities through informal networks of friends, family and neighbors — some 80% of jobs are never advertised.[2] Since racism segregates communities, schools and workplaces, this pattern leaves people of color out of the loop for many jobs, advancement opportunities, scholarships and training programs. Federal law requires widespread and public advertisement of such opportunities so that not only people of color, but also white women and men who are outside the circles of information, have an equal opportunity to apply for these positions.

Affirmative action also addresses preferential hiring programs. Court decisions on affirmative action have made it illegal for employers to require qualifications that are not relevant to one's ability to do the job. They have also mandated hiring goals so that those employed begin to reflect the racial mix of the general population from which workers are drawn. There is no legal requirement to hire an unqualified person. There is a mandate, when choosing between qualified candidates, that the hiring preference should be for a person of color when past discrimination has resulted in white people receiving preferential treatment.[3]

Sometimes people argue that affirmative action means the best-qualified person will not be hired. Affirmative action does not mean unqualified people should be hired. Rather, it means that qualified people who may not have the highest test scores or grades are still eminently ready to do the job. Employers have traditionally hired people not only for their test scores, but also based on personal appearance, family and personal connections, school ties and race, gender and religious preferences, demonstrating that qualification or talent can be defined in many ways. These practices have all contributed to a segregated workforce in which whites hold the best jobs and people of color work in the least desirable and most poorly paid positions. Affirmative action policies serve as a corrective to such patterns of discrimination. They keep score on the progress toward proportional representation and place the burden of proof on organizations to show why it is not possible to achieve it.

It has been argued that affirmative action benefits people of color who are already well-off or have middle-class advantages, not the poor and working-class people of color who most need it. Affirmative action programs have benefited substantial numbers of poor and working class people of color. Access to job-training programs, vocational schools and semi-skilled and skilled blue-collar, craft, pink-collar, police and firefighter jobs has increased substantially through affirmative action programs. Even in the professions, many people of color who have benefited from affirmative action have been from families of low income and job status.[4]

Another argument raised against affirmative action is that individual white people, often white males, have to pay for past discrimination and may not get the jobs they deserve. It is true that specific white people may not receive specific job opportunities. We tend to forget that millions of specific people of color have also lost specific job opportunities as a result of racial discrimination. To be concerned only with the white applicants who don't get the job, while ignoring the people of color who don't get it, shows racial preference.

If we look at the composition of various professions such as law, medicine, architecture, academics and journalism, or at corporate management or higher-level government positions — or if we look overall at the average income levels of white men — we see that people of color are significantly under-represented and underpaid in every category. People of color don't even hold a proportion of these jobs equal to their percentage of the population. White men are tremendously over-represented in almost any category of work that is highly rewarded except for professional athletics.[5]

We should note two other aspects of this dynamic. We have seen how all white people benefit from racism. Yet white men receive more of the economic and other benefits of racism than white women of the same socioeconomic status. Men still make more than women for comparable work, are given better educational opportunities, have more leisure time and are accorded higher status than women.

The second and equally important part of this dynamic is that not all white men are equal. Business leaders are able to exploit male workers by appealing to common bonds and common fears among white men. They have played on white male fears of losing their jobs (and their manliness, which is defined differently, but no less exclusively, in the computer industry than in trucking or construction) to keep them working hard, claiming that only white men had the strength, skill, intelligence, independence, strength of character and virility to do the job. White workers have felt pride and increased self-esteem in their working abilities and felt personally threatened by the presence of people of color and white women in the workplace. Their ability to fight against low wages, unsafe working conditions, the restructuring of their jobs and plant closures has been diminished, even while they thought they were protecting their jobs by supporting race riots, anti-immigration laws, attacks on affirmative action and workplace discrimination, harassment and exclusion. It is not in the best interests of poor, working- and middle-class men to collude with well-off white men against affirmative action.

Affirmative action programs have been effective in many areas of public life because they open up opportunities for people who would not otherwise have them, including white women and working-class white men. Attacks on affirmative action are part of a systematic attempt to roll back progress in ending discrimination and to curtail a broad social commitment to justice and equality. Attacking affirmative action is self-destructive for all of us except the rich.

There are so many subtle and not-so-subtle ways to eliminate people of color from the job application process, it is not surprising that employers have found ways around affirmative action unless it is tied to visible hiring and promotion targets. In a society with such overwhelming evidence of racism, we must assume that individuals and organizations will resist efforts to end it. For instance, in 2008 the Equal Employment Opportunity Commission received over 95,000 employment discrimination complaints and had a 70,000 caseload backlog.[6] We have to set goals and enforce and monitor standards because it is the only way we can measure compliance. These are the mechanisms we need to ensure that affirmative action is more than a facade.

Affirmative action is not a cure-all. It will not eliminate racial discrimination, nor will it eliminate competition for scarce resources. Affirmative action programs can only ensure that everyone has a fair chance at what is available. They cannot direct us to the social policies we need to pursue so we do not have to compete for scarce resources in the first place. In the larger picture, we must ask ourselves why there aren't enough well-paying, challenging and safe jobs for everyone. Why aren't there enough seats in the universities for everyone who wants an education? Expanding opportunity for people of color means expanding not only their access to existing jobs, education and housing (affirmative action), but removing the obstacles that cause these resources to be limited (social justice).

In 1996, confronted with Proposition 209 (which would have eliminated affirmative action programs in California if it were passed), a group of white men in Oakland came together to discuss ways that we could add our efforts to those of people of color who were defending affirmative action. We were angry that racism continued, angry that affirmative action was being curtailed and angry that white men were being portrayed as the victims of affirmative action programs. As a group, we felt that since we had benefited so directly from affirmative action programs it would be hypocritical to deny these benefits to people of color just when they had finally gained access to them. We named ourselves Angry White Guys for Affirmative Action and began a campaign to address white people on the issue. We chose the name to challenge the conventional thinking that all white men were racist, reactive and resentful of affirmative action.

When we gathered for meetings of Angry White Guys for Affirmative Action, our goal was not to understand our privilege, but to use our status as white men to counter the racist attacks on communities of color. Working closely with organizations led by people of color, we mapped out a strategy to reach white people in the urban and suburban areas around us. We gave talks and conducted workshops, wrote editorials, stood on street corners with our banner, conducted a walk of hope between urban and suburban churches and synagogues, educated white people about the history of affirmative action and about the deceptive and manipulative tactics being used to attack it. And we talked about our own experiences as beneficiaries of affirmative action, challenging the myth of a level playing field. (See the chapter on white benefits in Part II of this book for my personal account.)

Affirmative action has been a symbol of white people's acknowledgement of and serious commitment to eradicating racial discrimination. It has been interpreted as such by most people of color. It is crucial that, at this stage of

Questions and Actions — Affirmative Action

1. List some of the obvious and subtle ways that people of color may be discriminated against in the hiring, promotion and benefits processes at your workplace or other workplaces you encounter in your daily life.
2. Which of these areas do you have some control over or participation in as a worker, manager or client/consumer?
3. What is the role of any labor organizations related to your workplace regarding affirmative action? Does the membership of the organization reflect the diversity of the community?
4. How are people recruited to the organizations you are involved in?
5. How might these recruitment practices discriminate against people of color?
6. Have there been charges, lawsuits or public action against discrimination in any institution you use (a bank, school, city government, retail store or manufacturer)? How was it resolved? Did you ignore or feel angry about the disruption? Did you support the action against discrimination by:
   a. Joining the action?
   b. Boycotting the store or product?
   c. Writing letters of support?
   d. Encouraging your friends, family or co-workers to be supportive?
7. What would the composition of your workplace look like at all levels if it truly reflected the racial diversity of the community?
8. Affirmative action is a tool for full inclusion and equal opportunity for all people, not only people of color. Go back through these questions and substitute women, lesbians and gay men, people with disabilities, seniors or young people for people of color.
9. What fears, doubts, questions or concerns do you have about affirmative action? Where do your fears come from? What could you do to answer your questions? Who could you talk with about your concerns?
10. Have you ever been chosen for a job, training program, college-level program or housing opportunity for which you were less qualified than others? Have you ever been given preference because of family connections, economic background, age, race or gender?
11. Think again about Question 10 and try to understand ways that family connections, economic background, race, age or gender may have given you benefits compared to other applicants.
12. Besides numerical goals, what measures would you suggest be used to monitor racial and other forms of discrimination?
13. How are you going to respond to people who say that affirmative action unfairly discriminates against white males?
14. List three things you can do to defend or strengthen affirmative action programs in your workplace, community or state.
15. Choose one that you will start doing.

backlash against the gains of the last three decades, we don't abandon one tool that we know works.

The hypocrisy is clear when white people who say they support equal opportunity attack affirmative action, yet want to leave intact the basic economic and racial injustices it is designed to correct. Ask people who oppose affirmative action how they propose to eliminate racial discrimination. You can learn a lot about their underlying beliefs from their answers.

Notes

1. See the affirmative action timeline in Marquita Sykes. *The Origins of Affirmative Action*. National Organization of Women, 1995. [online]. [cited February 28, 2011]. now.org/nnt/08-95/affirmhs.html.

2. Jessica Dickler. *The Hidden Job Market*. CNNMoney.com, June, 2009. [online]. [cited February 26, 2011]. money.cnn.com/2009/06/09/news/economy/hidden_jobs/.

3. *Stanford Encyclopedia of Philosophy*, rev. 2009, s.v. "Affirmative Action." [online]. [cited February 28, 2011]. plato.stanford.edu/entries/affirmative-action/.

4. Gertrude Ezorsky. *Racism and Justice: The Case for Affirmative Action*. Cornell, 1991, p. 64.

5. See, for example, the Chicago United 2010 Corporate Diversity Report which estimated that it would take "well beyond" 89 years to see proportionate representation of minorities in executive jobs in the Chicago area: 2010 Chicago Diversity Profile. *Human Capital and the Cost of Recession: A Survey of Corporate Diversity in the Chicago Metropolitan Area*, Chicago United, 2010. [online]. [cited February 28, 2011]. chicago-united.org/pdfs/2010-Corp-Diversity-Profile.pdf.

6. Tresa Baldas. "EEOC Will Get $23 Million to Reduce 70,000-Case Backlog." *The National Law Journal*, December 15, 2009. [online]. [cited February 26, 2011]. law.com/jsp/article.jsp?id=1202436345429.

At Work

WHITENESS HAS LONG BEEN RELATED TO RACISM in the workplace and economy. As David Roediger explains in his book *The Wages of Whiteness,* part of the campaign to entice white male workers into industrial jobs during the 19th century was to rationalize that at least they were not slaves. They could keep their white masculinity intact, even while giving up their economic independence, because (they were told) being a worker in a factory was not the same as being a slave working for a master.

Male industrial workers eventually borrowed the language of slavery to describe their "waged slavery." They played on similarities between their work situation and that of slaves, at the same time trying to keep the differences clear so they could preserve industrial jobs for whites. The relationship of racism to work issues is complex. In general, early white industrial workers were manipulated by racism, and in turn, they used racism to gain economic benefits. In turn, employers manipulated racism in white workers to instill in them a false sense of pride and opportunity which they then used to hold themselves separate from male workers of color.[1]

W.E.B. Du Bois was one of the first historians to note the impact racism had on both blacks and whites in the South. Because of slavery, there was no major labor movement to protect the region's 5 million poor whites, who owned no slaves, from being heavily exploited by the 8,000 largest slave owners. The availability of cheap slave labor undermined white workers' ability to bargain for higher wages and better working conditions. More recently, Michael Reich has demonstrated that, where the gap between the wages of blacks and whites is greatest, wages of whites are the lowest and profit to the wealthy the highest. He describes how racism works in the workplace:

Wages of white labor are lessened by racism because the fear of a cheaper and underemployed Black labor supply in the area is invoked by employers when labor presents its wage demands. Racial antagonisms on the shop floor deflect attention from labor grievances related to working conditions, permitting employers to cut costs. Racial divisions among labor prevent the development of united worker organizations both within the workplace and in the labor movement as a whole. As a result union strength and union militancy will be less the greater the extent of racism.[2]

Work in the United States is still highly segregated by class, race and gender. The overall economy, as well as most large organizations, is vertically segregated as well. Upper-middle- and upper-class white men have access to the jobs with the most money, power and status. Women, working-class whites and people of color are strung out on the economic hierarchy, but are found disproportionately at the bottom in the least secure, most unsafe, poorly paid jobs.

The immediate impact of racism on working people of color is economic. Profits from racism, or *super-exploitation* as economist Victor Perlo describes it, are the profits that employers make when they underpay workers of color. In other words, super-exploitation is the wage differential between white workers and workers of color, multiplied by the number of workers in private enterprises. Perlo notes that the profits from racism against all minorities grew from $56 billion in 1947 to $197 billion in 1992 (expressed in 1995 dollars). When the earnings of white workers are compared with those of specific other groups, we find that the profits from super-exploitation (the gap in earnings between the groups) more than doubled from African American workers, and increased tenfold from Latino/a, Native American and Asian American workers.

In addition, racism benefits employers and hurts white workers because any low-waged segment of the workforce exerts significant downward pressure on *all* wages. Perlo concludes his chapter on racism and work by stating that the extra profits employers gained from racism — either directly at the expense of minority workers, or indirectly at the expense of white workers — came to approximately $500 billion in 1995.[3]

Winning the broader struggle for economic democracy is crucial for truly ending racism, and a key to achieving economic justice is solidarity between white workers and workers of color, between US workers and workers from other countries. Racism undermines both levels of solidarity.

During the 1990s, problems in the Mexican, Japanese and Southeast Asian monetary systems made the interdependence of the world economy evident. What may not be so clear to us in the United States are the brutal living conditions in non-Western countries that result from the economic policies imposed by the International Monetary Fund (IMF), the World Bank and other US-dominated institutions. The colonial practices of European countries, beginning in the late 15th century and later taken up by the United States, have concentrated international power and wealth in the hands of white people and have given us the ability to dictate the economic fortunes of much of the rest of the world.

One way to challenge these patterns is to organize against new attempts by US financial interests to consolidate further their dominance through such trade agreements as North American Free Trade Agreement (NAFTA), General Agreement on Tariffs and Trade (GATT), Multilateral Agreement on Investment (MAI) and Free Trade Agreement of the Americas (FTAA). Treaties like NAFTA and GATT make it easy for companies to move production to locations with the lowest wages, lowest labor standards and least environmental regulation. These trade agreements falsely encourage us to believe that our own (white) US jobs will be protected at the expense of those of people of color in other countries. In reality, we get played off against foreign workers and are able to exert even almost no control over labor-related policy in the US.

We have created an *international* racial hierarchy of wealth, power and control that mirrors our internal one. This international hierarchy subjects us to economic and cultural exploitation camouflaged by racist justifications that blame workers of color and foreign capitalists of color for our declining standard of living and social problems instead of blaming decision makers in our corporate boardrooms.

We are not powerless against multinational corporations if we overcome our training in racism to work together with people from other countries. We can challenge the dumping of toxic waste and unsafe products in other countries; the exploitation of foreign workers by US companies; the sexual exploitation of women of color overseas by US tourists, corporate and military personnel; the economic policies of the IMF and the World Bank; the displacement of local agricultural production to grow export crops for the United States; the manipulation of unequal trade and other agreements; the scapegoating of foreign workers for US-generated problems and the scapegoating of foreign capitalists of color, such as the Japanese, Chinese and Arabs, when British, Canadian and German capitalists go unmentioned.

Many of us work for these same corporations and can challenge their policies from within. We all have specific opportunities to confront racism where we work.

To identify where you have the most leverage related to your work, it is important to make an assessment of your workplace. Use the following questions. Talk with others, particularly people of color, to help you do the assessment.

Look to the leadership of the people of color you work with, if there are any. They know where the racism lies in your organization. They may be quite clear about what kind of solidarity they need from white co-workers. Ask them how they see things and what their priorities are.

You will need to work with other white workers, building a core group dedicated to eliminating racism. Many of your white co-workers may not have questioned the racism in your workplace. They need information and support for making changes in workplace practices and environment. You may meet with solid resistance from others who feel they have something to lose from eliminating racism. Challenging them will require strategic thinking.

Many workers have such pressing financial and emotional needs they may not understand at first why racial equality and economic justice need to be a priority. The information provided in this book can help you devise effective strategies to show them the costs of racism in their lives.

A good way to begin, once you have the information you need, is to ask questions. "Why is this person of color paid less than that white person who was hired more recently?" "Why aren't there any people of color at management level?" "Why don't people of color stay with this organization very long?" "What effect does that kind of comment (e.g., a racial put-down) have on other people around here?"

Asking questions raises issues for people to think about. Sometimes that alone will encourage other people to make some changes. Often you'll get excuses, justifications or cynicism in response. Those responses will let you and others see how white people are thinking about racism and what level of awareness they have. It will also help you map out where you'll meet resistance to further actions.

It is generally not useful to label people as racist. If you attack people personally, they will probably counterattack. Everyone within the organization will feel unsafe. You will do better to document racism within the organization, build alliances and propose concrete changes. You want to focus on policies, practices and procedures.

• •

- What is the mission of the organization or business you are working for?
- What is the relationship of the mission to communities of color?
- What are the needs of those communities?
- How do white people hold power in your organization?
- The most important question to ask might be, what long-term changes will be made in who holds power and how decisions are made?

• •

Eliminating racism is not a question of economic cost but of injustice. However, when you organize against specific forms of racism, it can be a useful short-term strategy to point out the economic benefits of the changes desired or the economic costs of the old patterns. What does it cost an organization when there are high turnover rates for personnel who are people of color, when clients of color are not well served, or when the leadership talent of people of color is not used? What does it cost when there are discrimination lawsuits, strikes, boycotts or government investigations because of racism within the organization? Organizations have different levels of vulnerability to such costs.

Each particular fight against racism is part of the long-term struggle. Even when it is unsuccessful, it can educate and organize other workers. Our long-term goal is to create a broad movement of people committed to eliminating racism in all aspects of our lives.

I am not going to romanticize the power of workers; in most circumstances multinational companies can play off workers from many sites against each other. However, keeping the issue of race- and gender-based exploitation on the table in every workplace struggle will further the move toward economic justice. Doing so keeps people of color and white women in leadership positions, demonstrates the interconnected ways that people are exploited and produces the informed solidarity that is essential to the success of any struggle for economic justice.

Assessment — At Work

1. Who, by race, gender and class, has the power to make decisions about hiring, firing, wages and working conditions in your workplace? Who gets promoted and who doesn't? Are there upper levels (glass ceilings) beyond which some groups of people (i.e., people of color, white women) cannot go?

2. Is hiring non-discriminatory? Are job openings posted and distributed? Do they attract a wide variety of applicants? Are certain groups excluded? Does the diversity of your workplace reflect the diversity of the wider community?

3. Do layoffs, reassignments, workplace closures or other cutbacks disproportionately affect people of color?

4. What are the salary differentials between the lowest- and highest-paid workers? Are salaries for comparable work equal?

5. Are there *invisible workers* — people who cook, clean or do maintenance, for example — who are not generally noticed or not paid well?

6. Do the board of directors and the top-level management of your employer include significant numbers of people of color?

7. What is the racial composition of the group of people that actually owns your workplace? Who makes money from the profits of your work?

8. Are there jokes, teasing, put-downs or harassment of people based on race, gender, sexual orientation, age, religion or other differences?

9. Has there been or is there any racial or sexual harassment or discrimination, or charges of such or investigations by any outside agency about such things? Do people of color describe discrimination or harassment at your workplace?

10. Does your organization provide products or services to people of color? If it does, is the clientele treated with respect and dignity? Do staff members make racial comments about clients? Is there any discrimination in how people are served or treated?

11. Do the advertising and publicity images that your employer produces convey a multiracial image or do they reinforce racial or sexual stereotypes?

12. Are there any workplace groups such as unions or affirmative action committees that monitor or respond to racial discrimination? Are they effective? Are they supported or hindered by management? Do they challenge or do they support racism?

13. Is your employer part of a larger organization, with manufacturing or other facilities at other sites? Are those sites in communities of color? If they are, are workers paid the same as, and treated equally to, workers at your site?

14. Has your employer closed down or moved facilities to areas of the United States or to other countries in order to pay workers less or to avoid unionization, workplace safety regulations or other oversight?

15. Does your company produce any kinds of toxic waste? If so, in which communities is the waste dumped?

Notes

1. Roediger et al *The Wages of Whiteness.*
2. Michael Reich. *Racial Inequality.* Princeton, 1981, quoted in Victor Perlo. *Economics of Racism II.* International, 1996, p. 159.
3. Perlo, *Economics of Racism II,* p. 171.

At School

MOST OF US SPENT A CONSIDERABLE AMOUNT of our childhood in school. Our children still do. Social activism is needed to create equal opportunity in the educational system, which is a major gatekeeper for the distribution of the social and economic benefits of this society.

Most students in the United States are still attending segregated schools. Within schools, students are segregated by race and tracked by class or by smaller divisions of economic difference. Segregation and tracking destine most students for particular socioeconomic roles in their adult lives.

The top 10% of school districts (primarily white and suburban) spend 10 times more than the bottom 10% (primarily urban, where students of color are congregated). The difference between spending $40,000 per pupil and $4,000 is huge. When this is multiplied by the number of students in a classroom or school, the impact is enormous. That money buys fewer students per teacher; classroom necessities like books, pencils and paper, not to mention computers; art and music classes; recreational equipment; teacher's aides, special events and field trips and, in the long run, the best teachers. Students are given a direct measure of their social worth and future chances by the amount of money they see being spent on their education.[1]

Given the economic and educational realities of this society, it makes sense for us to give our children the best education possible. That is why, when white parents can afford it — and sometimes even when we can't — we move to school districts with better schools, work hard to get our children into better schools within the district or send them to private ones. We shouldn't feel guilty for doing so. But insofar as many children of color are abandoned to the disaster of inadequately funded public schooling, our individual actions do contribute to the overall gap between white children and children of color.

. . . .

- Find out per student expenditures in your district and others.
- What differences do you find? Where does the extra money come from?
- How can you work with others to develop new school-funding strategies?

. . . .

However, education is more than money. It includes teachers, curricula, school buildings, safety to learn and many other factors. Racism affects the quality and quantity of each of these resources. Although students of color make up more than 42% of the student population,[2] the percentage of teachers who are white is increasing and presently approaches 84% (of that 75% is female).[3] This means that few students of color have role models of their own ethnicity, and few white students have contact with people of color in positions of authority. Many white teachers carry with them subtle and not-so-subtle biases against people of color. Researchers have found that teachers give higher grades to children of their own race, and white teachers give significantly lower grades to black and Latino/a students.[4] White teachers may also exhibit greater aggression, overt friendliness coupled with covert rejection and avoidance or simply offer less assistance to students of color while being completely unaware of their prejudice.[5]

. . . .

- Who is teaching in our schools?
- How are they trained?
- What do they do in the classroom?
- How does racism in schools affect teachers of color?

. . . .

The answers to these questions can guide us to action. For instance, knowing about changing teacher demographics leads us to work against changes in educational policy, such as the National Teacher's Exam and longer teacher education courses that present unnecessary obstacles to teachers of color and contribute to their increasing exclusion from our classrooms.

We also need to eliminate racism in the curriculum. School curricula in the United States have a European/US historical focus that emphasizes the development of ideas and political processes from Greece through Rome and Europe to the United States. "Western" knowledge actually includes ideas and developments from every part of the world. The Greeks themselves acknowledged the source of their learning, and made many references to their Egyptian mentors.[6] Textbooks often present other world civilizations as if they only became significant when they were discovered by or interacted with white Westerners. Cultures from other geographic regions are presented superficially, particularly in the lower grades, through their food, holidays, traditional clothes and little else.

Our curricula also omit the history of white colonialism as colonialism, and they don't address racism and other forms of exploitation. People of color are marginally represented as token individuals who achieved great things rather than as members of communities of resistance. The enormous contributions that people of color have made to our society are simply not mentioned.[7] For example, Arab contributions to mathematics, astronomy, geology, mineralogy, botany and natural history are seldom mentioned. The Arabic numbering system, which replaced the cumbersome and limited Roman numeral system, along with trigonometry and algebra, which serve as cornerstones of modern mathematics, were all contributions from Muslim society.[8]

As a result, children of color do not see themselves at the center of history and culture. They do not see themselves as active participants in creating this society. The roles played by their foreparents have simply been written out of history, giving both white children and children of color distorted understandings of their own heritages.

We need to challenge all aspects of racism in educational curricula, including, but not limited to, literature classes in which only white authors are presented; the exclusion of poor and working people from written histories; the exclusive use of white cultural examples for math problems and the omission of racism as a pervasive and central component of lessons in history, social studies and other subjects.

There are further questions we need to ask.

• How are students treated?
• Are students of color systematically harassed, disciplined or tracked by teachers or administrators?
• Does the school have anti-racist policies in place, and are these known and enforced?
• How are students prepared to deal with racism?

Social scientists once thought that if white students and students of color just had contact with each other, prejudice would diminish. They have since found that contact by itself doesn't necessarily eliminate prejudice. White people often simply claim that the people of color they know are different. In any case, most white students don't go to school with students of color. Because of tracking, even those who do may not share the same classes or social networks.

Many people are already involved in the struggle to make our schools more democratic, safer and less racist. These efforts include two kinds of interventions.

The first approach is to help individual students of color succeed in spite of the limited opportunity provided by their family or community. Tutoring programs, scholarship funds, special training programs — these are effective in helping specific individuals acquire higher education or better jobs. Such programs do not address the systemic inequality between the educational opportunities of white students and students of color. On the contrary, the results of these programs, a few successful people of color, are often used by whites to put down the rest of the community and blame those who don't succeed.

The second approach is to attack the structural roots of inequality. People are organizing around the issues of school funding, curriculum development, resource allocation, teacher training and the control and administration of educational programs. Such activity is probably already occurring in your community, and you can join. If it isn't happening, get together with concerned parents, teachers and educational activists to get something going. The questions we must keep asking ourselves as we analyze the status quo or evaluate changes we want to make are:

- What are the effects of these policies on students of color?
- Who is going to benefit from the changes?
- How can we achieve greater equality of opportunity?

Notes

1. Linda Darling-Hammond. "Structured for Failure: Race, Resources, and Student Achievement." In Markus and Moya, *Doing Race,* p. 300.
2. US Department of Education, Institute of Education Sciences. "Public Elementary and Secondary School Student Enrollment and Staff Counts From the Common Core of Data:

School Year 2008-09." August 2010. [online]. [cited February 28, 2011]. nces.ed.gov/pubs2010/snf200708/findings.asp.

3. US Department of Education, Institute of Education Sciences. "The Condition of Education 2010. Indicator 27 Characteristics of Full-Time Teachers 2010." [online]. [cited February 28, 2011].nces.ed.gov/programs/coe/2010/section4/indicator27.asp.; Karen Zumwalk and Elizabeth Craig. "Who Is Teaching? Does It Matter?" In Marilyn Cochran-Smith et al. *Handbook of Research on Teacher Education: Enduring Questions in Changing Contexts.* Routledge, 2008, pp. 404-423.

4. Amine Ouazad. *Assessed by a Teacher Like Me: Race, Gender, and Subjective Evaluations.* Centre for the Economics of Education, 2008. Quoted in Markus and Moya. *Doing Race,* pp. 67-68.

5. F. Crosby, S. Bromley and L. Saxe. "Recent Unobtrusive Studies of Black and White Discrimination and Prejudice: A Literature Review." *Psychological Bulletin,* 87 (1980). Quoted in Lisa Delpit. *Other People's Children: Cultural Conflict in the Classroom.* New Press, 1995, p. 115.

6. Martin Bernal. *Black Athena: The Afroasiatic Roots of Classical Civilization.* Rutgers, 1987.

7. See Bernal. *Black Athena;* Weatherford, *Indian Givers* and Ivan Van Sertima, ed. *Blacks in Science: Ancient and Modern.* Transaction, 1986.

8. Seyyed Hossein Nasr. *Islamic Science: An Illustrated Study.* World of Islam Festival Publishing, 1976, pp. 75–88.

Healthcare

THE US HEALTHCARE SYSTEM IS SO RIDDLED WITH RACISM that tens of thousands of people of color die needlessly every year because of its inadequacies. Others are permanently disabled, live with remediable conditions or suffer seriously inferior quality of life. The impact of race is felt in every area from basic accessibility to healthcare, through adequacy of coverage, treatments prescribed, prenatal care, cultural sensitivity of care, availability of specialized treatments and physical proximity to hospitals, to under-prescription of routine diagnostic tests and painkillers and over-prescription of amputations and sterilization. Former US Surgeon General David Satcher has labeled these disparities "institutionalized racism."[1]

The cumulative impact is devastating to people of color. To give just one example for the African American community, which is the best documented, it is estimated that blacks suffer over 91,000 *excess deaths* a year — that is 37% of all black deaths.[2] Excess deaths are deaths from health conditions that are preventable or treatable and are therefore unnecessary or avoidable.[3] In other words, all other factors being equal, 91,000 black people die each year because of racism. Because of this, African Americans have a life expectancy four and a half years less than white Americans.[4] For parts of the Latino/a and Southeast Asian communities, life expectancy and healthcare status are equally low, and in many Native American communities, they are even lower. Obviously not all the deaths of people of color are attributable to racism, but it is well-documented that tens of thousands are.

Race and gender clearly make a difference in how patients are diagnosed and treated. In one study, medical residents viewed a video showing a white male and a black female patient (the students did not know they were actors), who described identical systems of chest pain indicative of heart disease. Seventy-four percent of the students believed the white male had heart disease, but only 46% believed the black female.

Another study of Medicare patients found that only 64% of black patients receive potentially curative treatment for early stage lung cancer, while 77% of white patients receive it, leading to survival rates of 34% for whites and just 26% for blacks after five years. A UCLA study found that Hispanics in emergency rooms in Los Angeles are twice as likely as white people in comparable circumstances to end up with no pain medication — not even a Tylenol. Over 30 years' worth of studies show that people of color who arrive at a hospital while having a heart attack are significantly less likely to receive Aspirin, beta-blocking drugs, clot-dissolving drugs, acute cardiac catheterization, angioplasty or bypass surgery.[5]

Racism in the healthcare system is also an international problem. The example of the drug development, pricing and delivery systems shows how people of color in economically exploited countries suffer needlessly from policies that ultimately benefit white people in developed countries, and financially benefit an even smaller number of the white Western elite.[6]

Pharmaceutical companies do not develop many treatments to cure diseases that primarily affect people in economically exploited countries (and kill millions of people annually). Of the 1,556 new drugs marketed between 1975 and 2004, only 21 were indicated for neglected diseases (including malaria and tuberculosis, but not HIV), and a mere 10 were directed at neglected tropical diseases which affect over a billion people annually.[7] The main emphasis of drug company research programs is "lifestyle drugs" for conditions like obesity, baldness, face wrinkles and impotence. Although the companies complain that otherwise research would be unprofitable, the worth of the five largest pharmaceuticals is twice the combined GDP of all sub-Saharan Africa.

Drug companies defend their profits at the cost of millions of lives in Africa, South America and Asia. For example, GlaxoWellcome threatened legal action against the Indian company Cipla for trying to provide Ghana and Uganda with a cheap version of Combivir, two drugs developed in the US with public funding. Nearly 40 companies took the South African government to court to prevent its making low-cost generic equivalents of certain AIDS drugs available to people who could not otherwise afford to be treated for AIDS. This lawsuit was dropped only after there was a large international outcry in response to the fact that about 5.7 million South Africans are HIV-positive, and most will die much sooner without access to low-cost drug treatments.[8]

Brazil is a country that shows a significant saving of life is possible with more humane drug availability policies. In the early 1990s, the country had the fourth-largest number of reported cases of HIV/AIDS in the world. The government began to import, produce and distribute large quantities of anti-retroviral drugs, which lowered the price for a year's treatment to $600, compared with $10,000 for the drug company's version of the drugs. This policy has reduced the number of AIDS-related deaths by 38%. However, the United States government, at the urging of pharmaceutical companies, threatened retaliatory measures if the policies were not discontinued.[9]

All people should have a basic right to adequate healthcare. Of course economic factors also play a role in who has access to healthcare in the US, and we need to address the concerns of many white people who suffer from inadequate care. But we have seen that race is an independent variable, and we need to develop race-specific remedies that address the systemic ways that people of color are denied, have limited access to or experience inadequate medical care, leading to needless suffering and death.

Notes

1. Much of the following information is summarized in an article by Neil Rosenberg. "Separate and Unequal: US Practices a System of Medicine that Shortchanges Minorities and Women." *Milwaukee Journal Sentinel,* April 16, 2001.

2. W. Michael Byrd and Linda A. Clayton. *An American Health Dilemma: A Medical History of African Americans and the Problem of Race, Beginnings to 1900.* Routledge, 2000, p. 29.

3. Abstract of: James Macinko and Irma T. Elo. "Black-White Differences in Avoidable Mortality in the United States, 1980-2005." *Journal of Epidemiology and Community Health,* April, 2009. [online]. [cited February 27, 2011]. jech.bmj.com/content/early/2009/04/12/jech. 2008. 081141.abstract.

4. US Centers for Disease Control and Prevention. *Health, United States, 2009.* Publication #DHHS 2010-1232, January 2010. [online]. [cited February 27, 2011]. cdc.gov/nchs/data/hus/hus09.pdf.

5. For an in-depth look at racial disparities in healthcare, see Brian D. Smedley et al. *Unequal Treatment: Confronting Racial and Ethnic Disparities in Health Care.* National Academies, 2003. [online]. [cited February 27, 2011].books.nap.edu/openbook.php?record_id=10260&page=R1.

6. The examples in this chapter are taken from Jordi Martorell. "Drug Companies Putting Profits Before Millions of People's Lives." March 9, 2001. [online]. [cited February 27, 2011]. marxist.com/drugs-companies-profits090301.htm.

7. P. Chirac and E. Torreele. "Global Framework on Essential Health R&D." *Lancet,* Vol. 367 (May 13, 2006), pp.1560–1561. [online]. [cited February 28, 2011]. dndi.org/images/stories/pdf_scientific_pub/2006/chirac_lancet05132006.pdf.

8. Martorell. "Drug Companies Putting Profits Before Millions of People's Lives."

9. Indira A.R. Lakshmanan. "The Rising Cost of AIDS Drugs Threatens Brazil's Free Treatment Program." *New York Times,* January 3, 2007. [online]. [cited February 27, 2011]. nytimes.com/2007/01/03/world/americas/03iht-aids.4090052.html.

The Police

JUST AS TEACHERS HAVE THE MIDDLE-CLASS FUNCTION of training young people for their future roles in the economic hierarchy, police officers, security guards, prison wardens and immigration officials have the working-class function of disciplining those who don't follow the rules. Teachers are primarily women because women have been traditionally trained to be caretakers of young people. Police officers and other security personnel are primarily men because men have been traditionally trained to enforce class, gender and racial roles. Both occupations are primarily white because their function is also to train people of color to accept their place in society and to punish them when they don't. People in these roles act as a buffer between people of color and the rest of the white community.

For these reasons, white people have a very different relationship to the police than do people of color. Middle-class economic status also influences our experience; we are more respectful and trusting because the police are protecting our property and upholding our values. If we are poor or working-class, we have more likely experienced harassment from the police and have less at stake in their role of maintaining the status quo.

As a middle-class white child, I was raised to trust the police and to look upon them as a source of help. The ensuing decades have worn off much of that trust, but in general, I do not expect to be stopped and searched arbitrarily by law enforcement. People of color, particularly young African American and Latino men, are very likely to be stopped and searched by the police for no apparent cause. This doesn't just happen to young men hanging out on the street. If the police think you look suspicious — and to some police, any man of color looks suspicious — you may be stopped even if you are with your family, even if there is no apparent cause for suspicion, even if you are just driving by somewhere.[1]

Police brutality is part of a much longer history of white working-class male policing of communities of color that began with colonial militias attacking Native Americans and continuing through slave patrols, state militias, private security forces, race and anti-immigrant riots and vigilante groups such as the KKK. Local and county sheriffs and police were particularly diligent in harassing, falsely arresting and locking up men of color, often selling them into virtual slavery to industrial corporations in the North and West or cotton plantations, coal mines and steel mills in the south. Police have often been part of vigilante groups in their off hours or have hired themselves out as security guards and prison wardens as alternative or supplemental employment.

Every year there are hundreds of reports of *police brutality* — the excessive use of force well beyond what is required in a situation. A Human Rights Watch report documented that police brutality is disproportionately directed at people of color.[2] The cities in major metropolitan areas pay out tens of millions of dollars a year in settlements for such cases, yet that is only the tip of the iceberg because it costs so much money to even bring a lawsuit and many people are scared to do so.[3] The results of police brutality investigations in many cities are frequently not even released to the public. Young people, youth advocates and citizen groups across the country continue to push for full police review and accountability.

The examples of police use of "excess force" are disturbingly widespread.[4] For example, on May 10, 2009, Christopher Harris was outside Seattle's Cinerama Theater when an officer charged at him and slammed his head into a wall, leaving him in a coma. In Orlando, Florida, police officer Fernando Trinidad was caught on video allegedly pushing a woman down a set of stairs in a club during April, 2007. He arrested her for assault and battery. On May 11, 2009, a deputy in Palmdale, CA, shot a 15-year-old boy who was playing "cops and robbers" with a toy gun. The child had been reported to police as someone riding a bicycle and brandishing a weapon.[5]

There are a number of other forms of police abuse of power such as false arrest, intimidation, racial profiling, political repression, surveillance abuse, harassment, sexual abuse and corruption. Such behavior has a devastating impact, particularly on the Native Americans, Latino/as and African American communities. It is also the conduit for a large number of young people of color into the criminal justice system, discussed in the next chapter.

Most people of color know of someone who was stopped arbitrarily by the police; many know someone who was shot without justification. Hundreds of thousands of people have seen the footage of the Rodney King beating or the cell-phone-recorded murder of Oscar Grant.[6] At this time in our history, the police are seen as the representatives of white power in communities of color. When they trample people's rights, they are acting in our name. When they are protecting the lives and property of white people at the expense of those of people of color, they are a visible tool used by white people to enforce a racial and economic hierarchy.

The racism behind much police brutality makes people of color unsafe in two ways. First, they are vulnerable to attack from the police. Second, knowledge of police brutality prevents many people of color, particularly women, from seeking protection from non-racial crimes such as domestic violence. Many women of color are understandably hesitant about handing their men over to a racist and violent police force and a discriminatory criminal justice system, even though their refusal to do so might increase their own vulnerability to violence.

Many white people are afraid of being robbed, beaten, raped or burglarized. Some of us have been already. Most of the crime we experience is committed by other white people, often by people we know. When there are racist patterns to police practices, we are even more at risk because the police are looking in the wrong direction.

This is not to say that white people are never robbed by people of color. You may even know someone who was. You have certainly read about someone who was, because the racial bias of the news media presents us with a disproportionate number of these cases, giving them wide publicity, which in turn exacerbates our fears.[7] We then allow the police to continue their practices, justifying their "excesses" by attributing them to rogue officers who, it is claimed, are the exception.

When we don't respond strongly and actively to police brutality in our communities, we increase polarization and justify the anger of people of color who say that the police represent the interests of white people. If we want to deal with racism we have to rein in, retrain and redirect the police so they don't initiate acts of violence in our name. More multicultural awareness for police, or more community policing, are not enough.[8] How should we redirect the police? Most acts of physical and sexual violence are between people who know each other. Police response to incidents of domestic violence, child sexual assault and rape are crucial indicators of the safety of our communities. White-collar crime and high-level drug importation and distribution are more devastating to our lives and pocketbooks than petty thievery and small-scale drug dealing.

Where do the police devote their time and attention? How do they allocate resources? How well are they trained, including training in racism, domestic violence, community relations and community building? These are the kinds of questions we need to ask. Here are some places to start.

When you see the police stop people of color, slow down and drive around the block. Let them know you're paying attention. Don't assume that because the detained are people of color they must have done something wrong. Don't assume that because you respect the police, they respect everyone in the community.

Get together with other concerned citizens to monitor police activities.

The single biggest deterrent to police abuse is an alert community. Good community-based policing can help make all our lives safer. And we can each help ensure that police action does not further racial violence.

Assessment — The Police

1. Is there an independent police review board or commission in your community? How effective is it?
2. Are there allegations of police brutality or civil suits against the police or sheriff's department? What is their status, and how have law enforcement officials responded? What is the history of allegations, lawsuits and police response in your local police and sheriff's departments?
3. Are the police and sheriff's departments fully integrated? Are members trained to deal with a multicultural population? How do they respond to different kinds of calls? Do they work well with community agencies and organizations?
4. Is the response to family violence racially biased? Is there a policy of mandatory arrest for incidents of domestic violence? Are reports of child sexual assault and rape investigated and prosecuted vigorously and without discrimination?
5. Is community policing used by the police department? How is the community involved? Are people of color from within the community represented and empowered?
6. Are the police and sheriff's departments in your area currently enforcing or participating in programs which reinforce immigration laws? How does this impact immigrant communities? How does it impact the ability of police to conduct routine law enforcement activities?
7. White adults and adults of color can collude to blame and criminalize young people for high crime and drug abuse rates. This conveniently ignores the responsibility adults have for youth safety, education, family support and recreational opportunities. Do the police in your area respond without prejudice and undue force to the needs of young people in your community? (Ask young people.) How can young people be more involved in police-community relations?

Notes

1. See the chilling account of a police attack on a private party: Mandisa-Maia Jones and Valerie Willson Wesley. "Anatomy of a Party Gone Wrong: When Police Brutality Hits Home." *Essence*, December 1991.

2. Human Rights Watch. "Shielded from Justice: Police Brutality and Accountability in the United States." July 1, 1998. [online]. [cited February 28, 2011]. hrw.org/en/reports/1998/07/01/shielded-justice.

3. Charlene Muhammad. "The High Cost of Police Brutality." *New America Media*, February 27, 2009. [online]. [cited February 28, 2011]. news.newamericamedia.org/news/view_article.html?article_id=c1fdb31f21e60db0bbcafd26de8071a1.

4. Police brutality is not limited to attacks on people of color. Lesbians, gays, bisexuals, transgendered people, immigrants, sex-workers, political activists and working-class people are vulnerable to similar treatment.

5. All these cases and many others are documented on the website brainz: "30 Cases of Extreme Police Brutality and Blatant Misconduct." [online]. [cited February 28, 2011]. brainz.org/30-cases-extreme-police-brutality-and-blatant-misconduct/.

6. Oscar Grant was a 23-year-old African American father who was murdered in 2009 by a Bay Area Rapid Transit cop while waiting for a BART train. He was shot in the back while laying face down on the platform. The officer was convicted on a charge of involuntary manslaughter.

7. Bill Yousman. *Prime Time Prisons on US TV: Representation of Incarceration.* Peter Lang, 2009, pp. 41-44.

8. Community policing refers to the practice of assigning police to specific neighborhoods so they can get to know the area and the people.

The Criminal Justice System

MOST OF US DON'T HAVE AN ACTIVE, EVERYDAY ROLE in the criminal justice system, but we do have some influence on what happens within
it. Our advocacy for crime legislation, the death penalty and particular police
practices such as immigration enforcement, as well as our funding of prisons,
jails and "wars" on crime and drugs, all play a part in how people are treated
on a daily basis by the legal system.

Wealthy white people have controlled the US legal system since colonial
times. Our country's founding legal documents were written by the small percentage of white men who owned property, and they limited most legal rights
and the ability to use the criminal/legal system to men of property.[1]

When slavery was legally ended after the Civil War, the criminal/legal system took over the role of controlling the African American population from
the slave patrols and vigilante groups of the previous era. When Jim Crow
laws were passed in the South during the last two decades of the 19th century,
they included a set of laws aimed at introducing a new form of slavery, the
convict labor system. White people criminalized behaviors that they believed
could be used to ensnare newly freed slaves by intimidating them and forcing
them into debt peonage for white-owned agricultural and industrial enterprises. It became a crime to be hired by an employer without a discharge paper
from a previous employer, and even walking down the street without proof
of employment was a crime. In a harbinger of the current operation of the
child welfare and foster care systems, orphans and the children of black people
deemed inadequate parents could be apprenticed to their former masters.

The legal system entrapped blacks at every turn, and then the local sheriff
would lease the prisoner to a farm, corporation or public employer. Brutally
treated, unable to escape, almost always tortured, starved and usually literally
worked to death in just a few years, newly freed slaves were re-enslaved, but

this time by a system that had no economic interest in keeping them alive. Workers were leased, used up and then replaced by a new round of "criminals." Like tenant farmers and sharecroppers, if they did stay alive, the workers were continually subjected to never-ending rounds of indebtedness to whoever leased them. State governments made tremendous amounts of money from this system, and the coal mines, steel mills, timber operations and vast cotton plantations — literally the entire economy of the South — was dependent on their labor. Many of these enterprises were owned by northern companies and financiers: the steel was shipped to northern manufacturers and the cotton to northern textile mills.[2]

The system of false or flimsy arrest and prosecution of men of color and their subsequent sale to corporate enslavement continued into the 1940s and 50s. Much progress was made to eliminate this system, but even in the 1970s and 80s, there were still slave labor camps in the South. With the passage of the Justice System Improvement Act of 1979, legal barriers to exploiting prisoner labor for profit were removed, and once again prisoners were coerced into working for corporate profits. Looking for workers they could pay less even than those in majority world countries, companies such as Dell, Microsoft, Eddie Bauer, Starbucks, McDonalds and Victoria's Secret moved into the prison labor employment business.[3]

Two reports released in spring 2000 showed that at every stage of the US criminal justice system — from arrest through plea bargaining to sentencing — African Americans and Latino/as get tougher treatment than whites.[4]

The total population under supervision in prison, jail, on parole or probation grew from 1.8 million in 1980 to 7.3 million in 2008.[5] This 400% increase compares with only a 3% increase in the number of violent offenders. Of that 7.3 million, 2.3 million were in prison or jail — 60% for non-violent offenses and 25% percent for non-violent drug offenses.[6]

There are well over one million African Americans behind bars, out of a total prison population of 2.3 million. In 2009, nearly 60% of those arrested for a violent criminal act were white, but we would never know that from looking at the makeup of the prison population because so many people of color are convicted for non-violent drug offenses.[7]

In a clear example of racism in the criminal justice system, an October 2010 report found that in California, in the 25 cities surveyed, police arrested blacks at rates between 4 and 12 times greater than they arrested whites for marijuana possession, even though US government data consistently show that whites use marijuana at higher rates than blacks do. Young black men, targeted by the police for racial profiling and harassment, end up entangled in the criminal/legal system for low-levels of possession and with a drug offence on their record that limits their future job opportunities in ways that young white men who also use marijuana rarely experience.[8]

The increased criminalization of communities of color through racial profiling, the "war on drugs" and mandatory minimum sentencing has had a severe impact on African American women and Latinas — they have become the fastest-growing group of people coming into prison. The number of women in prison has now risen to over 200,000 with over a million under supervision by the criminal/legal system. Over 50% of the women incarcerated are women of color, and up to 80% of these women are there for non-violent crimes, primarily drug possession.[9] Almost all of them are poor, and 80 to 90% of them have experienced male violence in the form of child sexual assault, rape or domestic violence.[10]

Another problem with the criminal justice system is subtle racism rooted in the structure of the probation system. A study by University of Washington sociologists found a consistent bias in probation officers' written reports on young black and white offenders with the same backgrounds, offenses and ages. The officers routinely described blacks as bad kids with character flaws, while they wrote about white offenders as victims of negative environmental factors such as exposure to family conflict or delinquent friends.[11]

The combination of racially biased perceptions and racism built into the structures of the criminal justice system contributes to the fact that blacks under the age of 18 make up 16% of their age group in the US, 28% of those young people arrested, 30% of those sent to juvenile court, 38% of those detained in juvenile jails and 30% of those found guilty of being a delinquent. Black youths account for 35% of all juveniles tried in adult criminal courts, 38% of those sent to juvenile facilities and 58% of juveniles confined in adult prisons.[12]

This has harsh consequences for the youth themselves and for the entire community. As Mark Soler, president of the Youth Law Center in Washington DC, remarked, "These disparities accumulate, and they make it hard for members of the minority community to complete their education, get jobs, and be good husbands and fathers."[13]

Racism also plays another role. Sentencing is different depending on the race of the victim. White victims are considered more valuable, and those who harm them are given harsher sentences. As Richard Morin, writing in the *Washington Post*, reported:

> A black man is run over and killed by a drunken driver.
> A typical sentence: two years in prison.
> A white man is run over and killed by a drunken driver.
> A typical sentence: four years in prison
> A white woman is run over and killed by a drunken driver.
> A typical sentence: seven years in prison.

In the same article, Morin cited a report by Edward Glaeser and Bruce Sacerdote which led him to conclude that, holding constant all other key factors about the crime, the killer and the victim, "murderers who kill black victims receive 26.8 percent shorter sentences than they would have received if the victims had been white."[14]

In January 2000, George Ryan, the Republican governor of Illinois, put a halt to executions in that state after Northwestern University journalism students discovered that several death row inmates were actually innocent. Since 1977, Illinois has exonerated 13 death row inmates and killed 12. The *Chicago Tribune* examined the almost 300 death penalty cases in Illinois since the death penalty was reinstated and found that half of the 260 cases that were appealed were ultimately reversed.[15] Only five nations — China, Iraq, Iran, Saudi Arabia and the US — account for 85% of the world's executions. Some states and most countries have long abandoned the need to penalize people with death. The death penalty has been proven ineffective as a deterrent, racially and economically biased, cruel and unusual punishment and a diversion from the pressing issues of racial and economic justice.

We have become a policed society. The fastest-growing male occupations are security guards, police, immigration officials and prison wardens. There are over 884,000 police officers and detectives and another 1 million private security guards in the US.[16] Tens of thousands of police are members of heavily armed, military-trained SWAT teams deployed primarily in communities of color.[17] We now routinely find metal detectors and security in airports, government buildings, schools and other public facilities.

A policed and criminalized society is a tremendous drain on our resources. Incarceration costs run over $55 billion a year and have shifted expenditures away from education and other social services.[18] The State of California, which used to be second in education spending per student in the US and now is 49th, has built 21 prisons in the last 30 years and only one university. It costs, on average, $23,000 a year to incarcerate a prisoner and much less to send him or her to a university. It is calculated that a reduction by half in the incarceration rate for people with non-violent drug offenses would result in a savings of $16.9 billion, most of that savings going to state and local governments who could invest instead in public services.[19]

Between police brutality, the racial and class biases in the criminal justice system, the increasing surveillance of our daily lives and recent anti-terrorism legislation, we are seeing civil rights being eroded in the US. By not standing up against the attacks on, and the criminalization of, communities of color, we are sliding down a slope of more white fear but less safety and rights for all of us.

We need to look within the criminal justice system to understand and eliminate the ways that racism blames and then punishes youth of color. Young people of color don't grow, make, import or transport drugs; white adults do. Young people of color don't manufacture and sell guns nor do they move jobs and stores out of neighborhoods; white-led corporations do. Young people of color don't keep information about birth control, sexually transmitted diseases, drugs and violence away from young people; white adults do. Young people of color don't decrease funds for education while increasing spending on war and prisons; white adults do. As white adults, we need to take responsibility for the policies and decisions that set young people of color up to fail and then punishes them for their lack of success.

We also need to look at the broader social context to understand the root causes of violence and criminal behavior. We know what the answers are for crime prevention — well-paid and safe jobs, challenging and supportive educational opportunities, recreational activities, adequate healthcare and adequate economic and psychological family support services. We must measure every dollar we spend on prisons and jails, which can never be a

- Would you want white youth to be treated as harshly as youth of color are now?
- What about your own children, grandchildren, nieces, nephews or the children of friends?
- Should 13- and 15-year-olds be treated as adults and imprisoned for life?
- What responsibility does our society have for their behavior?

long-term solution, against the other ways we know we can make a dent in the levels of violence we all fear. As an individual, you can become involved with efforts to end the death penalty, fund rehabilitation, shift funding from prisons to schools and stop the building of new prisons.

Notes

1. Feagin and Hernan. *White Racism,* p. 189.
2. For this account, I draw heavily on the excellent documentation provided by: Douglas A. Blackmon. *Slavery by Another Name: The Re-Enslavement of Black Americans from the Civil War to World War II.* Anchor, 2008.
3. Heather Ann Thompson. "Rethinking the True Horror of Convict Leasing: African Americans' Forced Labor." *Against the Current,* no. 147 (July/August 2010), p. 33; Heather Ann Thompson. "Blinded by the 'Barbaric' South: The Ironic History of Penal Reform in Modern America." In Matthew Lassiter and Joseph Crespino, eds. *The Myth of Southern Exceptionalism.* Oxford, 2009.
4. Leadership Conference on Civil Rights. *Justice on Trial: Racial Disparities in the American Criminal Justice System.* [online]. [cited February 28, 2011]. civilrights.org/publications/justice-on-trial/; Vince Schiraldi and Building Blocks for Youth. *The Juvenile Justice System in Black and White.* Center for Children's Law and Policy. [online] [cited March 2002]. cclp.org/building_blocks.php.
5. Bureau of Justice Statistics. *Correctional Populations.* [online]. [cited February 28, 2011]. bjs.ojp.usdoj.gov/content/glance/tables/corr2tab.cfm.
6. John Schmitt et. al. "The High Budgetary Cost of Incarceration." Center for Economic and Policy Research, June 2010. [online]. [cited February 28, 2011]. cepr.net/documents/publications/incarceration-2010-06.pdf.
7. US Department of Justice, Federal Bureau of Investigation. "Crime in the United States 2009, Table 43." September, 2010. [online]. [cited March 8, 2011]. www2.fbi.gov/ucr/cius2009/data/table_43.html.
8. Harry G. Levine et al. "Arresting Blacks for Marijuana in California: Possession Arrests 2006-08." Drug Policy Alliance, October, 2010. [online]. [cited February 28, 2011]. drugpolicy.org/library/arrestingblacks.cfm.
9. Women's Prison Association, Institute on Women and Criminal Justice. *Quick Facts: Women and Criminal Justice — 2009.* [online]. [cited February 28, 2011]. wpaonline.org/pdf/Quick Facts Women and CJ 2009.pdf .
10. 80% of women in prison report incomes of less than $2,000 per year in the year before their arrest, and 92% report incomes under $10,000.
11. George S. Bridges and Sara Steen. "Racial Disparities in Official Assessments of Criminal Offenders: Attributional Stereotypes as Mediating Mechanisms." *American Sociological Review,* August, 1998.
12. National Council on Crime and Delinquency. "And Justice for Some: Differential Treatment of Youth of Color in the Justice System." January, 2007. [online]. [cited February 28, 2011]. nccd-crc.org/nccd/pubs/2007jan_justice_for_some.pdf.
13. Fox Butterfield. "Racial Disparities Are Pervasive in Justice System, Report Says." *New York Times,* April 26, 2000.
14. Richard Morin. "Justice Isn't Blind." *Washington Post,* September 3, 2000, p. B05.

15. Manning Marable. "Halt the Machinery of Death." *Colorlines,* February, 2000.
16. Bureau of Labor Statistics. *Occupational Outlook Handbook, 2010-11 Edition.* [online]. [cited March 8, 2011]. bls.gov/oco/ocos160.htm#projections_data and bls.gov/oco/ocos159.htm#projections_data.
17. Manning Marable. "Race-ing Justice: The Political Cultures of Incarceration" *Souls,* Vol. 2, no. 1 (Winter 2000), p. 10.
18. N.C. Aizenman. "The High Cost of Incarceration." *The Denver Post,* February 29, 2008. [online]. [cited February 28, 2011]. denverpost.com/ci_8400051#ixzz12Gr3mnT7.
19. John Schmitt et. al. *The High Budgetary Cost of Incarceration.* Center for Economic and Policy Research, June 2010. [online]. [cited February 28, 2011]. cepr.net/documents/publications/incarceration-2010-06.pdf.

Religion

SPIRITUALITY REFERS TO OUR EXPERIENCE OF BEING CONNECTED to a reality greater than ourselves. Religions are the organized social structures in which some of us put spirituality into practice. We are all spiritual beings. Many of us are also connected to a particular religious institution through our upbringing or through current affiliation.

Most white people who are part of an organized religion in the United States are Christian, so I am going to focus this discussion on Christianity. If you are a white person who is Muslim, Jewish, Buddhist or pagan, or who belongs to a new-age spiritual community, much of this chapter will be relevant to you as well (with some adaptations).

The major denominations of the Christian church have contributed to racism and anti-Jewish and anti-Muslim oppression in both Europe and the United States for many centuries. Colonization, genocide and slavery by the Spanish, English, Dutch, Belgian and French empires were given explicit, divine sanction by official statements from the church. For example, in 1455 the Pope allowed Christian rulers "free and ample faculty"

> To invade, search out, capture, vanquish, and subdue all Saracens and pagans whatsoever, and other enemies of Christ wheresoever placed, and the kingdoms, dukedoms, principalities, dominions, possessions, and all movable and immovable goods whatsoever held and possessed by them and to reduce their persons to perpetual slavery, and to apply and appropriate to himself and his successors the kingdoms, dukedoms, counties, principalities, dominions, possessions, and goods, and to convert them to his and their use and profit.[1]

Christian denominations, religious orders and individual churches owned slaves and ran Indian boarding schools in which Native children were kidnapped, beaten and molested and large numbers were starved to death.[2]

Today, Christian institutions promote racist foreign policy on the basis of a US manifest destiny to save other countries by bringing them "freedom," "free markets" and democracy; they support domestic policies that punish people for their sins rather than provide for their needs.[3]

At the same time, many individual Christians and church leaders have been inspired by Christian teachings to work for social justice. In other words, the Christian church and its teachings have been used by Christians both to support slavery, genocide and economic exploitation and to resist it.

This is not the place for a detailed discussion of Christian history or theology. Nor can the important role that faith plays in white Christian resistance to racism be addressed. It is important that we build on the inspiration our religious faiths give us to work for social justice, while resisting racism in our religious institutions. Use the following questions to guide you in these tasks.

Assessment — Religion

1. What did you learn about people of color, Jews and Muslims in Sunday school or sermons?
3. Is your religious community all white? Is the leadership all white?
4. What is the history of your church's practice of establishing missions in, or sending missionaries to, areas of the US or to other parts of the world such as Africa and Asia?
5. What attitudes are expressed about people of color during discussion of missionary work, charity or social problems?
6. What connections, if any, are made in your church between sin, evil and the lives or situations of people of color or people who are Jewish or Muslim? What Christian virtues are used to make negative judgments about people of color (e.g., "We are hardworking, but they are lazy")?
6. What religious or historical role do the Jewish people have in your church's teachings? How may that role have contributed to anti-Jewish oppression?
7. What do you know about the history of resistance to racism in your religion or denomination (e.g., abolitionist or civil rights struggles)?
8. What Christian values did you learn that might direct you to work against social injustice? What values specifically inspire or support anti-racism work?
9. Where does racism appear in your current religious organization
   a. In the leadership?
   b. In the theology?
   c. In the membership?
   d. In the educational curriculum?

Assessment — Religion *cont.*

e. In the practice of the church as a community institution that owns land, employs people, develops projects and allocates resources?

10. How is your religious group actively addressing racism
    a. as a priority by the membership and by the leadership of the church?
    b. as a problem in the community and/or within the church?

11. Does your church have an active committee or program to address racism?
    a. Is it equipped and authorized to make real changes?
    b. What has it accomplished?
    c. Where has there been resistance?

12. How can you be more involved?

You probably participate in other institutions besides work, school and church, such as social service agencies, recreational clubs, youth service organizations or volunteer agencies. Think about these institutions also; ask yourself some of the questions from the previous chapters. What do you notice? Where are you going to become involved?

Notes

1. Papal Bull *Romanus Pontifex,* (Nicholas V), January 8, 1455. [online]. [cited February 28, 2011]. nativeweb.org/pages/legal/indig-romanus-pontifex.html.

2. There are many accounts of Christian churches (orders such as the Franciscans) and Christian universities (such as Georgetown University) owning slaves. For an account of the slave-owning Presbyterian churches of Virginia, see Jennifer Oast. "'The Worst Kind of Slavery': Slave-owning Churches in Prince Edward County, Virginia." Journal of Southern History, November 1, 2010. [online]. [cited March 1, 2011]. faqs.org/periodicals/201011/2195260991.html. For information about Christian-run boarding schools and their impact, see Ward Churchill. *Kill the Indian, Save the Man: The Genocidal Impact of American Indian Residential Schools.* City Lights, 2004.

3. For a detailed account of the active involvement of one particular Christian institution, The Family, in US foreign and domestic policy, see Jeff Sharlet. *C Street: The Fundamentalist Threat of American Democracy.* Little, Brown and Company, 2010.

Foreign Policy

RACISM IS ONE OF THE FOUNDATIONS OF UNITED STATES foreign policy. During the colonial period, policy was directed against European competitors such as England, Spain and France, and against Native Americans, particularly those on the Atlantic coast. White Christians saw themselves as Chosen People in a Promised Land, and Native peoples were labeled Canaanites, Moors and animals — all inferior beings in this Christian worldview.[1]

The concept is *American exceptionalism* — the belief that the United States has a higher calling, a moral responsibility and a providential (God-given) destiny to conquer and rule over people of inferior races such as Native Americans and Mexicans.[2] The desire of capitalist leaders for the perpetual expansion of markets is easily justified by the inferiority of the people whose land is desired. These people of color are simply in the way of progress, modernity and the superior morality and intelligence of the white Christian race.

US foreign policy based on expansionism, exceptionalism and racial (and therefore moral) superiority has been remarkably consistent throughout our history. We have fought wars against white Christian Europeans only with great reluctance and for specific reasons of defense. We have continually fought wars throughout the rest of the world, believing that, as superior people, we must provide other countries with our superior forms of religion, morality, democracy, economic and legal systems. When these people refused our generous gifts, we quickly sent in the marines, concluding that it was easier to kill great numbers of them rather than accommodate their own desires for independence and self-sufficiency.

Since our brutal attempt at exterminating Native Americans and our invasion of Mexico, US foreign battles have taken place further from our shores. Just since World War II, the US has killed or directly sponsored and financed the killing of millions of Asian, Latino/a, black and Arab people in countries such as Korea, Vietnam, Indonesia, Laos, Cambodia, Iran, Iraq, Nicaragua, El Salvador, Chile, Brazil, Somalia, the Congo, South Africa, Palestine, Afghanistan — the list seems interminable. Because they are people of color, the number of those killed, maimed, injured or displaced is rarely counted and certainly not mourned. The deaths of US soldiers are tracked assiduously, and their lives and sacrifice honored. Just as white people don't generally notice or mourn the deaths of Latino/a, African American, Native Americans and Asian Americans killed in US cities by violence, lack of affordable housing and healthcare and environmental pollution, we do not account for those we kill overseas to maintain access to their valuable resources. When Madelaine Albright, then UN Ambassador under Clinton, was confronted with the fact that US sanctions of Iraq were estimated to have cost the lives of 500,000 Iraqi children, she replied, "I think that is a very hard choice, but the price, we think, the price is worth it."[3] Could she possibly have said this in reference to white children?

And yet 15 years and two full-scale invasions later, do we know, even within a range of 100,000, how many Iraqis have been killed as a result of our foreign policy decisions? Or how many Afghanis?

Even our foreign *aid* is based on racist assumptions that nations which have been colonized and depleted by Western imperial powers now need us to

---

Assessment — Foreign Policy

1. Do you believe that the US is a generous country?
2. How do you think people in other countries such as Haiti, Iraq, Afghanistan, Vietnam or the Congo see our country?
3. Consider a country that the US has invaded or intervened in during your lifetime. How many people in that country died as a result of our interventions? What were the reasons given for our intervention? How was the belief in manifest destiny part of the justification for intervention? What role did racism play?
4. In what ways are the deaths of US soldiers shown greater concern than the deaths of civilians killed by US soldiers in other countries?
5. In what ways does this mirror the way that the abduction and murder of white children in the US is shown greater concern than the abduction and murder of children of color?
6. Is there any way, even slightly, that you believe that the life of a US soldier is more valuable than an Iraqi woman or child killed by our troops?
7. Is there any way, even slightly, that you believe that the life of a white child in the United States is more valuable than the life of an African American, Latino/a or Native American child?

"help" them get back on their feet because they are unable to do it themselves. These "relations of rescue," whether individual or national, are used to justify interventions which are rarely beneficial to those receiving such "help."[4] A recent example of this dynamic is response to the devastating earthquake in Haiti. The charitable response of individuals in the US was needed, substantial and well-intended. But the US, after years of economic policies that deliberately impoverished the nation and supported military dictatorships — including participation in deposing the democratically elected president, Jean Bertrand Aristide — used the crisis to send in large numbers of troops, slow down the distribution of international aid and set the stage for further economic exploitation. When aid was slow in reaching desperate people in need, it was easy to blame the Haitians for lack of infrastructure — infrastructure that had been deliberately sabotaged by US policies.[5] Confirming their sense of the US as a generous Christian nation, people could feel good about their charitable response, blame the Haitians for their problems and ignore the devastating centuries-long impact of US interventions in that country.

Notes

1. For an extended discussion of this chosen people metaphor and its influence on colonial policy and subsequently on US law, see Newcomb. *Pagans in the Promised Land.*
2. Godfrey Hodgson. *The Myth of American Exceptionalism.* Yale, 2009, p. 10.
3. Statement on CBS, May 12, 1996. [online] [cited March 2, 2011]. youtube.com/watch?v= FbIX1CP9qr4.
4. I borrow this phrase from Peggy Pascoe. *Relations of Rescue: The Search for Female Moral Authority in the American West, 1874-1939.* Oxford, 1990.
5. See, for example, Michael Chossudovsky. *The Destabilization of Haiti: US Sponsored Coup D'etat.* Centre for Research on Globalization, November, 2004. [online]. [cited March 2, 2011]. globalresearch.ca/articles/CHO402D.html.

Environmental Justice

O NE OF THE MOST CRITICAL NATIONAL AND INTERNATIONAL ISSUES we face is global warming, including such visible effects as ice cap melting, rising temperatures and sea levels, species and habitat destruction, unsustainable levels of consumption and an increasing number of extreme weather events. Neither the problems nor the solutions are race-neutral.

Environmental racism refers to any policy, practice or directive that differentially affects or disadvantages (whether intentionally or unintentionally) individuals, groups or communities based on race or ethnicity. It combines with public policies and industry practices to provide benefits for whites while shifting costs to people of color. Numerous studies have shown that heavily polluting industries in North America such as mining and manufacturing, garbage dumps, toxic waste sites, medical waste incinerators and congested freeways are located disproportionately in communities of color in urban and suburban areas and on Native American land.[1] Higher levels of air, water and land pollution lead directly to higher levels of asthma, cancer and other illnesses, i.e., increased mortality for children and adults. In addition, people of color are, in general, more likely to have jobs with higher exposure to contaminants such as pesticides, asbestos and other toxic chemicals.[2] Finally, people of color are most likely to experience lack of access to clean air and water and uncontaminated healthy food.[3]

At the international level, the United States is the largest per capita consumer nation on Earth — containing 4% of the world's population, the US consumes 22% of its products and produces 25% of the world's carbon dioxide emissions from fossil fuel.[4] US-based multinational oil, mining, agribusiness, lumber, fishing and manufacturing companies, along with their European, Japanese and Chinese counterparts, continue to pursue profits at all costs throughout the world. These companies destroy the environment and block efforts to cut back on consumption and address global warming. The US military is the largest and most destructive contributor to global heating through the production of its equipment and armaments, the transport and size of its personnel, its deployment of people — and the use of environmentally destructive weapons such as Agent Orange, white phosphorus, depleted uranium, land mines and cluster bombs.[5]

As I described earlier, US foreign policy is based on the disposability of people of color and the protection of white people. Our domestic policy mirrors this practice. Hurricanes Rita and Katrina were devastating but predictable events. Their damage was compounded by inadequately maintained levees and canals, dilapidated housing, poor emergency planning, police protection of white property and harassment of people of color, racially biased media coverage and racist municipal and state policies that gave priority to rebuilding white neighborhoods and tourist centers over the neighborhoods where people of color lived.[6] Both internationally and domestically, the exploitation and destruction of the environment is intertwined with the exploitation and oppression of people of color.

On the front lines of attack, communities of color have also been on the front lines of resistance. The people of the color-led environmental justice movement have been engaging in a creative and powerful struggle against environmental destruction and for the preservation of lives, land and cultures.

There is little controversy about the environment problems we face, but much about the solutions. Here again, racism affects what solutions are proposed and who gets to decide (for example, at the 2010 Copenhagen climate action meeting). Most mainstream environmental organizations, especially the largest and best funded, are run by white people. People of color (and majority world nations at the international level) have been systematically shut out of the conversations and decision making related to environment issues. Basic white racist assumptions continue to operate in the environmental movement. Some of these are:

- White people know what's best
- White people know how to get things done
- People without education, money and connections are not qualified to lead organizations and organizing efforts
- People of color have a limited and local point of view, while white people can see the broader picture

- The way to make change is through political influence, lobbying, advocacy, lawsuits and the courts rather than mobilization and organizing
- The way to address environmental problems is to educate the public and change individual habits of consumption. Power is located in the individual, not the collective

To use a metaphor developed by social justice activists Victor Lewis and Hugh Vasquez, imagine the United States as a huge passenger ship.[7] The ruling class is in first class on the deck enjoying all the amenities and thinking themselves protected from any hardship. Most of us are in second, third or fourth class. We may have moved down a class during the recent recession, but we are still getting by. Some of us are in fifth and sixth class and literally struggle to keep our heads above water. And many low-income people of color are at the very bottom of the boat in steerage, along with low-income white people, cleaning the rooms, preparing the food, serving and doing the laundry for those at the top.

The ship has a big hole in it, and those in steerage are living in water to their waist, struggling to stay alive. People higher in the ship may think they are immune to the water (pollution, climate change, natural disasters) pouring into the hole. But when the ship sinks — we all go down. Power and privilege may mitigate or postpone the impacts of environmental devastation, but ecologically all life is connected and interdependent.

The people at the bottom of the ship know the ship is sinking and have been organizing to save their communities and to fix the hole. The people at the top also know it is sinking, but they don't want to publicize the fact. They are clearly benefiting from the way things are set up; they fear exposing their incompetent leadership and corruption and losing their wealth and power by riling up the rest of the passengers. They continue to mishandle the ship (for example, the Gulf Oil disaster), driving too fast through dangerous waters, refusing to slow down or alter course (encouraging new deep-water oil drilling). Their actions contribute directly to the hole in the ship getting bigger.

Most of the rest of us are willing to go along with the ruling class. We don't give credibility to the voices at the bottom of the ship. We think we can rely on those in power to take care of us, or for advances in science and technology to fix things. Perhaps we are just in denial, minimizing the danger and assuming we'll be unaffected by what is happening. But increasing cancer rates,

Questions and Actions — Environmental Justice

1. Are you concerned by US wars in the Middle East over control of oil?
2. Have you and your family been affected by contaminants in the food you eat, the air, the water or the toys your children play with?
3. Do you know anyone who has died of cancer or other pollution-related illness?
4. Do you know anyone who has died of heart disease, diabetes or other illness related to lack of access to healthy food?
5. Do you acknowledge to yourself and others how serious this crisis is?
6. How is the health and well-being of communities of color in your area being impacted by environmentally related hazards?
7. How are they organizing around environmental issues?
8. How would you characterize the responses to environmental crises so far by corporations, the government and the media?
9. What solutions are being proposed? Are they adequate?
10. What powerful groups are resisting or sabotaging these solutions?
11. Do you support any environmental organizations? Are they mostly white? Is their leadership mostly white?
12. What kinds of solutions are they working for? Who is being left out of those solutions?
13. What are you doing to support systematic, institutional policies that change the way our society consumes, pollutes and relates to the environment?
14. What are you doing to listen to communities of color, support their leadership and work with them to sustain the planet and all life?

larger-scale natural disasters, constant war for control of declining oil fields and contaminated air, food and water belie the danger we're all in.

There are numerous sources of information about environmental racism and environmental justice; a few are listed in the online bibliography at PaulKivel.com. We cannot afford to be uninformed on these issues.

Notes

1. Robert D. Bullard. *Environmental Justice in the 21st Century.* Environmental Justice Resource Center at Clark Atlanta University, ND. [online]. [cited March 1, 2011]. ejrc.cau.edu/ejinthe 21century.htm. See the endnotes for extensive documentation of environmental racism and its health effects.
2. Researcher Harvey L. White states that "nonwhite workers are 50% more likely to be exposed to hazards in the workplace;" Harvey L. White. *Race, Class, and Environmental Hazards.* California Environmental Protection Agency, 2003. [online]. [cited March 2, 2011]. calepa. ca.gov/envjustice/Documents/2003/Appendices/AppendixB.pdf.
3. For example, the phrase *food deserts* has been coined to describe urban areas where people of color don't have access to healthy and affordable food because of corporate decisions to relocate grocery stores from city centers to the suburbs.

4. Natural Resources Defense Council. *Global Warming Basics: What It Is, How It's Caused, and What Needs To Be Done To Stop It*. [online]. [cited March 1, 2011]. nrdc.org/globalwarming/f101.asp.

5. International Peace Bureau. *The Military's Impact on the Environment: A Neglected Aspect of the Sustainable Development Debate*. August, 2002. [online]. [cited March 1, 2011]. sdissues.net/SDIN/uploads/Mil-Envir%20JOBURG%20version.doc.

6. Jean Hardistry. *Hurricane Katrina and Structural Racism: A Letter to White People*. October, 2005. [online]. [cited March 2, 2011]. jeanhardisty.com/blog_katrina.html; Lee Sustar. "Hurricane Katrina Exposes Racism and Inequality." Countercurrents.org., September, 2005. [online] [cited March 2, 2011]. countercurrents.org/cc-sustar010905.htm.

7. Personal communication.

Part VI

Democratic, Anti-racist Multiculturalism

Democratic, Anti-racist
Multiculturalism

I ENVISION A SOCIETY WHERE EACH PERSON IS VALUED regardless of gender, race, cultural background, sexual identity, ability or disability or access to wealth.

This society would provide adequate shelter, food, education, recreation, healthcare, security and well-paying jobs for all. The land would be respected and sustained, and justice and equal opportunity would prevail.

Such a society would value cooperation over competition, community development over individual achievement, democratic participation over hierarchy and control and interdependence over either dependence or independence.

The only way to actualize such a vision is to create a democratic, anti-racist, multicultural society in which no one is left out and no one is left behind.[1]

Any fourth-grade history textbook will tell you that living in a Western democracy commits one to a common set of legal rights and responsibilities that are supposed to apply equally to *all people*. *All people* means all people regardless of gender, race, class, physical condition, sexual orientation, religion, place of residence, length of time here, level of education and ability to speak English.

Beyond that, our differences are infinite. In fact, our diversity makes the US a strong, dynamic and creative nation.

We are not all the same. Other people do not look like you, think like you, cook like you, eat like you or act like you. For many of us, this is hard to accept. We are used to having things done in ways that are familiar and comfortable. Most of us have experienced tremendous upheaval and change in our lifetimes. We may not be anxious to invite more.

Being a multicultural nation does not mean that we all fit together easily, or that our differences complement each other. We should expect conflict and get good at it! Individually and as a nation, we need to develop tools for dealing with conflict without resorting to violence. The phrase *multicultural democracy* describes a process in which we all participate in making the decisions that affect our lives. It is a strategy toward full inclusion, participation and justice for all people.

When any strategy is turned into practice, however, it can fuel greater inequality or it can fuel further progress toward ending racism. Multiculturalism can be used to deflect attention away from racism or to dilute attempts at racial inclusion. And in examining how multiculturalism is conceived and put into practice, we need to look at who has power — who benefits, who pays and who really decides.

We already live in a multicultural society. This is not something we're striving for; much as some white people hark back to a whiter past, we have been a multicultural society from the beginning. However, our multicultural society is neither democratic nor anti-racist. We have much to do to achieve the goals I described above. In our daily lives, most of the organizations we are involved with are not even multicultural; they are segregated. One way to achieve racial justice is to build democratic, anti-racist multicultural organizations.

What does it mean for an *organization* to be democratic, anti-racist and multicultural? At a minimum, the membership, staff, administration and board of directors would all have to reflect the ethnic, gender, economic, religious and other diversity of the larger community. The organization would have to serve the needs of a broad-based section of the community. What the organization does, how decisions are made and who is served would have to reflect an inclusive process.

Our dominant Western tradition is based on *either/or* logic. Even complex racial matters get reduced to black-white contrasts, win-lose situations. We have seen how this simplified perspective distorts our perception of reality and can make our actions ineffective.

When people come together to make decisions affecting their lives, their differing perspectives, needs and desires will probably not reduce to an either/or choice. If we expect differences to lead to conflict, then we come in

- How would it make a difference in your interactions with other people if you always assumed there was a cooperative solution possible that would benefit all parties?

defensively, ready to protect our own interests. We won't be striving for common solutions that take into account everyone's needs.

The assumption of *competition* built into Western modes of thinking strongly influences our interactions with each other. Boys are particularly well trained by academic competition, sports and the military not to find cooperative solutions to problems. One reason they get into fights with other guys so often is the expectation that there can be only one winner. One reason they hit young women is they feel they cannot afford to lose to anyone, much less a "girl." This binary opposition, with one person on top, is expressed in many ways. We talk of winners and losers, champs and chumps, bullies and wimps. We don't teach people to negotiate, compromise or work out creative solutions. Instead, particularly for men, aggression becomes the best defense. Action precedes discussion.[2]

We need innovative ways of thinking about reality that embrace diversity, complexity and cooperation. Otherwise we are stuck in a competitive framework with all parties feeling that if they don't win, they will lose — and that they can only win if others lose.

Some people have suggested that we adopt a *both/and* way of thinking. In this framework, we assume that the needs and perspectives of different parties are not necessarily in conflict. Using this approach allows us to embrace the perspectives of both sides and draw up a solution that includes elements of each. This kind of thinking shifts the emphasis from fighting to negotiating.

People who employ both/and thinking understand that truth is not absolute. Truth comes from the understanding, traditions and experience of the people whose lives are involved. Different people have different experiences, and what is true for one person or culture may not be true for another. Although there may be simple truths in science (and even those are hotly debated), our social reality is much more complex. One mark of a mature person is the ability to accept differing opinions and ideas respectfully and without attack.

Both/and thinking is an improvement over either/or thinking because it helps people reduce conflict and develop cooperative solutions. Yet even both/and thinking assumes there are two sides that are mutually exclusive. There may be as many truths as there are people or groups involved in the process. How do we deal with three, four or eight different sides?

Beyond either/or and both/and thinking is *inclusiveness*. In a democratic, multicultural process, everyone is included. Each person's opinions are respected, and each person's needs are taken into account. Even more importantly, each person participates in making the decisions that affect their life.

Democratic, anti-racist multiculturalism requires time, inclusion and more complex decision-making processes than most of us are used to. Such processes necessarily take time because each person must have the opportunity to be heard. We need more versatile decision-making tools than simple majority rule or majority take all. We need to refine consensus models, systems of proportional representation and other group processes that are more inclusive than those we have relied upon so far.

Full inclusion can only occur if we don't throw anyone away. Our society tends to discard people whenever there is trouble. One common way we deal with conflict is to label some people as the problem and then try to make them disappear by locking them up, isolating them or segregating their communities. Often those thrown away are marginalized and have little political power. For example, labeling students troublemakers and kicking them out of school, which consigns them to a future with little prospect for success, is a way of throwing them away rather than working to include them. Locking up young people for long prison terms casts them out of society. We cannot throw some people away and then claim that we are being inclusive just because we have included everyone who is left.

A cardinal rule of conflict resolution is to attack the problem, not the person. More often we attack the people and leave the problem unattended. We talk about the poor rather than about poverty, the unemployed rather than the lack of jobs, the homeless rather than homelessness, women who are abused rather than male violence and violent youth rather than violence against young people. The people who are suffering the effects of discrimination or violence become the objects of our discussion but are not themselves participants in that discussion. Most of the solutions we come up with are based on blaming and then punishing the victims.

I don't think we can solve problems if we exclude the people who are experiencing those problems. When we do, we guarantee that the problem will remain. Living and working together in a democratic, anti-racist and multicultural society has to be based on inclusion.

Notes

1. My appreciation to Nell Myhand and Allan Creighton for this phrase.
2. For a discussion of male training, see Kivel, *Men's Work*.

Multicultural Competence

IN ORDER TO MAKE SURE THAT EVERYONE is not only present, but can also participate fully, we need to be what many people call culturally competent. *Cultural competency* is the ability to understand another culture well enough to be able to communicate and work with people from that culture.

We are all culturally competent in our own culture. We know the language, the nuances and the assumptions about how the world is defined and organized. We know where there are disagreements and differences and generally what the rules are for solving problems. Most of us know how to get around in our cultural neighborhood. Multicultural competence is fluency in more than one culture, in whichever cultures are part of your surroundings.

Culture is a vague shorthand word to name the complex ways that people who form a *community* (another vague shorthand word) interact with each other. There are usually cultural norms within a community, but cultural practices can change, can be contradictory and usually overlap with practices of other cultures. Cultures form around specific identities, geographies, beliefs and daily practices. Other factors besides our ethnicity and "race" influence the cultures we are a part of, our roles and experiences within them. Multiculturalism requires more than racial balance and inclusion. All members of the community must be competent to communicate with each other.

Learning to be sensitive to the cultural expressions of another group is not difficult, but does require time and energy. We must learn to observe, empathize and appreciate other people's ways of doing things to become culturally competent. Even beginning levels of such competency open doors to understanding different perspectives. People who are culturally competent in even one culture besides their own have a broader, richer and more accurate view of the world. They are able to work with others as full and equal partners.

It is difficult for white people to become multiculturally competent because we are the mainstream culture — we are in the culture of power. Wherever we look, we see ourselves — our language, values, images and history. We have learned how great European-based US culture is. Most of the heroes we studied were white men such as Shakespeare, Washington, Jefferson and Lincoln. We were taught that our values, form of government, literature, science and athletic accomplishments are not only the best of all, but also an entire level above any others. We have been trained to think that other cultures are less literate, less civilized, less efficient, less practical. It is impossible to make a good-faith effort to respect and learn about other cultures when we hold a core assumption that they are inferior to ours. Operating from that assumption, we naturally believe, even if at a very subtle level, that we, white people, are the ones who should be in control, who should make the important decisions.

The difficulty of valuing multicultural competency is increased for white people who are Christian. Christianity places such importance on the individual's relationship with Jesus that culture has often been seen as a distraction to faith. Since people who don't believe in Jesus are consigned to damnation, many denominations focus exclusively on saving the souls of non-Christians. The primary value in understanding another group's language is to translate the New Testament and win them over to God. This perspective makes it difficult for many Christians to respect and value the beliefs and cultural expressions of non-Christians.

Many white people — women, people with disabilities, people who are poor or working-class, Jews, Muslims, lesbians, gays and bisexuals — are already competent in two or more cultures. They understand mainstream US culture and are fluent in their own. Sometimes this understanding gives them the impetus to challenge the cultural assumptions of whiteness. It can give them insight into how the dominance of one culture oppresses and exploits people outside the mainstream. However, white cultural dominance puts pressure even on alternative cultures to be white. These cultures often accept white norms and fail to be inclusive.

Furthermore, the more economically privileged we are, the more racially isolated we tend to be. We have less opportunity to learn from different cultures. The people of color we do come in contact with are in less powerful roles or are in jobs that provide services for us. We are trained to value them less and to devalue the contributions of their cultures. Without a good understanding of how racism has set up this hierarchy of status and sense of entitlement, we don't have much incentive to value or understand other cultures.

US culture has drawn from many different cultural traditions. We have valued them enough to appropriate their strengths and achievements. It is time explicitly, sincerely and publicly to acknowledge these contributions. It is not a question of valuing diversity, but of acknowledging rather than exploiting the contributions of all people to our society.

One way we retain our assumptions of white superiority while increasing our cultural competency is to split off the culture from the people who live it. White people have appropriated music, art, spiritual practices and stories from other cultures while killing or excluding the people who created them.

For example, it is not difficult for a white person to become a connoisseur of jazz — learning to appreciate, collect and even perform the music — while remaining opposed to the full participation of African American people in society. It is possible for a white person to become an expert on the Dine, the Cherokee or the Pomo while supporting the federal government's exploitation of their culture and land. One of the ways that white people have traditionally become experts in other people's cultures is by participating in exploitation.

There is also the danger that we will use our knowledge of another culture to feel superior to the people whose culture it is. Even if we know a lot about the holidays, music or beliefs of another culture, we still have a lot to learn from the people who live it.

We need to use what we learn to be stronger allies for people of color. An ally is an advocate, a person who supports other people's right to speak for themselves, who resists the temptation to speak as an expert on their behalf. Other white people will ask us to speak or translate for, or have an expert opinion about, people of color we know, have studied or lived with. We will be pressured to use our knowledge and professional expertise against those whose lives it is based on. If we do not defer to the leadership of people of color and defend their ability to speak for themselves, we will end up using our expertise to promote ourselves. Only if we are clear that we do not want to reinforce white dominance can we resist the temptation to profit from the accomplishments of people of color.

If we are not careful, cultural competency can also become a substitute for full inclusion. I previously mentioned that the teaching profession is still overwhelmingly white. It is crucial that every white teacher becomes multiculturally competent, but white teachers and administrators who are anti-racist must not rest on their competency laurels. Schools will remain fundamentally racist until people of color are full participants at all levels of the educational system. White educators who are anti-racist activists should be fighting for the training, hiring and retention of teachers, counselors and administrators of color because they know that, in the long run, nothing can replace the understanding and experience that they bring to the educational system.

Part of being multiculturally competent is realizing the limits of your understanding. It should make you less arrogant and more humble. It should provide you with skills for supporting the leadership of those from the cultures in which you are competent. As we become more multiculturally competent, we increase our effectiveness in working with diverse populations, but we cannot stand in the place of people who are experts in their own culture.

Making multicultural processes work is essential to our success as a 21st-century society. The United States faces complex social challenges. Diverse experience, complex approaches and critical thinking are tremendous assets. We must learn how to value the experience and understanding that people of color possess. Diversity is essential to the vitality, strength and maintenance of our society. Valuing diversity is not just a personal preference. Nor is it something we can choose not to do. We have no choice but to draw on the rich and multifaceted experience of all peoples in the US if we all are to survive and thrive. The goals of multicultural competency are increased understanding, respectful communication and full inclusion of all people, not cultural competence by itself. We are striving for a democratic, anti-racist multiculturalism in which all people are part of decision-making processes.

Anti-racism

WHY DOES ANTI-RACISM and other anti-oppression activism have to be one of the components in a multicultural process? Isn't it enough that we are inclusive and democratic, that we value diversity and are culturally competent?

If we were starting out today without 500 years of history, we might be able to ignore racism. However, when we come together in a multicultural environment, it is in a context of white, Christian-based racism. Even if we are all included, even if we listen, value and respect each other, and even if we focus on the challenges we face, we still need to address this legacy.

Anti-racism is the process of actively and consistently confronting racism wherever it occurs. The only way to build a democratic multicultural society from a society dominated by racism is through a commitment to use anti-racist analysis and action.

We have seen how white people hold power in ordinary interactions and in institutional settings and receive unequal and unjust benefits from the social system. We bring this history of inequality and injustice and our training in racist assumptions of power and privilege with us wherever we go. All too often, people who are proponents of multiculturalism refuse to acknowledge or address the persistent effects of racism on our ability to create an inclusive process.

Other dynamics of racism also make it difficult to achieve our goals. For instance, people of color, Muslims and Jews carry with them varying levels of distrust, unease and internalized racism from their prior experiences. In addition, there are the many levels of institutional racism that influence particular situations. Unless we pay explicit attention to the specific, ongoing dynamics of racism, it will inevitably sabotage our efforts to build an inclusive, diverse and respectful society.

The first efforts to create a multicultural event, program or staff may be greeted with great anticipation as well as fear. Whether it's a new employee of color, a new policy, inclusion of new material in a program or even one new song or book in a curriculum, pent-up feelings hoping for and fearful of change can interfere with the normal process of interaction and evaluation. That person, policy or item can become the test of whether multiculturalism will work. These high stakes may well jeopardize the long-range prospects for successful change, as white people quickly judge something or someone as less than perfect and therefore as a failure. If we pay attention to the way that racism undermines the considered responses of both white people and people of color, we are better able to work with these dynamics.

A clear anti-racist agenda can also help prevent multiculturalism from being watered down. It is possible to use our emphasis on inclusiveness to divert attention from racial issues. Concerns of gender equality, sexual orientation, physical access or even religious pluralism can become dominant issues while the struggle against racism is ignored. This dynamic occurs in part because white people tend to treat any other inclusion issue as a white issue. This is another manifestation of racism.

Even if we disagree with or are violently opposed to homosexuality, for example, it is often more comfortable to talk about lesbian and gay rights if we have created a white context. We define issues of disability, gender, class and sexual orientation as white issues, not having to do with race. (Most of us would probably say these issues are racially neutral, but in a racist society *neutral* means not taking into account the reality of racism and therefore is a code word for *white*.) In trying to be so broadly inclusive, we end up excluding people of color with disabilities, women and lesbians of color, gay men and bisexuals of color. Without a strong and continuous focus on racism, we can end up with a group of heterosexual white men and women, white lesbians, white gay men, white people with disabilities, white Jews and some people of color who "represent" their racial groupings. This setup perpetuates racism under the guise of multiculturalism. We do need to focus on complete inclusion, but we cannot let that become a substitute for dealing with racism.

The effects of racism will linger with us for a long time, even if we immediately instituted massive changes to create a democratic multicultural nation. Unchallenged, racism makes a mockery of our values. It turns multiculturalism into the same kind of false promise that integration has been, camouflaging the continuing dominance of white people in our society. A commitment to anti-racism encourages us to pay attention to the effects that racism continues to have so that we can take action against them.

The word *democracy* implies more than a cultural democracy where every culture is represented. We also need to make sure it includes the concept of economic democracy, that this multicultural agenda includes the goal of ending economic injustice. For example, we have already noted how sections of the African American, Latino/a, Asian American and Jewish communities have been given economic opportunities in exchange for supporting the status quo. Without an economic analysis we can continue to support injustice while appearing multicultural.

There are many ways that inattention to the distribution of wealth can subvert our efforts at democracy. For instance, we might bring only middle- or upper-class people of color into the organizations we are involved with, and this will do little to redress the unequal participation of broad groups of poor and working-class people of color. We can become professionals, specializing in multicultural or diversity trainings, and not change the segregation in our schools, neighborhoods and workplaces. Diversity training now supports an industry generating millions of dollars a year for professional trainers. Multiculturalism without attention to issues of wealth and power can become a form of collusion among professionals, both white and of color, to maintain control of the movement to end racism and to benefit themselves.

Multiculturalism supports each person or group's articulation of their economic, political and cultural needs and concerns. It also demands that people work toward solutions that are inclusive and for the good of everyone. We each must learn to address the entire agenda, not just our own concerns.

This collaboration is inherently difficult because our society is large and complex, and no one can represent the interests of very many others. People of color have come together around racial identities in response to political and economic exclusion. People can act as if these racial boundaries are well drawn and clear, even though we know that they are not. We may find ourselves negotiating for the participation of people from particular racial groups in an organization, even though we know such homogeneous groups with clearly defined agendas do not exist. We must begin by focusing on the racial configurations that have developed under racism while understanding they are temporary, artificial and dictated by history.

This means that people cannot represent "their group." A Korean American cannot speak for all Korean Americans, much less for Asian Americans or people of color. People speak as individuals, perhaps sharing interests with others. When we bring a group of diverse individuals together, each person must be allowed to speak from his or her own understanding, experience and integrity, not as a representative of some group or constituency. We don't want multiculturalism to degenerate into a collection of individuals jockeying for power by claiming to represent different constituencies. We don't want to become complacent and believe that we understand the needs of a community of people after hearing from a few "representatives." We must avoid the tendency to think of multiculturalism as a device for representing the interests of different constituencies; we must insist that our organizations be diverse enough to reflect the diversity of the larger society.

We also need to be looking out for the interests of whoever is not included in the process. We can't represent them. But we can push to have the broadest possible inclusion. We should be thinking seriously about how the needs and interests of anyone not already involved can be taken into account, how their voices can be heard. In this sense, multiculturalism is a strategy toward full inclusion, i.e., democracy. If any policy, practice or program labeled multicultural increases exclusion, tokenism, false representation or the unequal distribution of resources, then it is not an effective strategy for ending racial injustice.

You can become an advocate for democratic, anti-racist multiculturalism in every setting you participate in. Pick a formal or informal group that you are a part of, and use the following questions to sharpen your strategic thinking.

Questions and Actions — Anti-racism

1. Describe the group you are thinking about in terms of composition, purpose and decision-making process.
  a. Is it multicultural? Who is involved and who is excluded?
  b. Is it democratic? Who holds power and how are decisions made?
  c. Is it anti-racist? Is racism talked about and dealt with effectively within the group?
2. What needs to change?
  a. Who needs to be brought into the group to make it more inclusive?
  b. How would the group need to change to be truly open to their participation?
  c. How could the group be more democratic?
  d. What forms of racism need to be dealt with?
  e. Who can you talk with about these challenges?
  f. Who might be allies in changing the dynamics of the group?
  g. What is one thing you will do to begin this process?
  h. What fears or concerns do you have about raising these issues?
  i. What will you and the group lose if you don't raise them?

Integration and Tokenism

MANY PEOPLE OF COLOR HAVE EXPRESSED CONCERN that multiculturalism will become (or already is) a new form of integration and tokenism. Unless we are vigilant it certainly can become so.

Integration is based on the belief that people of color have been segregated from the mainstream of US society and need to be incorporated into it for full participation. Even before the *Brown v. Board of Education* US Supreme Court decision in 1954, the discussion about racial equality in the United States revolved around integration.

White belief in the importance of integration is based on the assumption that there is one mainstream, normal set of (white) values, practices and procedures that other people can learn and adapt to. We assume that people of color want to be included in the mainstream but have previously been excluded because of prejudice and discrimination-racism.

There is real cause for concern about the exclusion of people of color from mainstream institutions in the United States. To a great extent, people of color and white people live separately, pray separately, go to different schools, do different jobs and socialize separately. Insofar as people of color are not only separate but unequal, this is a tragedy of injustice, as the Supreme Court ruled in 1954.

Integration is not necessarily the solution to racism. Integration assumes that people of color will adapt to a white mainstream way of doing things and that the institutions they integrate into will accept them as equal participants. Many people of color feel that having to give up culturally specific ways of thinking, acting and relating to others in order to "integrate" simply maintains white power. Our question needs to be: "Integration into what, on whose terms?"

When we assume that the terms and the institutions are fixed, we are advocating not integration, but assimilation — continued control by those who have traditionally held it. For example, under pressure from African Americans, many traditionally white colleges and universities integrated their classrooms in the 1960s and 1970s. When students of color started to demand participation in decisions about the curriculum and policies, these same institutions reacted by calling the students ungrateful and irresponsible. When students demanded that the faculty and administration include people of color, with the power to make decisions, school officials dismissed such demands as impossible.[1]

Today, over 30 years after integration of those schools, most public and private school administrators, deans and professors are white. Obviously most college and university student bodies are integrated to varying degrees. Just as obviously, white people remain at the center of power and decision making. This "you can join us, but we're going to keep control" form of integration does not deal with the fundamental inequalities of racism.

Not everyone wants to be integrated, and few people want to be assimilated. Some people of color are cynical about the ability of white people to fully accept them as equals. Others are sceptical about most white people's willingness to seriously question their own privilege. Many people of color have rich cultures, practices and identities they don't want to give up. There are some Native Americans and black nationalists who want cultural and political sovereignty. Still others are only willing to integrate into democratic, multicultural and explicitly anti-racist institutions because these will protect them from further racism.

We need to develop a much more sophisticated view of racial progress in which we don't make assumptions about what people of color want or don't want. In some cases, for some people, integration is an appropriate strategy. In other cases, it may be a step backwards. In still others, it may be a way to sidestep demands for justice. Integration can only be a strategy for justice and equality, not a goal. As a goal, it too often leads to tokenism and isolation.

Tokenism (small or insignificant change in lieu of fundamental transformation) can play out in many ways. When people of color demand greater power and participation, they meet with white resistance at each stage. White people seldom voluntarily give up control or willingly look at how we resist change. If people of color push hard enough, we slowly and reluctantly accept their participation. We meet each stage with cries of "We've already done so much, what more do they want?" or "They're so unappreciative of what we've done; they'll never be satisfied until they control everything" or "We're moving as fast as we can." All the tactics of denial, minimization, blame and counterattack discussed in Part I are marshaled to justify a slow pace toward equal participation.

The first and simplest stage of tokenism occurs when a small and insignificant number of people of color are allowed to integrate a school or workplace. Or we add a few names and pictures of people of color to a textbook or a wall. We treat people of color and their contributions as an exception. People of color are extremely isolated in these situations and acutely vulnerable to personal abuse. They do not have much support and usually succeed only if they assimilate by thoroughly internalizing the values of the institution.

Another early stage of token integration occurs when white people include only those people of color who fit a certain mold or support the traditional values of an institution. Any who might challenge traditional patterns are screened out, isolated or fired. People of color are accepted for their decorative role and to deflect concerns about discrimination or diversity, not as full participants.

This is also the stage where white people quote or point to particular, usually conservative, people of color in academia or politics — such as Shelby Steele, Ana Chavez, Clarence Thomas, Elaine Chao or Thomas Sowell — to give a seal of approval to our policies and statements.

These tactics may not work. There may be significant numbers of people of color who are demanding equality. We will then seek input from people of color. We allow them to speak out or testify, we study the situation, we do research and we remain in control. This process creates the illusion of participation, but there is still no sharing of power.

This stage might be coupled with another form of tokenism that involves paying attention to racism only when people of color are in the room, outside the door or in the streets. When they are not visibly present, it is business as usual. Racism is viewed as a problem for people of color and only of incidental concern to the main business of the organization.

If these tactics don't succeed in quelling protest, white people will give up some control, but only in special areas that are deemed culturally appropriate to people of color. We may allow them to teach in ethnic studies departments but not in the sciences, or to write about news in their community but not about mainstream events.

These are just some of the ways that white people control the participation of people of color and prevent a democratic multiculturalism from developing. Each involves a token form of integration in which white people retain ultimate power and control.

Many organizations can look multicultural from the outside, covering up their resistance to redistributing power and resources. To break the patterns of white control, we must see through our own tactics and understand why the democratic and anti-racist components of multiculturalism are crucial. Most importantly, white people must be willing to share power.

We should be actively organizing to create a democratic, anti-racist multicultural process in our workplaces, schools, police and fire departments, religious organizations, athletic clubs, unions and city, state and national governments. We must keep four key questions in mind:

1. Is this organization multicultural?

2. Is it democratic?

3. Is it anti-racist (and anti-sexist, etc.)?

4. What are you going to do about it?

Notes

1. I personally witnessed this response by the administration of the small liberal arts college I attended in the late 1960s towards the African American students' requests for a black studies program. For a detailed account of the resistance of elite educational institutions to respond to demands for racial justice and the pressure on people of color to assimilate to them, see: Richard L. Zweigenhaft and William G. Domhoff. *Blacks in the White Establishment?: A Study of Race and Class in America.* Yale, 1991, chapters 2-4.

Organizational Change and Accountability

I ROUTINELY GET REQUESTS FOR WORKSHOPS ON RACISM, diversity and multiculturalism from diversity coordinators, members of a diversity team or someone in the HR department of an independent school, community-based non-profit or institution of higher education.[1]

These requests are one result of the success of the civil rights movement, although the person making the request is probably not aware of this. The existence of their job, and their access to the education that enables them to be credentialed to do the job, were the result of the demand that institutions be integrated, responsive to the needs of communities of color, and that their staff and those they serve be representative of the general population. I receive these calls for talks and consulting because, to some extent, individuals and organizations are still affected by the call for racial justice, however much that call has diminished. People still feel a pressure to address issues of racism in their organizations, however little they understand what those issues really are.

However, the legacy of the movement and the tremendous backlash against its achievements has led many to define racism superficially, reducing it to trainings and workshops, calls to "get along" and respect our differences. The core issues of institutionalized power, systemic racism, economic, political and social disparities in opportunities and outcomes — the continuing existence of white privilege and racial injustice — are now denied, minimized, ignored and even justified. Instead of receiving requests for information and training about how to achieve organizations with full participation and empowerment of people of color, dedicated to eliminating racism both within themselves and in the greater community, I receive requests for a one-day training on diversity. I could certainly fly in, take the money and fly out. However, that would be completely unaccountable on my part because I know that I would be colluding in a deception: the illusion that one talk, workshop or training would shift how racism operates in an organization

My first question to people who call is "Why do you want a one-day training on diversity/racism?" We proceed to have a conversation about what they want to accomplish. Their goals are usually quite circumscribed. They often want white people to be educated, more sensitive, more supportive of efforts to address racism. This is a small goal within an organization or institution that was founded to benefit white people, has white people in control, has no deep organizational commitment to racial justice and probably is unwilling to dedicate significant resources to eliminating the racism within it.

My experience has led me to conclude that talks and trainings only make sense in an organization that is committed to serious organizational change. Otherwise they are window dressing — ineffective and possibly even damaging to the cause of racial justice. They lead individual participants to believe they have done something. They allow organizations to claim they are serious about racial justice. They provide the illusion to the public that something has changed. But business continues as usual.

I am not interested in furthering the illusion of anti-racism work where it is not happening. Therefore, through a series of questions, I try to indicate what I think needs to be in place for a talk or training to make a difference:

1. How will the training relate to preceding and ongoing efforts to create a practice of racial justice within the organization?
2. Is there sustainable leadership at the highest levels for this effort?
3. Is a serious commitment to diversity built into the core mission of the organization?
4. Is there a strategic plan for diversity within the organization at all levels, and/or is it an integral part of the overall strategic plan?
5. Is there an adequate, sustainable and dedicated budget for long-term anti-racism work?

Basically I am asking "Is this organization serious and committed to working towards racial justice?" I am not willing to settle for a verbal assurance. I want to see concrete indications that the money, commitment, leadership and sustainability of the project is in place so that it has some chance to succeed. If the organization is ready, then we can talk about trainings, hiring and retention practices, organizational culture, accountability to various communities served, allocation of resources and leadership development.

Almost always when I ask these questions, I am met with a polite response indicating that the person I am talking with had not thought about any of these things. They say something about taking this information back to their director/the diversity committee/the board — and I never hear from them again.

Few organizations are serious about anti-racism work in their organizations, which is why most remain toxic environments for people of color, providing them with limited opportunities to thrive and succeed. Opportunities which do exist come with an unacknowledged requirement to assimilate and be submissive within an impenetrable culture of whiteness. These organizations are unaccountable to communities of color, and no matter how much they claim to do on behalf of those communities, they leave the structural problems of racism unaddressed and white institutional power intact.

Those of us who are educators, trainers and consultants on issues of diversity and multiculturalism and who are committed to the struggle for racial justice need to ask ourselves some hard questions:

1. What is our role when affirmative action is being attacked by politicians and devastated by the courts, violence against Muslims and immigrants is increasing and welfare mothers and young men of color are being blamed for a variety of social ills?
2. What is our role when large-scale unemployment, environmental degradation, deterioration of public services and the deflation of the housing bubble have disproportionately affected the jobs, housing and living conditions of people of color?

As diversity professionals, we are also facing tightening economic constraints within our field. Many consultants are having increasing difficulty finding work, reputable training centers have closed their doors for financial reasons and more and more training is being conducted by in-house staff in corporations, schools and community-based organizations. Although multicultural training has become a multi-million-dollar profession, the context of that work is still largely marginal, maintained by networks of consultants, increasingly besieged professional staff within large organizations and overworked, isolated teachers without adequate support or resources.

1. How can educators and trainers be accountable to communities of color?
2. How do we maintain the political integrity of this work within increasingly conservative and embattled organizational environments?

3. How are the participants in our trainings connected to social justice activism?

4. What role does anti-racist action play in our work and in our lives?

Since our work occurs in an extremely polarized and unequal economic hierarchy, and in an increasingly segregated and racially polarized society, we can only begin to answer these questions by analyzing the effects of our work on the communities of color we claim to serve.

In other words, who benefits from our work?

To answer this question honestly, many of us would have to admit that although our work may benefit many individual people, including many people of color in the bottom 80% of the economic pyramid, in the larger scheme of things, our work and the organizations we work for maintain the status quo, perpetuating the inequalities of the pyramid. Our work primarily benefits the top rungs, the managerial and ruling classes. Our jobs may help many people have greater access to job and educational opportunities, promotions and training and greater access to social services, but often they do not challenge the distribution of power, wealth and resources which maintain the basic structure of inequality in the US. Many of us work in the middle area of the pyramid, providing a buffer zone between the frustration, pain and anger of the people at the bottom and the concentration of wealth and power at the top. We may keep people and their hopes alive, but without giving them enough information, material resources and skills to seriously challenge the racial hierarchy.[2]

We should not be surprised by this situation. Multicultural educational work developed partly as a response to the demands of the civil rights movement and its anti-racist allies. However, the growth of a group of professionals who do multicultural, diversity, unlearning or other trainings, as opposed to anti-racist organizing, was partly a progressive response to incorporating grass-roots demands for inclusion and diversity, and partly a reactionary response to deflect further such demands. During the 1960s and 1970s, there was a more liberal social climate and more immediate grassroots pressure on institutions. Multiculturalists had more leverage to fight for changes within organizations.

More recently, the question of how we can all get along, work together, succeed as a team and hear everyone's voice superseded the questions of who has power and how can it be shared more equitably. With less external social pressure, organizations were quick to take racism off the agenda and to put team building and celebrating diversity in its place. Today, in the second decade of the 21st century, teachers and trainers currently have even less leverage to challenge this backlash, although that does not mean we have none.[3]

Even from within large organizations and institutional structures, it is possible to work for social justice. It is possible to serve the interests of the poor and working-class, people of color and women, lesbians, gays, bisexuals and trans people and people with disabilities. But doing so is not without risk.

We each need to determine the amount we can risk financially against the spiritual and emotional risks we bear by not standing by our commitment to social justice. These are strategic decisions that we cannot make in isolation from the inside of the organization(s) we work for. Our work is part of a much wider network of individuals and organizations working for justice on the outside. To make effective decisions about our own work, we need to be accountable to those groups and their actions and issues. This accountability[4] then becomes a source of connection which breaks down our isolation and increases our effectiveness as social justice activists.

There are three questions we need to ask ourselves in the current political context:

Who supervises my work?

I don't mean who employs us or funds us, although that is an important consideration in a conservative political climate when jobs are scarce. Who are the grassroots activists of color who advise us, review our work and with whom we consult? I think it is particularly critical for those of us who are white to be accountable to people of color so that our work doesn't inadvertently fuel the backlash or otherwise make it more dangerous for them. But regardless of our ethnicity or race, we need to be accountable to people who are on the front lines of struggles for racial justice and who have leadership positions in local communities of color.

Am I involved in community-based anti-racist struggle?

If we are not fighting for affirmative action, for immigrant rights, against environmental dumping in communities of color, against police brutality, or for access to healthcare or for anti-racist policies and practices within our own institutions, what are we modeling? How are we learning? What informs our work? Can we be accountable to communities of color if we are not politically involved ourselves in some aspect of anti-racist struggle?

Are current political struggles part of the content of what I teach?

Do we connect the participants in our networks, classes and trainings to opportunities for ongoing political work? Do we bring current grassroots political struggles into our activism and organizing, or do we teach about diversity and multiculturalism without dealing with the issues that most directly affect the lives of people of color? Do we give participants tools and resources for getting involved in the issues people of color identify as most immediate for them, whether those be public policy issues such as immigration, affirmative action, welfare, healthcare or workplace, neighborhood and community issues such as jobs, education, violence and toxic waste? When they leave the (class)room after our training or workshop, can they connect what they just learned to the racism people of color experience in their lives? Are we responsive to their needs for survival, safety, economic well-being and political action?

Who we are accountable to is a crucial concern in a contracting economy during conservative political times in which racial, sexual and homophobic scapegoating and backlash are widespread. We may be discouraged about the possibility of doing effective anti-racist work in this context. But this is also a time of widespread organizing and resistance to the backlash.[5] It can be a time for us to realign clearly with those organizing efforts and reclaim the original vision of racial justice and equality which brought our work into being. A focus on organizational and institutional change within a framework of accountable practice is essential to any work for racial justice.

Notes

1. I do not work for corporations or the military because I don't think systemic change can come from organizations whose mission is inimical to social justice.
2. For more on these dynamics, see my article "Social Service or Social Change?" in Incite! Women of Color Against Violence, ed. *The Revolution Will not be Funded: Beyond the Non-profit Industrial Complex*. South End, 2007, pp. 129-150. Also available under articles at paulkivel.com.
3. For more on the history of this work, see "Part I The Rise of the Non-Profit Industrial Complex." in Incite: Women of Color Against Violence. *The Revolution Will Not Be Funded*. South End, 2007.
4. Other resources on accountability: Bonnie Berman Cushing et. al. *Accountability and White Anti-racist Organizing: Stories from Our Work*. Crandall, Dostie & Douglass Books, 2010; Jen Margaret. *Working as Allies*. Auckland Workers' Educational Association, Winston Churchill Fellowship Report, August, 2010. [online]. [cited March 2, 2011]. awea.org.nz/

allies_north_america; Lynne Davis. *Alliances: Re/envisioning Indigenous-non-Indigenous Relationships.* University of Toronto, 2010.

5. You can find contact information for a variety of social justice organizations at PaulKivel.com.

Home and Family

ALTHOUGH YOUR FAMILY MEMBERS may all be white and your neighbors appear so, there may well be people of other cultures, people in interracial families, people of mixed heritage or people who are passing as white among your friends. People of color may also be providing childcare, cleaning, maintenance or healthcare services for you, your children or other relatives. Our environment is seldom as white as we assume it to be because we generally don't notice people of color when their presence doesn't challenge our sense of their proper role.

Our homes are less separable from the greater community than they have ever been. They are connected to the outside world via TV, computer games, the Internet, toys, CDs, radio, books, magazines, the daily newspaper and direct market catalogues. Each of these provides a vehicle by which racism can enter your home, but they also give you opportunities to respond to it.

Talking about racism is not easy for most of us to do. Few of us grew up in homes where racism or other difficult and emotional issues were mentioned at all. We come from backgrounds of silence, ignorance or a false belief that to talk about racism is to further it. When talk about race did occur, some of us experienced conflict with family members because we disagreed over racial issues. We can acknowledge these past experiences and create an atmosphere in our own homes where we can openly and respectfully talk about issues of race, gender or class.

- Do you talk about racism where you live?
- When you and other family members watch a movie, discuss the news or talk about daily events, do you notice and discuss racism?

It is challenging to raise white children in the highly racist society we live in. When babies are born, they are unaware of racial difference and attach no intrinsic value to skin color. We know that they begin to notice racial differences and their effects between the ages of two and four.[1] Throughout their childhood, they are bombarded with stereotypes, misinformation and lies about race. Without our intervention, they may or may not become members of extremist groups or commit hate crimes, but they may well become white people who accept the injustice, racial discrimination and violence in our society and perpetuate racism through their collusion. That is why we must begin teaching them at an early age to embrace differences and to become anti-racist activists. We can start this process by assessing our home and family environment for evidence of racism.

Do the calendars, pictures and posters on your walls reflect the diverse society we live in? Are there books by women and men, lesbian, straight and gay people from many different cultures? Are there magazines from communities of color? We don't get extra points if there are. Nor are we trying to create an ethnic museum. But paying attention to our environment broadens our perspective and counters the stream of negative racial stereotypes that otherwise enter our home through the media.

It is even more important to discuss racism and to pay attention to our home if we have children. As responsible parents, we need to think about the toys, games, computer games, dolls, books and pictures that our young ones are exposed to. It is not just children of color who need Latino/a, Asian American, Native American and African American dolls. It is not just children of color who are hurt by computer games that portray people of color as evil, dangerous and expendable.

I am not recommending that you purge your house of favorite games and toys or become fanatical about the racism you find in your child's life. Children don't need to be protected from racism. They see it all the time. They need to be given critical thinking tools for recognizing, analyzing and responding to the different forms that racism takes. Discussing the racism (or sexism) in a children's book or movie, helping them think about the injustices of racism and providing alternative anti-racist materials — all these contribute to your children's awareness and their ability to respond to injustice.

Our children need opportunities to listen to the experiences of people of color.[2] Placing our children in multicultural childcare settings, encouraging multiracial friendships, reaching out to co-workers and colleagues who are of diverse backgrounds and choosing professionals like doctors and dentists who are people of color are all ways to broaden our children's experience. Our society is so highly segregated that any of these efforts may turn out to be more complex than we imagined. But that complexity also can become material for understanding how racism operates and for introducing our children to the issues.

If our neighborhood or school is segregated, we can still introduce our children to a multicultural world experience that breaks down stereotypes. The best and often most accurate way is to read what people of color write about their lives. Many new children's books realistically portray the lives of adults and children who are African American. There are a substantial number of books about the lives of Latino/as and Jews. Books by Native American, Arab American, Asian American and Muslim writers for young people may be harder to find, but there are some good ones available.[3] Many of us, especially if we live or visit large cities, have access to photo exhibits, live musical performances, museums and cultural centers where we can take our children. Hearing and seeing examples of other people's diverse experiences is extremely valuable for our children.

If we understand that we live in a multicultural society, we will begin to question any situation where people of color are not present. For example, if our children are in a Scout troop, sports team, Math Olympics team or a religious school class that is all white, we will ask ourselves, "Why is this group all white? Are there any barriers that keep children of color out?" Then we might question the curriculum or program. "Is it multicultural? Does it reflect the diversity of the larger community? What values are being taught? Are issues of racism being addressed? Are other groups excluded, such as girls or gay youth?"

Children notice differences in people and how they are treated. Many of us want to teach children not to judge people in biased and unkind ways, and therefore, we may downplay the significance of differences. But this can sometimes lead children to conclude that avoiding discrimination means avoiding differences. On the contrary, we want children to notice differences and similarities in people and to notice when differences lead to people being treated unfairly because of them. As early childhood teachers Ann Pelo and Fran Davidson have discovered, "Children who notice differences and who are comfortable with them can identify discrimination more clearly and can explore the unfairness that arises from biased understandings of difference. This is the beginning of activism."[4]

When we notice and remark on the ways that people are separated and treated differently, we validate our children's own perceptions and encourage them to build a sharper awareness of how racism works. When my son was caught shoplifting a couple of years ago, the store manager called me and released him to my care without calling the police and having him arrested. Of course my son was scared when he was caught and was relieved that he was not taken to jail. He was fined and banned from the store, but did not get an arrest on his record. Afterwards, when we talked about this incident, I asked him how Charles, an African American friend of his, might have been treated if he had been the one caught shoplifting. I didn't tell him he would have been treated differently. I asked him what difference he thought it might make. We had a thoughtful discussion of what might have happened if the store had called the police, how his friend might have been treated, what it would have meant if he had an arrest record. I brought this up not to make him feel guilty or lucky, but to give him practice in noticing that race makes a constant difference in how people are treated.

It is hard to know at what age we should begin talking about institutionalized racism and the history of racial injustice, because we don't want to overwhelm our children. I think that, certainly by age six to eight, young people are capable of understanding patterns of discrimination such as slavery, the Jewish holocaust or the genocide of Native Americans when the information is presented to them in age-appropriate ways. They can begin to see the differences between individual white responses to people of color and government or corporate policies.

I think it is crucial that we be honest with our children about racial inequality in the larger society. When we are answering their questions about poverty, homelessness or AIDS, we can discuss the ways that racism makes people of color more vulnerable to these problems and less able to access resources and support. We can point out how people of color are blamed for having these problems while the large number of white people in the same situation are not blamed as much — or perhaps not at all. For instance, there are substantial numbers of white people on welfare in the United States, but the media most often present images of welfare mothers who are black, not white.[5]

Biased representations of people of color reinforce the unstated belief that white people are superior. In almost every interpersonal and institutional setting, the assumption is that white is better because white people are in charge, white images are taken for granted, white history is taught in our schools and white people receive more respect. This instills in white children a sense that they are entitled to respect, power and inclusion, and can even justify disrespect for, violence towards and exclusion of people of color. Our children need to hear from us that white is not superior, that all white people are not smarter, nor do they work harder than all people of color. Young people will understand this once they have a grasp of how racism works as a system, a set of interlocking institutions that deny equal opportunity in education, housing and jobs to people of color.

When we talk about poverty, for example, we can discuss job discrimination and unequal funding for education. This will help our children understand the social roots of individual problems. Whether the issue is race, gender, economics or disability, nothing is more important than to give our children insight into the systemic nature of power, violence and blame at a level at which they can absorb it. We do this not to excuse abusive or destructive behavior, but to put it into context and to help our children move beyond blaming individuals for social problems.

It empowers white children when they see that they have a role to play in ending racism and all forms of social injustice. White people fight against hate crimes, police brutality, housing and job discrimination and environmental racism. There are probably local people, possibly members of your extended family or community, who are also models of white people who have been allies to people of color in the fight for racial justice. We can give our children models of white people (particularly young white people) who have resisted racism so that they know it is *racism as a system* that is the problem, not every white person.

At the same time, we can help our white children recognize that white people in general have been resistant to acknowledging and ending racism. We need to be honest about our own role and the roles of our foreparents. Many of us have relatives who did not support the civil rights movement or the struggles for racial justice by Latino/as and Native Americans. Adult whites, either actively or passively, are the biggest supporters of racism in the US. Some of us have family members who are today speaking out against or acting against equal opportunity, immigrant rights, affirmative action and religious tolerance. These stories need to be told as well.

Young white people need to see that they can choose to support racist policies or they can choose to become anti-racist activists. We can present all sides — the complex dimensions of white responses to racism — so that our

Questions and Actions — Home and Family

1. Were people of color and racism talked about in your childhood home? Think about particular incidents when they were. Who initiated discussions, and who resisted them? Was there tension around it? What was the general tone?

2. Were Jews, the Jewish holocaust or anti-Jewish oppression talked about? Think about particular incidents. What was the general tone? Who initiated discussions, and how was tension handled if there was any?

3. Was there silence in your home on issues of racism or other forms of oppression? What did you learn from the silence?

4. Was there conflict within your family because of racism (over integration, interracial or interfaith dating, music or busing)? Think of particular incidents. How was the conflict dealt with?

5. Were there people of color who cared for you, your parents, house or yard? If so, how were they treated? How did their presence and your family's attitudes toward them influence you?

6. As a child, what stories, TV shows or books influenced you the most in your attitudes about people of color? About people who were not Christian? What do you carry with you from that exposure?

7. Talk with your partner, housemates and friends about these issues. Notice the whiteness of your surroundings out loud to family and friends. This needn't be done aggressively or with anger. You don't need to attack other people. Ask questions, notice things out loud, express your concerns and give other people room to think about and respond to what you say.

8. Bring up feelings or thoughts about reading this book at dinner or other family time. What is difficult or awkward about doing this? What is the response?

9. Do an assessment of your home including the following items:

a. books	f. magazines	k. toys
b. posters	g. newspapers	l. art materials
c. cookbooks	h. videos	m. religious articles
d. calendars	i. games	n. sports paraphernalia
e. paintings	j. computer games	o. music

10. What would you like to remove?

11. What would you like to add to what you have? Try to go beyond the tokenism of putting up pictures of Martin Luther King, Jr. or LeBron James or adding a book or two to your children's collection. Explore the roles and contributions of people of color in areas where you and other family members share an interest — such as sports, science, music, books or movies.

12. Are women well represented in the items in your home? Are poor and working-class people? Are people with disabilities? Are Muslims, Jews and Buddhists? Are lesbians and gay men? Are children? Are the creations of children themselves included?

13. Do you employ people of color? How well are they paid? How well are they treated? How do your children respond and relate to them? How will you talk with your ☛

children about these relationships? How will you balance these relationships with friends and neighbors from different cultures who are not employees? Are your children exposed to professionals such as teachers, doctors and dentists who are people of color? How could you increase such exposure?

children will see that they have moral choices to make. When they understand how racism is institutionalized, they will know that they are not responsible for it, but they are responsible for how they respond to it. Will they stand for racial justice and equal opportunity? Will they stand with people of color? Their answers to these questions will begin to form through the ways we raise them.

You might want to initiate family discussions about racism by talking about this book and how you don't want your home to support racism. You can solicit their help in doing an assessment of your home and thinking about how different games, books, videos or posters might be racist.

Let your children help decide what to do to make your home different. It is one thing to create an anti-racist, multicultural environment by yourself. It is an entirely different level of education, empowerment and activism to include your children as valued participants in the process. The goal is to acknowledge and celebrate the diversity of people and cultures in our society.

Obviously, this kind of assessment and interactive process should address issues of gender, class, disability, sexual orientation and religious and cultural difference as well as race. We don't want to foster stereotypes that people of color are not also women, poor or working-class, people with disabilities, lesbian, gay or bisexual and/or Muslim, Buddhist or Jewish. These differences are inseparable. When dealt with in a context of social justice, young people are quick to develop principles of fair treatment and equality, eager to become co-participants in creating a healthier environment and challenging injustice. They may well end up inspiring and leading us with their readiness to challenge authority, take risks and stand up for fairness.

These are small personal steps, but they have two important consequences. The more contact we have with people of color and with images and information about them, the more we are motivated and equipped to challenge racism. We are able to see more clearly the tremendous gap between average white perceptions about people of color and their actual lives and communities. This awareness can guide our action and enrich our lives.

Second, we prepare our children to notice how racism operates and to become champions for racial justice. *Uprooting Racism* provides resources and a bibliography to enhance your parenting skills and continue this process.

Notes

1. See, for example, Debra Van Ausdale and Joe R. Feagin. *The First R: How Children Learn about Race and Racism.* Rowman & Littlefield, 2001.
2. The following paragraphs are adapted from my book *Boys Will Be Men.*
3. One useful resource to begin with is Daphne Muse. *The New Press Guide to Multicultural Resources for Young Readers.* New Press, 1997.
4. Ann Pelo and Fran Davidson. *That's Not Fair! A Teacher's Guide to Activism with Young Children.* Red Leaf, 2000, p. 31.
5. US Department of Health and Human Services, Administration for Children and Families. *Table 8 Temporary Assistance for Needy Families — Active Cases: Percent Distribution of TANF Families by Ethnicity/Race October 2007 – September 2008.* [online]. [cited March 4, 2011]. acf.hhs.gov/programs/ofa/character/FY2008/tab08.htm.

For the Long Haul

R ACISM IS NOT GOING TO END TOMORROW OR NEXT YEAR. Every delay and
setback saps our strength and strains our hope. It is easy to despair, easy
to give up. How do we nurture and sustain ourselves for what may well be a
lifetime struggle? How do we keep alive the vision of racial justice and multicultural democracy that guides our action?

The first step is to stop and think about how we are taking care of ourselves
for the long term. Our guilt, desperation, anger, fear, the immediate pressure
of events or even our enthusiasm may make it difficult for us to think about
how to keep going after this next action, campaign or crisis.[1]

If we are not thinking about how to nurture ourselves in the coming years,
we are probably also not thinking strategically about the future. We may have
become bogged down reacting to everyday events. We may have lost sight of
our goals, not noticed how the world is changing and forgotten that we are
going to have to renew ourselves to remain effective.

We need to create time in our overworked, overcommitted lives to reflect
on the future. Some of us do this best alone, others with friends and family. In
either case, we must start with time for reflection.

Reflection is a spiritual practice for some of us. Any spiritual practice that
connects us to a reality greater than our individual lives — that connects us to
other people, to animal and plant life and/or to a larger energy in the world
— can increase our respect for life and our valuing of difference. It can renew

> • Take a moment to think about how you center your energy or calm yourself amidst
> the pressures and stress of your daily routines. How could you strengthen this part of
> your life?

and guide our pursuit for a better world. We each have, or can find, our own unique way to reflect and connect.

We also need to take care of ourselves physically and emotionally. We need to live as if we wanted to be alive when our visions are realized. It goes without saying that we need to eat, exercise, relax, have fun, play, enjoy and smile. Yet how many of us don't take these parts of our lives seriously until we can't continue our work because of exhaustion or poor health? How do we expect to continue in the struggle? What are we modeling for the young people around us?

For people from a white Christian background there may be a big divide between work and leisure. Taking care of oneself, goofing off and having fun may seem self-indulgent, even sinful. Some people can turn exercise and other forms of recreation into work, diminishing some of their value. These attitudes can also make it difficult to exult in the singing, dance, drama and other celebratory rituals that can be so renewing to our lives.

Reclaiming or developing cultural rituals can heal and reinvigorate us. Rituals build community, connect people and inspire new visions and strategies. Singing or going to hear music; writing, reading or listening to a poem; participating in a holiday ritual; sharing a meal with friends — we need to allow ourselves the cultural activities that nurture our souls.

Mainstream male, white and Christian traditions push people to be rugged individuals. The message is "Go it alone." This assumes there is an individual path to salvation and that people shouldn't make mistakes or ask for help. As a result of this message, we can become isolated and feel scared, confused or lost. We may not know where to turn for support. Many of us find it easier to support others than to ask for help. We have to overcome our pride and fear to admit that we can't do things all by ourselves. We can't fight racism alone. We can't create social justice by ourselves.

Friends, family members and community networks keep us connected, supported and inspired. They help us maintain perspective on who we are and what we can do. Working with others aids us in evaluating what we can

- What activities help you connect to a greater reality?
- How could these activities support your work for social justice?
- How might you create more time for reflection in your life?

Questions and Actions — For the Long Haul
1. Who are family and friends you can talk with about doing racial justice work? Who will you talk with first?
2. Who are co-workers who might help you form a racial justice action/support network? Who will you talk with first?
3. Do you know or know of people of color who you want to talk with about fighting racism? List the one you will talk with first. Ask if they have time and is willing to do this with you.
4. Name one network, action committee or support group that you are going to join.
5. What kind of cultural events, rituals or celebrations bring you together with others? Which ones renew your spirit?
6. How can you honor and a celebrate the efforts of those who have preceded you?

or cannot take on, what our share is. Taking care of ourselves through healthy lifestyles, rituals, cultural activities and support networks builds and sustains a community of people dedicated to the struggle for social justice.

Finally, we need to celebrate our successes, no matter how small; our victories, no matter how tenuous. Although racism is still a central constituent of our society, we have made progress, and some things have changed. They have changed because multitudes of courageous people of color and white allies have fought, resisted and refused to be overwhelmed by racism. They have changed because the human spirit is indomitable and we each share that spirit. We can only sustain our efforts by building on and celebrating the achievements of the people who have contributed to getting us as far as we are today.

Notes

1. Two good resources on taking care of ourselves spiritually as well as physically are Claudia Horowitz. *The Spiritual Activist: Practices to Transform your Life, Your Work, and Your World.* Penguin, 2002; Laura Van Dernoot Lipsky and Connie Burk. *Trauma Stewardship: An Everyday Guide to Caring for Self While Caring for Others.* Berrett Koehler, 2009.

Conclusion

A FEW YEARS AGO, MY COLLEAGUES AT THE OAKLAND MEN'S PROJECT and I did a five-day workshop in Ohio in which we focused extensively on racism. Six months later, we were back for a two-day follow-up with the same participants. To start the workshop, we asked them to talk about how the previous workshop had affected them.

I sat listening to several people describe how the workshop had changed their understanding of racism, how it had affected their relationships with co-workers and how it had sensitized them to racial injustice in their community. I was pleased that our work had a positive impact, but was a little uneasy without knowing why. Finally a white man, Mark, who works at a large social service agency, began to speak:

> That workshop has influenced me in more ways than I can say.
> But I think it made the biggest difference at work. This fall we
> needed to hire five new staff, and I made sure that three of those
> five people were people of color because our staff has been mostly
> white until now.

"That's it," I said to myself, realizing what had been missing from the others' accounts.

It is important for us to unlearn prejudice, broaden our understanding of racism and learn to recognize racist acts when we see them. But unless we are actively involved in the fight against racism, we haven't taken it far enough. Mark understood that he needed to take his awareness and turn it into concrete action. He changed his workplace. He didn't just try to get one person of color into the organization, because he knew that one person would be isolated and probably not last long. He wanted to make a significant impact, so he focused on the difficult but reachable goal of making three of the five new hires people of color.

Mark was not a high-level manager or director. When I talked with him later, he described in more detail what he had done. It had taken him many discussions, both one-on-one and with the full staff, to convince his peers and supervisors how important it was to hire qualified people of color. He had prepared a staff presentation about racism, looking at the agency, its staff, policies and clientele. He had lobbied long and hard, at some personal risk, to convince people that they needed to address racism concretely in their hiring practices. He had helped with the job search and interviewing so that qualified candidates would be found. Now he was supporting the new staff.

We don't always have the visible impact Mark had in fighting racism. Even if he had not been able to diversify the staff, he would have made a difference. By raising the issue of racism within the organization, he was questioning established patterns and expectations. He challenged everyone to rethink how hiring was done and what the implications were for the organization and for the community.

Sometimes change doesn't come in the first round, but in the second, third or fourth. Change starts with one person questioning, challenging, speaking up and doing something to make a difference. We can each make that sort of difference.

As Jewish poet Marge Piercy writes at the end of her poem "The Low Road"

> It starts when you care to act,
> It starts when you do it again after they said no.
> It starts when you say WE
> And know who you mean,
> And each day you mean one more.[1]

We can make a difference because each of us is already part of the community where racism exists and thrives. We are connected to neighborhoods, workplaces, schools and religious organizations. Our connections, our relationships, our positions in these organizations give us leverage to change them. Every time we add another white ally to our network, we increase our leverage. And every time white people step up as allies to people of color, that leverage increases the possibility of achieving racial justice.

I end by returning to questions I asked at the beginning of this book.

- What do you stand for?
- Who do you stand with?
- Do you stand for the idea that all people are created equal?
- Do you stand for the idea that everyone deserves life, liberty and the pursuit of happiness?
- Do you stand for the idea that no one should be discriminated against because of their race, religion, gender, sexual identity, sexual orientation, ability or other factors?
- Do you stand for the idea that, as Dr. Martin Luther King, Jr. said, "an injustice against one is an injustice against all?"
- And, even more importantly
- Do you stand with people of color who are still being discriminated against, marginalized and excluded from jobs, housing and educational opportunities?
- Do you stand with people of color who are experiencing increasing levels of hate crimes, racial profiling, police brutality and governmental surveillance and intervention?
- Do you stand with people of color who are still suffering and dying disproportionately from inadequate healthcare, toxic waste in their communities, violence and governmental neglect?
- If you stand for justice — and, if you stand with those who are under attack, then what are you going to do about it?

Notes

1. Marge Piercy. "The Low Road," from *The Moon Is Always Female*. Knopf, 1980.

Bibliography and
Other Resources

THE AUTHOR AND PUBLISHER have decided to lower the cost of this book (by $3) and to keep the resources up to date by providing an online bibliography and other resources for the reader at PaulKivel.com.

Below is a sample of what you will find there:

Bibliography

Bonilla-Silva, Eduardo. *Racism Without Racists: Color-Blind Racism and the Persistence of Racial Inequality in the United States,* 2nd ed. Rowman & Littlefield, 2006.

Lui, Meizhu, et. al. *The Color of Wealth: The Story Behind the US Racial Wealth Divide.* New Press, 2006.

Markus, Hazel Rose and Paula M.L. Moya, eds. *Doing Race: 21 Essays for the 21st Century.* Norton, 2010.

Magazines

Colorlines – colorlines.com

Rethinking Schools – rethinkingschools.org

Teaching Tolerance – tolerance.org

Film Distributors and Resources

California Newsreel – newsreel.org

Media Education Foundation – mediaed.org

Organizations and Websites

Antiracism Net – antiracismnet.org

Evaluation Tools for Racial Equity – evaluationtoolsforracialequity.org

National Network for Immigrant and Refugee Rights – nnirr.org

Poverty & Race Research Action Council – prrac.org
Teaching for Change – teachingforchange.org
US for All of Us — No Room for Racism – usforallofus.org

Conferences

Facing Race – arc.org/content/blogcategory/63/203/
White Privilege Conference – uccs.edu/~wpc

Full bibliography and other resources available at PaulKivel.com.

Index

Cuban Americans, 173, 225
cultural competency, 284
cultural hegemony, 177
cultural identity, 55, 106-108
culture of poverty, 70
culture of power, 47-50

D
danger, sense of, 80-86.
    See also fears.
Dawes Act (1887), 214
death penalty, 264
democracy, 102, 280, 290
denial, xv, 11, 15, 60, 67
deportation, 176, 182, 201, 202,
    203, 226, 229
discrimination, 44-45.
    See also affirmative action;
    reverse discrimination.
diversity training, 296-302
Doctrine of Discovery, 213
domestic violence, 2, 56, 63, 64, 83,
    91, 93, 96, 163 258, 263.
draft, 37-38
drug companies, 254
drug use, 163, 258-259, 262-263,
    265
Du Bois W.E.B., 242
Dyson, Michael Eric, 38

E
economic power, 78-79
economic pyramid, 43, 78, 140
economic status, 11, 70-71, 145,
    158, 256
education, 31, 36, 37, 44, 82.
    See also academic professions;

school systems; teacher
    demographics
either/or thinking, 281-282
Electoral College, 230-231, 233
entitlement, 51-54, 107, 285-286
environmental racism, 274-278
Equal Employment Opportunity
    Commission, 238
eroticization of difference, 89-94,
    154
ethnic cleansing, 215-216
European ancestry, 3, 25, 103, 150,
    193, 194, 198
exclusion, from jobs, 32, 35
ex-felons, and voting, 231-231,
    234

F
family environment, 303-310.
    See also happy family myth.
family violence.
    See domestic violence.
farming, 39, 199, 213, 215, 216
Feagin, Joe, 23
fears, 1-2, 56, 80-88, 112, 162,
    238
Filipinos, 150, 168
films, influence of, 28-29, 62, 179,
    181
Finns, 19
Florida, voting in, 229, 231, 232
foreign aid, 272-273
foreign policy, 5n3, 182, 199,
    271-273.
    See also immigration policies;
    military force (US).
frontier myth, 106

Terrell, Mary Church, 92
terrorism, 181-182, 187, 202-203
terrorist, as code word, 71
third world (as a term), 103
Thompson, Nicholas, 232
tokenism, 293-294
trade agreements, 175, 199, 244
trade unions, 32
Treaty of Guadalupe Hidalgo
    (1848), 175
Truth, Sojourner, 92
two-party political system, 230,
    232-233

U
underclass, 69-70
unintentional damage, 62
US Census Bureau, 173
US Constitution, 66, 155, 160, 213,
    220-221, 230, 231
US Immigration and Customs
    Enforcement (ICE), 182, 198,
    202
US Internal Revenue Service, 202

V
verbal abuse, interrupting, 130-133
Veterans Administration (VA), 33,
    34-35, 36, 41n2
victims, 4-75
Vietnam War, 37-38
violence,
    justification for, 3, 17, 83, 85,
        153-155
    by men, 59-65, 90-92.
    See also domestic violence.
Virginia, 18, 159, 231

voting irregularities, 229-230
voting rights, 198, 223, 229-234.
    See also citizenship.

W
Walker, Alice, 3-4
Washington, George, 153-154
wealth, in the US, xviii, 32, 41,
    78-79, 221-222, 290.
    See also economic pyramid; land
    use issues.
web of control, 142-146
welfare mothers, 70, 306
Wells, Ida B., 92
West Indies, xi, 18, 152, 158
white, as a label, 3, 8-14
white body, ideal of, 29-30
white culture of power, 48-49
white extremist groups, 181-182,
    193, 257
whiteness, 8-11, 17-27, 107
white racism, defined, 2
Wilson, James Q., 232
Wing, Bob, 232-233
women of color, 89, 212
women's groups, 91-92
work issues, 242-247.
    See also hiring programs;
    teacher demographics.
World Bank, 199, 244
World War II, 25, 34-35, 171, 216

Y
Yemenis, 180
youth of color, and criminal justice
    system, 263, 265

About the Author

Paul Kivel, social justice educator, activist and writer, has been involved in racial justice work for over 40 years. He is an accomplished trainer and speaker on men's issues, racism and diversity, challenges of youth, teen dating and family violence, raising boys to adulthood and the impact of class and power on daily life. His work gives people the understanding to become involved in social justice work and the tools to become more effective allies in community struggles to end oppression and injustice and to transform organizations and institutions.

Kivel is the author of numerous books and curricula including *Men's Work, Making the Peace, Helping Teens Stop Violence, Build Community, and Stand for Justice, Boys Will Be Men, I Can Make My World A Safer Place* and most recently *You Call This a Democracy?: Who Benefits, Who Pays,* and *Who Really Decides.*

If you have enjoyed *Uprooting Racism*, you might also enjoy other

BOOKS TO BUILD A NEW SOCIETY

Our books provide positive solutions for people who want to make a difference. We specialize in:

Sustainable Living • Green Building • Peak Oil
Renewable Energy • Environment & Economy
Natural Building & Appropriate Technology
Progressive Leadership • Resistance and Community
Educational & Parenting Resources

New Society Publishers

ENVIRONMENTAL BENEFITS STATEMENT

New Society Publishers has chosen to produce this book on recycled paper made with **100% post consumer waste**, processed chlorine free, and old growth free.

For every 5,000 books printed, New Society saves the following resources:[1]

35	Trees
3,158	Pounds of Solid Waste
3,475	Gallons of Water
4,533	Kilowatt Hours of Electricity
5,741	Pounds of Greenhouse Gases
25	Pounds of HAPs, VOCs, and AOX Combined
9	Cubic Yards of Landfill Space

[1]Environmental benefits are calculated based on research done by the Environmental Defense Fund and other members of the Paper Task Force who study the environmental impacts of the paper industry.

For a full list of NSP's titles, please call 1-800-567-6772 *or check out our website* at:

www.newsociety.com

NEW SOCIETY PUBLISHERS
Deep Green for over 30 years